Win
Every Day

I have had the honor of going from being one of the lost at an evangelistic outreach to sharing the stage with Steve and others, so I know the impact of event evangelism. Steve's passion for helping lead people from all walks of life to Christ is what he lives for. I believe that this exciting new book will be a great resource in helping people be victorious in their everyday lives.

John Birmingham
Executive Director, Warriors In The Workplace

America needs a straight-talk dose of Wingfield reality more than ever. The devotions in *Winning the Race Every Day* deliver rock-solid, daily biblical advice with a kick in the pants. Here are 365 days of Steve Wingfield wisdom harvested from more than 25 years of Christ-centered outreach.

Michael Coleman
Chaplain, Racers for Christ

I have been blessed and inspired by Steve's devotions. His teachings are spiritually sound and presented with illustrations and a down-to-earth approach that I find refreshing. I'm stronger in my Christian walk as a result of Steve's influence.

Danae Dobson
Speaker and author of 24 books

Steve Wingfield has taken his popular daily devotionals and put them into a great book titled *Winning the Race Every Day*. I am sure that this book will be a tremendous blessing to anyone seeking victory in his or her life by getting closer to God.

Dell Hamilton
NASCAR team owner

As someone who has been around racing fans for more than 12 years, I believe *Winning the Race Every Day* will be a tremendous resource for race fans and everyone else who reads it. Steve communicates real issues to real people as well as anyone with whom I've ever worked. This book will be an effective follow-up tool at the tracks and will help people walk more closely with Christ on a daily basis.

Leo Johnston
Leader Singer, CrossCountry the Band

I know that the desire of Steve's heart is for everyone to follow Christ daily. *Winning the Race Every Day* will be a great help to every person who uses it in his or her daily walk with Jesus. God is awesome, and He wants victory for all His children.

24 Blake Koch
SR² Motorsports and NASCAR Nationwide Series driver

Devotion in motion! This book explodes with practical ideas and information that will engage the imagination of anyone who commits to a faithful daily reading. Guys, especially, are sure to find empowerment on every page.

Benita Long
Author of *Come to the Table* and *Share the Bounty*

Winning the Race Every Day—what a perfect way to describe Steve's passion for people! His daily "Pit Stops" are powerful and come straight from his heart. It's been my privilege to know Steve as my mentor, friend and partner in ministry. The heart he has for evangelism has forever impacted me, our community and our church. May God use the words of this book to help you win the race every day!

Tim McAvoy
Senior Pastor, New Beginnings Church, Harrisonburg, Virginia

Steve Wingfield, my friend and partner in evangelism, is always moving forward in his effort to reach the lost, wherever they may be. His Victory Weekend ministry to racing fans is a new and powerful evangelistic movement. May this book be an impacting source of inspiration toward achieving God's victory in your life.

Luis Palau
Founder, Luis Palau Association

Steve Wingfield has always stood firm in evangelism and Christian living. In *Wining the Race Every Day,* he helps people address a need in the Christian life by showing how God can help them win the race every day. Steve has been used greatly to preach the gospel at many NASCAR events, and his daily "Pit Stops" reflect his commitment to soul winning. Every day you need a "Pit Stop" to refuel and be reenergized to live for God. May reading this book help you win the race every day for God.

Elmer Towns
Co-founder, Liberty University, Lynchburg, Virginia

Winning the Race Every Day
Keep Your Drive Alive

STEVE WINGFIELD

Regal

For more information and
special offers from Regal Books, email us at
subscribe@regalbooks.com

Published by Regal
From Gospel Light
Ventura, California, U.S.A.
www.regalbooks.com
Printed in the U.S.A.

All Scripture quotations, unless otherwise indicated, are taken from the *Holy Bible, New International Version®*. Copyright © 1973, 1978, 1984 by International Bible Society. Used by permission of Zondervan Publishing House. All rights reserved.

Other versions used are
ESV—Scripture taken from the *English Standard Version,* Copyright © 2001.
The *ESV* and *English Standard Version* are trademarks of Good News Publishers.
ISV—Scripture taken from the *Holy Bible, International Standard Version*.
Copyright 1998 by the Learn Foundation, Yorba Linda, CA. Used by permission of Davidson Press. All rights reserved internationally.
KJV—*King James Version.* Authorized King James Version.
NASB—Scripture taken from the *New American Standard Bible,* © 1960, 1962, 1963, 1968, 1971, 1972, 1973, 1975, 1977, 1995 by The Lockman Foundation.
Used by permission.
NKJV—Scripture taken from the *New King James Version.* Copyright © 1979, 1980, 1982 by Thomas Nelson, Inc. Used by permission. All rights reserved.
NLT—Scripture quotations marked *NLT* are taken from the *Holy Bible, New Living Translation,* copyright © 1996, 2004, 2007 by Tyndale House Foundation.
Used by permission of Tyndale House Publishers, Inc., Carol Stream, Illinois 60188. All rights reserved.
Phillips—*The New Testament in Modern English*, J. B. Phillips, Translator.
© J. B. Phillips 1958, 1962. Published by Harper-Collins.

© 2013 Steve Wingfield
All rights reserved.

Library of Congress Cataloging-in-Publication Data
Wingfield, Steve (Stephen)
Winning the race everyday / Steve Wingfield.
pages cm
Includes bibliographical references and index.
ISBN 978-0-8307-6716-8 (trade paper : alk. paper)
1. Devotional calendars. I. Title.
BV4811.W594 2013
242'.2—dc23
2013010395

Rights for publishing this book outside the U.S.A. or in non-English languages are administered by Gospel Light Worldwide, an international not-for-profit ministry. For additional information, please visit www.glww.org, email info@glww.org, or write to Gospel Light Worldwide, 1957 Eastman Avenue, Ventura, CA 93003, U.S.A.

To order copies of this book and other Regal products in bulk quantities, please contact us at 1-800-446-7735.

CONTENTS

Foreword 7

Preface 9

Introduction 11

January: Standing Firm 17

February: Obeying the Call 49

March: Being the Doxology 79

April: Representing Christ Well 111

May: Communing with God 143

June: Trusting the Lord 175

July: Telling Our Story 207

August: Investing Treasures 239

September: Running with Endurance 271

October: Living in the Light 303

November: Rejoicing in God's Unfailing Love 335

December: Producing Lasting Fruit 367

Endnotes 399

DEDICATION

I dedicate this book to my wife, Barbara, my daughter, Michelle, and her husband, Howard, along with Phin, Lars, Katie Ann, Field and Jude; my son, David, and his wife, Havilah; and to Salah—who have all played key roles in helping me represent Jesus as a way of life. I also must thank Elaine Starner for taking what I wrote and making it better!

FOREWORD

God loved you enough to send His one and only Son to be your Savior. Jesus paid the debt for all your sins, and He not only wants you to live with Him eternally in heaven, but He also wants you to enjoy the journey. In John 10:10 Jesus said, "I have come that they may have life, and have it to the full." The word "abundant" means that life is intended by God to be full and meaningful, with purpose and direction.

God wants you to be a spiritual winner! My friend, Steve Wingfield, has written *Winning the Race Every Day* to help you grow spiritually by helping you get to know Jesus better.

Learning to know Him by spending time with Him on a daily basis will enable you to be a better follower of Jesus. We are running the race of our lives and I pray this book will help keep you on track. This track is paved with forgiveness. If you are a spiritual wreck or have just experienced a fender bender, don't give up! Read 1 John 1:9: "If we confess our sins, He is faithful and just and will forgive us our sins and purify us from all unrighteousness." Confess your sin and ask Jesus to forgive you. Then get back in the race!

Steve Wingfield has faithfully served the Lord for over 40 years and lives the principles that are found in this book.

It is my prayer that this powerful devotional will help you maintain a daily time with the Lord. I believe it will enable all who read it to be better followers of Christ.

98 Michael McDowell
Phil Parsons Racing
NASCAR Sprint Cup

PREFACE

You hold in your hands the product of a lifetime of experience and several concentrated years of preparing daily radio and web broadcasts called *Keep Your Drive Alive*. I have lovingly distilled almost three years of *Keep Your Drive Alive* offerings into this book.

It is my heart's desire that *Winning the Race Every Day* will be a motivational tool for you and the friends, neighbors, coworkers and family members with whom you may share it. We also plan to make the book available to the fans who respond at our Victory Weekend ministry events at NASCAR racing events around the country.

Some early readers have told me that they can almost hear me reading the book to them as they go through it. I hope that is true because I want the words that I broadcast to have life enough to penetrate hearts and minds and make a soul difference for God's kingdom.

This book represents the fulfillment of many, many years of wanting to share what God has shown me over the decades as I have been trying to serve Him to the best of my ability. I hope it shows.

I am often quoted as saying, "Represent Christ well today." That is what I diligently sought to do with this book and I fervently hope that it will help you do that as well.

My hearts desire is that God will use *Winning the Race Every Day* to strength you as you run! May we all hear these words one day: "*Well done!*"

Steve Wingfield
Harrisonburg, Virginia

INTRODUCTION

> Do you not know that in a race all the runners run, but only one receives the prize? So run that you may obtain it. Every athlete exercises self-control in all things. They do it to receive a perishable wreath, but we an imperishable.
>
> 1 CORINTHIANS 9:24-25, *ESV*

Like many people in America, I grew up loving and playing sports. At times in my life, I studied only because I wanted to be on a particular team and maintaining a certain GPA would keep me eligible for play. I was sports crazy.

Scripture teaches us that "there is nothing new under the sun" (Ecclesiastes 1:9), and it's my opinion that God put competition into the human DNA at the very beginning of our history. Athletic contests have been around for many centuries. Admittedly, some allow the spirit of competition to swell out of control; but good healthy matches, races, and rivalries can be lots of fun.

Today, NASCAR is the most popular spectator sport in the United States. That statement may surprise you if you do not follow the sport, but I assure you it is true! Born and raised in Virginia, I grew up in the heart of NASCAR country, watching the Wood Brothers, Curtis Turner and Richard Petty become NASCAR legends as they repeatedly took the checkered flag at tracks like Richmond, Martinsville, Bristol and South Boston.

I enjoy the sport for many reasons, one of which is driver access; NASCAR drivers are real people who get up close and personal with their fan base. For the most part, they are good, down-to-earth men and women who love what they do and have not allowed success and fame to go to their heads. From my perspective, they are "salt of the earth" people, and I just enjoy being around them.

Whether it's NASCAR or a five-year-old's T-ball, however, each organized sport has rules to regulate the competitive spirit of the participants. Game officials, referees and umpires are on hand to make certain the game is played according to those rules. Every spectator, whether or not he or she is knowledgeable about the sport, understands that rules are to be followed and that the official is there to oversee the competition.

Of course, a child's T-ball game is probably much easier to officiate than the competition of cars racing around a track at almost 200 MPH. Shouting calls and making gestures would never work for NASCAR officials, so they communicate with drivers by use of colored flags, and each flag color has a specific message for the drivers. The flags cannot be missed, and every driver knows he or she must heed those waving colors.

Entering the Race

In the race we run for the duration of our lives, God desires to be our only official. He has many of the same flags for us that are so familiar in the NASCAR world. And if we pay attention to His flags, we will be much more successful in our race for the prize.

But before we talk about God's flags for us as we run our race, let's think about the flag *we* must wave before we "compete" for the eternal prize: a white flag. Although NASCAR has a different meaning associated with a white flag, we must wave this flag to give the universal signal of surrender. Before we can enter this race for the imperishable prize, we must acknowledge five things.

1. Grace

Salvation is a free gift from God; it is not earned or deserved. We cannot do enough good to earn grace. We do not receive grace by being baptized or by joining a church. Salvation comes only by believing and accepting God's free gift: "For by grace you have been saved through faith. And this is not your own doing; it is the gift of God, not a result of works, so that no one may boast" (Ephesians 2:8-9, *ESV*).

2. Sin Problem

We do not deserve grace, because we have a sin problem. Adam and Eve's sin in the Garden of Eden not only affected them but also every member of the entire human race, who inherited from them a sin nature. As we read in the Bible, all of us have that same nature: "All have sinned and fall short of the glory of God" (Romans 3:23).

3. God
"I have loved you with an everlasting love; I have drawn you with lovingkindness," says God in Jeremiah 31:3. Nothing we do will keep God from loving us. When we sin, we grieve the heart of God; but neither you nor I can ever do anything so bad that God will stop loving us. However, even though God loves everyone, He is also a god of justice; and His justice requires that He must punish sin. If we were allowed into heaven with sin, we would contaminate all of heaven. Now, that confronts all of humanity with a major problem: "The wages of sin is death" (Romans 6:23). We have all sinned, and our sin must be dealt with!

4. Jesus
God sent His only Son into the world, born of a virgin, to become one of us. Jesus was fully God and fully man. He lived a perfect life, and He never sinned; but He was born to die—the just would die for the unjust. When He said, "It is finished," as He hung on the cross, He was in effect saying "I have paid the price for sin." He was buried and three days later rose from the dead. Because He lives, we now can live and have the assurance of eternal life: "For God so loved the world that He gave His one and only Son, that whoever believes in him should not perish but have eternal life" (John 3:16).

5. Faith
Salvation is a free gift, and we must receive it by faith. We can never earn salvation by doing good works. It is not enough to intellectually believe. We must wave the white flag of surrender and trust in Jesus alone to save us. We have been disobedient and do not deserve such a gift. It is a free gift from God, and we can only receive it by putting our faith in Him. "If you confess with your mouth that Jesus is Lord and believe in your heart that God raised him from the dead, you will be saved. For it is by believing in your heart that you are made right with God, and it is by confessing with your mouth that you are saved (Romans" 10:9-10, *NLT*).

Once we have waved our own white flag of surrender, we enter a great race. We run a race for an eternal prize, one that will never rust, crumble, fall apart or disintegrate. Paying attention to God's flags and letting Him officiate in our lives will help us run this race with daily victories.

The Green Flag

The green flag starts every NASCAR race, and every driver knows what it means: Go! It's the signal every driver waits for, the focus of his or her whole being.

"Go" is also one of the Lord's favorite words. Each Gospel quotes Jesus' command to go, and the book of Acts echoes it repeatedly. The Lord did not want us to miss this important command!

The command to go is intended for every believer—Jesus waved the green flag for every follower, not just His original circle of disciples. All of God's children have been commanded, "Go!" We dare not miss the fact that Jesus expects us all to go! Some believers have convinced themselves that the command to go is only for missionaries or others in full-time Christian service, but that is a total misunderstanding of Jesus' green flag. *Every* follower of Christ is expected to go and represent Him in whatever sphere of influence each of us has:

> Go and make disciples of all nations, baptizing them in the name of the Father and of the Son and of the Holy Spirit, and teaching them to obey everything I have commanded you. And surely I am with you always, to the very end of the age (Matthew 28:19-20).

As my friend Pastor John Sloop says, "We must all use our Monday through Friday pulpits to represent Jesus."

The Yellow Flag

The yellow NASCAR flag advises caution—all drivers must slow down, because something hazardous has been spotted on the track. The Holy Spirit is our yellow flag. He may speak to us through the Bible as we read, through a still, small voice as we go about our days, through circumstances or through the words of a fellow believer.

When He waves the yellow flag, we must pay close attention and be on guard. "The Counselor, the Holy Spirit, whom the Father will send in my [Jesus'] name, will teach you all things and will remind you of everything I have said to you" (John 14:26). Our primary responsibility is to listen and obey every caution flag!

The Black Flag

By waving a black flag, a NASCAR official signals that a driver has disobeyed the rules of the race and must report to the pit area to suffer the consequences of breaking the rules. When we sin, God waves the black flag. God desires to live in relationship with all of His children, but sin breaks the communion we have with our heavenly Father. We must not ignore a black flag; we must pay attention to the voice of God and deal with our sins as soon as possible.

We deal with our sins by being honest with ourselves and with God, acknowledging that we have sinned and repenting of our disobedience. In His grace and love, God provides a way for us to do that: "If we confess our sins, he is faithful and just and will forgive us our sins and purify us from all unrighteousness" (1 John 1:9).

Years ago, Dr. Bill Bright taught me the concept of spiritual breathing. I have benefited greatly from this practice, and I hope you will also. God created our amazing human bodies. We breathe to sustain life. We take in oxygen, our body extracts what we need, and then we exhale and life continues. What happens when someone quits breathing? First, the person passes out; then, if the problem is not corrected, death results. That, my friend, is a good visible reminder of what sins do to us. Sins lead to death. Confession of our sins to God is a spiritual breathing out, getting rid of all the impurities. Then we breathe in, asking God to fill us with the Holy Spirit. God wants all of His followers to be filled with His Spirit (see Ephesians 5:18). A Spirit-filled life is the normal Christian life. We must practice daily spiritual breathing so that sins do not keep us from living normal Christian lives.

The White Flag

When we waved the white flag of surrender, we gave God control of our lives. When a NASCAR official waves a white flag, drivers know there's only one more lap to go, and staying in front means winning! Every driver will do everything within his or her power to finish strong.

One day God will wave the white flag on each one of us, and our finish lines will be in sight. None of us knows when we will see that flag waving. I don't know when I will see it wave for me. We each must keep our eyes on the goal and not be distracted from it. Each of us needs to finish strong, no matter if we have one last lap to go or one hundred more laps to go. Each of us needs to keep our eyes on Jesus, the One who brought us to these lives of faith and who promises to supply everything we need to run the race:

> By his divine power, God has given us everything we need for living a godly life. We have received all of this by coming to know him, the one who called us to himself by means of his marvelous glory and excellence (2 Peter 1:3, *NLT*).

> Therefore, since we are surrounded by such a huge crowd of witnesses to the life of faith, let us strip off every weight that slows us down, especially the sin that so easily trips us up. And let us run with endurance the race God has set before us (Hebrews 12:1, *NLT*).

The Checkered Flag

Finally, a NASCAR official will unfurl a checkered flag to indicate that the race is over and the first driver who crossed the finish line has won the race. Like a NASCAR driver, every one of us should strive to finish strong and take the checkered flag in triumph. And as each of us takes the checkered flag, I pray that we will be able to say:

> I have fought the good fight, I have finished the race, I have kept the faith. Now there is in store for me the crown of righteousness, which the Lord, the righteous Judge, will award to me on that day—and not only to me, but also to all who have longed for his appearing (2 Timothy 4:7-8).

JANUARY

Standing Firm

Be on guard. **Stand firm in the faith.**
Be courageous. Be strong.

1 CORINTHIANS 16:13, *NLT*

January 1

> The Lord is near. Do not be anxious about anything,
> but in everything, by prayer and petition, with thanksgiving,
> present your requests to God. And the peace of
> God, which transcends all understanding, will guard your
> hearts and your minds in Christ Jesus.
>
> PHILIPPIANS 4:5-7

We're beginning a new year!

As you look forward, take the words of Philippians 4:5-7 to heart. Don't worry about anything. Pray and tell God about your needs. Put the past behind you and look forward to the new year, because He will be working for your good in everything. Give thanks always for what He has already done.

The Lord is near. He is walking with you through every moment, every hour, every day of the year. Does that assurance wrap you in peace, my friend?

There will be battles and victories; there will be suffering and joy. God has promised, though, that if you pray, tell Him what you need, and give Him thanks for what He's already done, you will experience His peace.

His peace, far beyond your ability to understand, will be present no matter what is going on around you. Even when peace seems impossible, your heart and mind will be able to rest in Him.

Three things to remember each day this year: (1) Pray. (2) Tell. (3) Give thanks. And the peace of God will guard your heart and mind through all that this year brings.

Pit Stop
PLAN

Follow the three-step plan for peace this year: (1) Pray. (2) Tell God what you need. (3) Thank Him for what He's done.

January 2

Words for the new year from 1 Corinthians 16:13 (*NLT*):

- Be on guard.
- Stand firm in the faith.
- Be courageous.
- Be strong.

Be watchful. Be on your guard in Christ. The devil is out to trap and destroy. Ask the Spirit for discerning eyes and ears, and watch out for the enemy's tricks and lies.

Keep your eyes on Christ and stand firm in your faith. Know what you believe and why you believe it. Don't go the way of this world that says everything is fine and you're okay and you're going up the same mountain as everyone else and God's at the top and everything's going to be fabulous once you get there. No. Jesus said that no one could come to the Father except through Him. Stand firm.

Be courageous and strong. Jesus said that He was the only way, but the world will say you have to be tolerant—that everybody can have his or her own way to God. Stand firm. You don't have to be arrogant, but you can be humble and speak the truth in love and not compromise your beliefs. That's what He's asked each of us to do.

Do you have courage? Not in your own strength but in His strength you will win the battle. He's promised never to leave you, never to forsake you, and to be with you to the very end. He will give you everything you need for the task He sets before you.

Stand strong in Christ.

"Be strong and courageous, all you who put your hope in the Lord!"
(Psalm 31:24, *NLT*).

January 3

Are you prepared for the battles that lie ahead?

This time of year, many people struggle with depression and discouragement. Maybe Christmas didn't turn out exactly the way you hoped, or maybe you're feeling some apprehension about what might be coming in the new year.

Even if things look really good right now, hold on—the outlook will change. There *will* be battles ahead. Jesus said that we will have troubles in this world and that everyone who follows Him will suffer, but He also promised that He is much greater than the world. We have a word of promise that God, regardless of what we face, will be with us through everything.

I just want to remind you, as this new year begins, that the victory is yours in Christ!

> Now it is God who makes both us and you stand firm in Christ. He anointed us, set His seal of ownership on us, and put his Spirit in our hearts as a deposit, guaranteeing what is to come (2 Corinthians 1:21-22).

You need to be prepared for the battles, and I pray that God will equip you and strengthen you in your inner being so that you can be all that God wants you to be in the coming days. He wants you to be victorious this year; He wants to strengthen you; He wants to help you; He wants you to prosper and succeed in Him.

Thank God for the opportunity of knowing Him, serving Him and loving Him. Grab hold of His promises. Ask Him to equip you for the battles that lie ahead. Thank Him for His promise of victory.

Arm me for battle, Lord. I belong to You. Make me stand strong in Christ!

January 4

The wisdom of Proverbs 19:21 tells us, "Many are the plans in a man's heart, but it is the LORD's purpose that prevails."

You may have many plans for this new year—goals you want to reach and dreams you would like to make reality. And that's okay. But remember that it will be the Lord's purpose that prevails. So as you make your plans, consult God.

God has plans, too! He says clearly in His Word that He knew you before you were knit together in your mother's womb; He has plans for you; you were created for a specific purpose and you are chosen, called and appointed. That's one of the reasons for this devotional: to help you hear God's plans for you so that you can walk obediently and humbly with your Creator.

Pray this prayer today as you think about and plan for this new year:

Lord, I want to do Your will.
So I want these plans to be Your plans, not mine.
And I want to be available to be part of Your plans.
I want to do what You want me to do, not what I want to do,
so that I can represent You well wherever I go.

And then look forward to a great new year!

You have a part in God's work in this world! Ask Him to teach you how to represent Him well.

January 5

What are you facing today? What difficulty lies ahead of you? What problem are you struggling through? What trial or challenge looms ahead?

Through the apostle Paul, Jesus says that we can do all things if we trust in Him:

> I can do all things through Christ who strengthens me (Philippians 4:13, *NKJV*).

That's a really great word of encouragement. Does it say we can do some things? A few things? No! When we rely on Christ for strength, we can do *all* things.

No matter what comes today, Christ's going to give you the strength to face it. If you trust Him, you belong to Him. He lives in you. He has equipped you and filled you with His Spirit. And He is going to give you the strength you need today.

Nobody can defeat you in Jesus Christ, not even the devil and all his demons. Christ said that He would give you the strength to stand. Hold on to that promise today and live it out.

When you feel as if you don't have the strength you need, say, *Lord, I'm gonna claim that promise You gave me that I can do all things. Give me the strength to do this.*

And He will do it.

Pit Stop
POWER

The Lord says to His people, "I am the Lord, your God, who takes hold of your right hand and says to you, 'Do not fear; I will help you'" (Isaiah 41:13).

January 6

I stood in a prison cell in Philippi where Paul was supposedly held a prisoner. From that cell, he penned these words to the church:

> I will continue to rejoice, for I know that through your prayers and the help given by the Spirit of Jesus Christ, what has happened to me will turn out for my deliverance. I eagerly expect and hope that I will in no way be ashamed, but will have sufficient courage so that now as always Christ will be exalted in my body, whether by life or by death (Philippians 1:18-20).

What a great word from Paul! He knew that death was a possibility, yet he took courage from prayers offered for him and from help given to him by the Spirit of Jesus Christ. Whatever happened to him, his hope was that Christ would be exalted.

Take courage today. Maybe a serious health issue is plaguing you, family conflicts have erupted or you are even being persecuted because of your faith. Whatever your problem is, put your hope in Christ. Be courageous. Take heart, for through your prayers and the help of the Spirit of Jesus Christ, you will have full courage—and Christ will be honored.

"God did not give us a spirit of timidity, but a spirit of power, of love and of self-discipline" (2 Timothy 1:7).

January 7

My prayer for you is from Colossians 1:11:

> Be strengthened with all his glorious power so that you will have all the patience and endurance you need (*NLT*).

Shortly after I committed my life to Christ, a friend shared five things with me to help me in my walk with the Lord. I want to share them with you today.

First, set aside some time every day to spend with Christ.

Second, find a good church. You need the fellowship of believers.

Third, tell others what Christ has done for you. Represent Him well, not only with your words but also with your life.

Fourth, get involved in a small group—a band of brothers or sisters that will hold you accountable.

Fifth, if you have a family, set aside some time every day to read the Scriptures and pray together.

If you've committed your life to the Lord, His desire for you is spiritual growth and maturity. These five things will help you in your walk with Him and will help you as you seek to stand firm in your faith.

Pit Stop PRAYER

"Teach me your ways, O LORD, that I may live according to your truth! Grant me purity of heart, that I may honor you" (Psalm 86:11, *NLT*).

January 8

On this journey through life, we are to learn to stand. Ephesians 6:13 tells followers of Jesus Christ to "put on the full armor of God, so that when the day of evil comes, you may be able to stand your ground, and after you have done everything, to stand."

Are you standing strong for the Lord?

Remind yourself daily of the words in 1 Peter 5:8: "Be self-controlled and alert. Your enemy the devil prowls around like a roaring lion looking for someone to devour." The *King James Version* reads, "Be vigilant."

My friend, the devil really is walking around, seeking whom he may devour. And in order for us to stand when evil comes against us, we need to be on guard and be men and women of the Word. The Word equips us in our inner being. During Jesus' time in the wilderness, He used the Word to fight Satan's strong temptations.

Dr. Charles H. Spurgeon wrote, "A man who has his Bible at his fingers' ends and in his heart's core is a champion in [any conflict]."[1]

Jesus Christ wants to live through you and wants you to stand strong for Him. The Word gives you strength and encouragement and enables you to stand and represent Jesus wherever you are.

Keep your eyes on Him, hide His Word in your heart, and be vigilant.

The Bible says that the Word of God is the sword of the Spirit. Take up the sword, and the Spirit will use it for victory.

January 9

When the devil comes alongside you and tries to bring you down, what do you do?

God is able to give you the strength to stand firm. I cannot stand by my own strength; you cannot stand by your own strength. But each of us can stand in the strength of Jesus. On our own, there's no way we can win the battle; but if we put our faith and hope in God alone, we'll find that:

> No temptation has seized you except what is common to man. And God is faithful; he will not let you be tempted beyond what you can bear. But when you are tempted, he will also provide a way out so that you can stand up under it (1 Corinthians 10:13).

You are in a battle; the battle is real, and the devil wants to devour and destroy. Jesus said that He came to give us "life and have it abundantly" (John 10:10, *ESV*). But the enemy comes to steal and kill and destroy. That's the battle that's going on.

The victory is yours as you walk with Jesus! As you stand in Jesus, He gives you strength, He equips you, He fills you, and He empowers you so that you can be victorious. You know how this story ends: Because Jesus has already defeated sin, you're going to win!

Trust Jesus, clasp His hand in yours, and keep your eye on Him.

Pit Stop PROMISE

Jesus knows you have troubles in this world, but He promised that He will help you overcome anything the world throws at you (see John 16:33). If you remain in Him, He'll give you the strength for victory.

January 10

> When I think of all [the troubles that you might face in this world], I fall to my knees and pray to the Father, the Creator of everything in heaven and on earth. I pray that from His glorious, unlimited resources, He will empower you with inner strength through His Spirit (see Ephesians 3:14-16).

If you belong to Christ, He wants to work in your life to strengthen you so that you can stand strong for Him, so that you can mature in your walk with Him, and so that you can be victorious in this life.

Jesus didn't come into your life to die for you and then abandon you and let you live out your life in defeat. He came into your life to save you, to redeem you and to help you become everything He wants you to be. He has plans for you; there are things He wants to do in you and through you for His honor and His glory.

He will work by His power—not by your power or your creativity or your winsomeness. Thank God for all the gifts and talents He's given you, but remember it is His power working in you that enables you to be victorious.

As you go about your day today, just think about the fact that God, in the power of His Spirit, is in you to strengthen you so that you can be who He wants you to be.

God has put His Spirit within you and has begun a work in you. As you learn to know Him better and better, you become more and more what He wants you to be.

January 11

> Let your roots grow down into him, and let your lives be built on him. Then your faith will grow strong in the truth you were taught, and you will overflow with thankfulness.
>
> COLOSSIANS 2:7, NLT

Colossians 2:7 is a great word. How much courage this should give us!

Let your roots grow down into Him. What are you doing to send your roots down into God? Know His Word—study it, memorize it, meditate on it. Spending time with Him will send your roots deeper every day, and you'll grow in your walk with Him.

Let your lives be built on Him. Don't build your life on sinking sand. Build on the Rock that provides a solid foundation for your faith. The world builds on so many things that fade away; build on what will endure forever.

Your faith will grow strong in the truth you were taught. Jesus said that He is the truth (see John 14:6). If your roots are growing ever deeper into Him, your faith will grow ever stronger.

You will overflow with thankfulness. Today, let thankfulness overflow in your life. Thank God for His goodness, His provision and the fact that He left the glory of heaven and came to this earth to be your Savior so that you could live this life with courage and strength. Think about all He has already done for you—and He has plans for far more than you can even imagine. Let thankfulness overflow in your life!

Today, enjoy living in God's strength and courage.

> Jesus said that without Him, you can do nothing; but if you keep your eyes on Him, your joy will overflow and you'll produce much fruit and bring glory to God (see John 15:5).

January 12

What are you up against today? Maybe you see a mountain ahead of you and wonder, *Man, how am I going to deal with* that? It could be a deadline or a medical issue or a financial challenge. And before long, you just feel overwhelmed with anguish and frustration.

I want to encourage you to keep walking by faith. Now, I know you can't ignore the reality of what's going on around you. The mountain is still there, facing you, and you can't be the proverbial ostrich that sticks its head in the sand. But it's been my experience that, if I keep my eyes focused on Jesus and continue walking by faith, He can take me to the other side in victory.

Jesus is the author and finisher of our faith. He has promised that He will never leave us or forsake us and will see us through to the very end. We don't need to live in defeat and despair. He will help us conquer every mountain, because His plan is for us to experience victorious Christian living as a way of life.

You can't conquer the mountains on your own; you don't have the strength to do it. But Jesus does have the strength, and He wants to use His strength to conquer your mountains—if you will put your hope and your trust in Him.

If there's a mountain ahead of you today, call out to Jesus who is your strength, "O LORD, do not stay far away! You are my strength; come quickly to my aid!" (Psalm 22:19, *NLT*).

King David wrote, "As soon as I pray, you answer me; you encourage me by giving me strength" (Psalm 138:3, *NLT*). Pray! God's strength will help you climb that mountain.

January 13

We need to be in a constant state of prayer: "Pray without ceasing" (1 Thessalonians 5:17, *KJV*). But how do we do that? We can't be on our knees all day long.

What Paul means is that we live in an *attitude* of prayer. We commune with our Lord throughout the day. Whatever comes our way, our automatic response is to first take it to Him.

> *Lord, I need Your help.*
> *Lord, give me direction.*
> *Lord, I need Your guidance on this situation.*
> *Lord, how do I handle this?*
> *Lord, what should I do?*
> *Lord, give me the right words to say.*

Being in constant communication with God becomes a part of you, a way of life. You ask Him for and about specific things. You don't just let life happen to you. You don't take on life in your own strength and power, but you learn to live in such communion with God that you're always aware that He is with you. He is the friend who sticks closer than a brother or sister. He will never leave you. And He's there to strengthen and help you so that you can be all He wants you to be.

Pray without ceasing today.

Pit Stop
PRACTICE

When something exciting happens, the first thing we usually want to do is call a friend and share our good news. When we face a problem, we usually unburden to someone close to us. Well, God loves you with a love greater than that of any family member or friend, and He is with you every moment. Talk to Him about everything.

January 14

After His baptism, Jesus went into the wilderness and fasted for 40 days. He was physically tired and hungry when Satan came to Him with temptations.

Satan hits us at our weakest times, too. When we feel pressured or exhausted or overwhelmed, the enemy attacks.

When you are tempted, remember that the Holy Spirit is present with you. If you know Christ in a personal way, you are the dwelling place of God. And He has said that no temptation will ever come your way without Him giving you the strength to deal with it.

> "Get out of here, Satan," Jesus told [the devil]. "For the Scriptures say, 'You must worship the Lord your God and serve only Him'" (Matthew 4:10, *NLT*).

Take a lesson from Jesus. When you're tempted, even when you feel as if you're already defeated, say, "Get out of here, Satan. Leave me alone. I belong to Jesus." Those are powerful words, my friend.

Jesus is your Rock, and you can run to Him. He is your always present help in times of trouble, and He's stronger than any enemy!

"Resist the devil, and he will flee from you" (James 4:7, *NLT*).

Pit Stop — POINT TO PONDER

You have taken up the sword of the Spirit as you read the Scriptures in this devotional today. The Spirit will use that sword when the devil tempts you.

January 15

When I first went to Romania almost 30 years ago, the country was still under the rule of Communism. I met people who had been persecuted for their faith, and I saw a depth of commitment in them that I longed for. I'm convinced, even to this day, that this level of commitment comes only through endurance under persecution; it can't be experienced in any other way.

> Although the Lord gives you the bread of adversity and the water of affliction, your teachers will be hidden no more; with your own eyes you will see them. Whether you turn to the right or to the left, your ears will hear a voice behind you, saying, "This is the way; walk in it" (Isaiah 30:20-21).

You may not be persecuted in the same way my friends in Romania have been. But you do have to eat the bread of adversity and drink the water of affliction at times in your life. Trouble falls. It rains on the just and the unjust.

Through it all, you can depend on this: If you will keep your eyes and your heart focused on God, He will say to you, "This is the way, walk in it." What a way to live!

If you're facing adversity today—and even if things are going well—listen for His voice saying, "This is the way; walk in it."

Pit Stop
PROMISE

God says to His people, "I am the LORD your God, who teaches you what is best for you, who directs you in the way you should go" (Isaiah 48:17). Ask Him to teach you—in good times and bad.

January 16

Is your life built on a firm foundation? Or are you tossed and turned by all of your troubles and problems and everything else that life throws at you? If you build your life on Jesus and the Word of God, then—as John Keith wrote in his hymn "How Firm a Foundation"—you will have all of the strength of God with you at all times:

> How firm a foundation, ye saints of the Lord,
> Is laid for your faith in His excellent Word!
> What more can He say than to you He hath said,
> To you who unto Jesus for refuge have fled?
>
> Fear not, I am with thee, oh, be not dismayed,
> For I am thy God and will still give thee aid;
> I'll strengthen and help thee, and cause thee to stand
> Upheld by My righteous, omnipotent hand.
>
> When through the deep waters I call thee to go,
> The rivers of woe shall not thee overflow;
> For I will be with thee, thy troubles to bless,
> And sanctify to thee thy deepest distress.

Listen to God's promises to you, His chosen child: "Do not fear, for I am with you; do not be dismayed, for I am your God" (Isaiah 41:10). "When you pass through the waters, I will be with you" (Isaiah 43:2). "Never will I leave you; never will I forsake you" (Hebrews 13:5).

Oh, my friend, these are God's promises for all of us. Trust Him to be your firm foundation.

Pit Stop PROMISE

Listen to God's voice always saying, "Never will I leave you; never will I forsake you." Your faith can stand strong on that promise.

January 17

> He gives strength to the weary and increases the power of the weak. Even youths grow tired and weary, and young men stumble and fall; but those who hope in the LORD will renew their strength. They will soar on wings like eagles; they will run and not grow weary, they will walk and not be faint.
>
> ISAIAH 40:29-31

What a promise! If you're feeling weary, if you're feeling faint, if you think all your strength is gone, where do you turn? That's when you turn to the Lord, my friend.

Look to Jesus and live. And if you will spend time with Him and look to Him, He'll renew your strength. If you will look to Jesus, He will meet your every need.

You might be climbing a mountain of troubles and think you can't keep climbing even one more day. Maybe you've been tormented with questions or doubts. Perhaps you don't feel assured of your salvation. Or maybe things are going very well for you right now. Wherever you are, if you look to Jesus and ask Him to speak into your life, ask Him to show Himself strong in you, I promise you, He will answer your prayer.

Stop just a moment and say, *Lord Jesus, please speak to me. Please help me in whatever I face today.*

Pit Stop PRAYER

The Holy Spirit is a comforter, encourager, helper and teacher. Jesus sent that Spirit to live in you! Ask Him for help and comfort today.

January 18

A friend asked me to pray for him. When I asked him what to pray, he replied, "I just feel like the devil is tempting me and beating up on me."

Do you feel like that? Do you need encouragement because the devil always seems to be discouraging you? Do you feel surrounded and under siege by forces that are enemies of your soul?

Put on the armor of God every morning before you leave the house, my friend. Take some time today to read Ephesians 6:10-18, and then make a quick list that you tape on a mirror or by your door as a reminder, so you can say aloud, "Lord, I put on the helmet of salvation. I put on the breastplate of righteousness and the belt of truth and the shoes of the gospel. I'm taking up my shield of faith." And then, friend, pick up your sword—the Word of God.

After His baptism, Jesus went into the wilderness and fasted for 40 days. He was physically tired and hungry when Satan came to Him with temptations. But each time, Jesus began His rejection of the temptation by saying "It is written."

Scripture says that hiding God's Word in our hearts will help us withstand temptation. In Ephesians 6:17, Paul says that the Word is the sword the Spirit uses to defend against the enemy. To hide the Word within us, to be able to use that sword, we need to know what is written; we need to know what God's Word says.

So at the beginning of this new year, I challenge you to develop some new patterns. Spend time daily in God's Word. Hide it in your heart (remember God's promises and memorize some of the verses) and give the Spirit a sword sharp and true to use against the enemy.

As you read God's Word, make this your daily prayer: "Guide my steps by your word, so I will not be overcome by evil" (Psalm 119:133, *NLT*).

January 19

> Physical training is of some value, but godliness has value for all things, holding promise for both the present life and the life to come.
>
> 1 TIMOTHY 4:8

You know, I think that today physical training has been taken to the extreme. Don't get me wrong; fitness is a good thing. I try to go to the gym on a regular basis, and I walk and exercise daily. I believe we have to take care of our "tents" in which we live—these tabernacles God has given us to dwell in here on earth—and I do want to take care of this body. But one phenomenon of the current age is the explosion of fitness centers.

Scripture says that godliness is of far greater value than physical training, because one day the bodies in which we live are going to die while the real me and the real you will live on forever.

Godliness holds promise for both your physical life and your spiritual life. Because it is true that "[your] body is a temple of the Holy Spirit," you should take good physical care of it (1 Corinthians 6:19). But because your physical body will last no more than the span of your years here on earth, how much more important should be training that part of yourself that will live on in the next life. God wants to conform your inner being to the image of Christ. Becoming more like Christ is becoming more godly; and godliness has effects that will go on forever.

Today, look for specific ways you can be more like the Master. Then ask the Spirit to help you make whatever changes are necessary.

How can you keep fit spiritually? What kind of "fitness" regimen will help you train in godliness?

January 20

We have this hope as an anchor for the soul, firm and secure.
HEBREWS 6:19

How's your hope today? Are you a person of hope? If you know Christ and He is living in you, you have a hope that will anchor your soul and will keep you firm and secure, no matter what storms and battles you face. Do you remember the old hymn "In Times Like These": "In times like these you need a Savior, in times like these you need an anchor; be very sure, be very sure your anchor holds and grips the solid Rock!"

Where have you dropped your anchor? Is it holding? If you've anchored yourself to the Lord Jesus Christ, your anchor will hold, regardless of what comes. Wind, rain, storms, sickness, pain—whatever may come—the solid Rock will hold you.

Your hope is not built on your own strength or abilities. Your hope is not built on any security you can build yourself. If you're going through a tough time, it's easy to become discouraged if you're focusing on what's going on in the world around you.

But, my friend, you have a firm and secure hope. You can't have anything or anyone more solid to hold on to than the Lord Jesus Christ. He's promised never to leave you, never to forsake you, to be with you to the very end.

The question for you today is this: Is your anchor firm and secure in the Rock? Are you holding on to the hope that Jesus has given you as the anchor for your soul?

One of these days, you will face death, and you want your anchor to hold even then. Set your anchor deep in the solid Rock. He is the only One capable of securing you!

Pit Stop PROMISE

If you know Jesus, you can sink your hope anchor in Him. Jesus is the Rock who will always hold you secure.

January 21

Have you noticed that winning gracefully can be harder than losing gracefully? It was even necessary to create a rule in football against celebrating too much after a touchdown.

In his book *When the Game Is Over, It All Goes Back in the Box*, John Ortberg writes: "When I win, I'm tempted by arrogance, power, insensitivity, gloating, and wanting to relive my successes long after everyone else is bored by them. Graceful winners always remember what it feels like to lose. And they are caught up in something bigger than their own wins and losses."[2]

"Gracious winners always remember what it feels like to lose." You know, I can always pick out somebody who is struggling and be critical. Or I can look at that person and say to myself, *Except for the grace of God, there goes Steve Wingfield*. Where would I be today if God had not shown me mercy, if Jesus Christ had not loved me enough to pay for my sins?

The apostle Paul says that he worked harder than any other apostle, but only "by the grace of God I am what I am" (1 Corinthians 15:10). It was not his own effort but God's grace working through him that brought results.

Only the grace of God has brought you to where you are today. Thank God for His grace. Thank God too for His mercy, love and patience. Don't lose sight of who you could have been without Him. And then, make it your heart's desire to be all He created you to be.

Right now, thank Him for what He's done in your life.

Pit Stop
PRAISE

Lord, without Your mercy, I would have no forgiveness; without Your unconditional love, no healing; without Your promises, no hope or security. Without You, I am nothing. With a grateful heart, I give myself to You.

January 22

A suggestion for you today: Begin a new habit. Pray before you pray.

In Psalm 26:2, David says, "Test me, O LORD, and try me, examine my heart and my mind." That's a great prayer to pray—before you pray:

> *Lord, see if there's any wicked way in me. I want to pray with clean hands and a pure heart. Examine my heart and my mind, and if there's something that is blocking communication with You, convict me of it. If there's something I need to make right, let me know that, Lord, that I might pray with clean hands and a pure heart.*

If you confess your sin, God will forgive you and cleanse you from all its stain (see 1 John 1:9). If there are things in your life you feel guilty about, confess them to Him. Ask the Lord to forgive you. And then receive and accept His forgiveness so that, cleansed and forgiven, you can go before His throne and make your requests known to Him.

God wants you to pray with clean hands and a pure heart. And that can only happen through the blood of your Redeemer, Jesus Christ. He will cleanse you from every sin, He'll fill you afresh with His Spirit, and He'll clothe you in His own robes of righteousness so that you can come into the Lord's presence free and without stains.

Go to Jesus Christ today and ask Him for that cleansing of heart and mind.

Pit Stop
POINT TO PONDER

If you confess your sins, God not only forgives you but He also cleans away the stains left on your life.

January 23

Here's a great promise from 2 Thessalonians 3:3 (*NLT*): "The Lord is faithful; he will strengthen you and protect you from the evil one."

Jesus said that His Spirit living in us is greater than he who is in the world. The devil and all his demons cannot defeat us if we put our faith and trust in Christ alone.

Maybe you are down and discouraged today. Maybe you feel as though your prayers are bouncing off the ceiling. It's one thing to praise God on the mountaintop, but it's another thing to hold on to the reality that when you're walking through the darkest valleys He is there with you.

Even if your faith feels feeble today, the Lord is faithful! He *will* strengthen you. He *will* protect you from the evil one. "The LORD watches over all who love him" (Psalm 145:20).

If you are in need today, my friend, turn to the Lord. He's promised to meet your need. He's promised never to leave you, never to forsake you. Hold on to God's promises, and hold on to His hand.

Pit Stop
POINT TO PONDER

"Let us hold tightly without wavering to the hope we affirm, for God can be trusted to keep his promise" (Hebrews 10:23, *NLT*).

January 24

> Lift up your heads, O you gates; lift them up, you ancient doors, that the King of glory may come in. Who is he, this King of glory? The LORD Almighty—he is the King of glory. Selah.
>
> PSALM 24:9-10

Who is this King of glory? In his book *The Knowledge of the Holy,* A. W. Tozer writes:

> The doctrine of the Trinity ... is truth for the heart. The fact that it cannot be satisfactorily explained, instead of being against it, is in its favor. Such a truth had to be revealed; no one could have imagined it.[3]

You know, there are those who deny the Trinity. I read somewhere that those who try to explain it will lose their minds, and those who try to deny it will lose their souls.

When Jesus went back to heaven, He sent the Comforter, the third person of the Trinity, to meet your needs. Let Him take over the controls of your life. The Holy Spirit is not something to be feared. In fact, "Be filled with the Spirit" is a command from God (Ephesians 5:18).

Let the Spirit empower you, equip you, strengthen you. He wants you to experience the reality of all that the Spirit can give you.

Today, walk in the knowledge that the Holy Spirit lives in you!

Pit Stop
PROMISE

When you accepted Christ, you were born again. The Spirit gave that new life, and if you walk in step with Him, you will be transformed and fueled for victory by His power.

January 25

Listen to what Paul tells us in Romans 12:2:

> Don't let the world around you squeeze you into its own mould, but let God re-mould your minds from within, so that you may prove in practice that the plan of God for you is good, meets all his demands and moves towards the goal of true maturity (*Phillips*).

Are you maturing in Christ? Is it your heart's desire to become all that God created you to be?

Maturing takes place over a period of time. You are saved. And you are now being saved—that's the process of sanctification that takes place in your life as you grow in your walk with the Lord.

Our goal is true maturity in Christ. So keep your eyes on Him. Follow hard after Him. Spend time in His Word.

Take just a minute to read Romans 12:2 again.

Through the apostle Paul, God says that He has a plan, and part of that plan is that He will change us. One of my favorite verses is Philippians 1:6, the promise that God is going to carry on to completion the good work He's begun in you and in me. He began it; He's still working on me and you; and He will complete it. That's what He wants to do in your life and in mine.

So keep your eyes on God. Keep your eyes on His plan. Let Him shape you into the person He wants you to be, and He'll move you toward the goal of true maturity.

Pit Stop PROMISE

God is changing you, my friend, into what He wants you to be. Even on days when you think you have failed Him, He is working. He will not give up on you!

January 26

In Ephesians 4, Paul talks about Christ building up His Church, preparing His followers for works of service:

> Until we all reach unity in the faith and in the knowledge of the Son of God and become mature, attaining to the whole measure of the fullness of Christ. Then we will no longer be infants, tossed back and forth by the waves, and blown here and there by every wind of teaching and by the cunning and craftiness of men in their deceitful scheming (verses 13-14).

Attaining to the whole measure of the fullness of Christ. What would that be like, my friend, to know the full measure of Christ? This Scripture says plainly that He is moving us toward that!

We need to become mature, to grow in our faith, so that the enemy of our souls cannot deceive us.

If we learn to know Jesus better and spend time in His Word, we grow in our relationship with Him. And as we do that, we become more and more mature in our faith, and we will not be tossed about by every wind of doctrine that comes along. When we know what Scripture says and we stand firm on that, we are not misled by those who misrepresent Christ and His Word.

Check what you hear and read against the Word of God. Christ said He is the truth. As a follower of Christ, nourish yourself with His truth, desire to know Him better, and grow strong in your faith.

Pit Stop
POINT TO PONDER

Trying to divide your loyalty between God and the world will make you unstable and unable to grow toward a mature faith. Jesus said that He is "the way and the truth and the life" (John 14:6). If your loyalty is to His truth alone, you'll seek daily to know Him better, and your faith will mature and strengthen.

January 27

Make no mistake about it. We are in a battle. Whose side are you on? Are you going to stand on the Lord's side and win? Or are you going to be on the enemy's side and let him bring defeat and despair and death into your life?

The battle is real, my friend. Ephesians 6:10-11 encourages us to "be strong in the Lord and in His mighty power. Put on the full armor of God so that you can take your stand against the devil's schemes."

Just as God is the Creator who wants to make our life and testimony beautiful and wants us to experience His love, our adversary, the devil—Satan himself—is the destroyer. He's the thief, the enemy who's out to smash every beautiful thing God created us to do and to be. That's the battle that rages.

Equip yourself for the battle. Study and put on the armor God has provided. He promises, "I'll give you the strength to win."

Walk through today and this year on the side of victory!

Pit Stop
POINT TO PONDER

James writes, "Who can win this battle against the world? Only those who believe that Jesus is the Son of God" (1 John 5:5, *NLT*). The One you trust is the Son of the Creator of the universe! He promises you His power to defeat the evil powers of the world. Your faith in Him brings you victory.

January 28

> Who shall separate us from the love of Christ? Shall trouble or hardship or persecution or famine or nakedness or danger or sword? No, in all these things we are more than conquerors through him who loved us.
>
> ROMANS 8:35,37

I love the apostle Paul's attitude. Paul was able to look at whatever situation he was in and see God working: "I have learned how to be content whatever the circumstances" (Philippians 4:11). He knew that nothing separated him from God's love and that God worked for his good in every circumstance.

Whatever circumstance you're in, God has called you to stand firm in Him. I've known many people who suffered severe illnesses, even unto death, and the testimony of their lives spoke to hospital staff and those who visited them. I am convinced God used their testimonies in a powerful way, maybe even more powerfully than if those people had been healed and gotten up out of bed and walked away.

I've traveled in many parts of the world where people are persecuted because they follow Christ, and there's a dynamic in their walk with the Lord that I haven't seen anywhere else. It's apparent to these people that in *everything*, they are more than conquerors through Jesus Christ.

What part of Romans 8:35 can you identify with today? What's present in your life? Trouble? Hardship? Persecution? Financial problems? Sickness? Death? In *everything*, you can have victory through Jesus Christ. Whatever situation you find yourself in, God wants to use you there, and no circumstance will ever separate you from His love.

Pit Stop
PROMISE

"Neither death nor life, neither angels nor demons, neither our fears for today nor our worries about tomorrow—not even the powers of hell can separate us from God's love" (Romans 8:38, *NLT*). Stand firm on that promise!

January 29

You have been our dwelling place throughout all generations. Before the mountains were born or you brought forth the earth and the world, from everlasting to everlasting you are God.

PSALM 90:1-2

What an awesome thought it is to know that God thought about you and me and all of creation even before anything was created. Isaac Watts's hymn "O God, Our Help in Ages Past" captures this theme:

> O God, our help in ages past,
> Our hope for years to come,
> Our shelter from the stormy blast,
> And our eternal home.
>
> Under the shadow of Thy throne,
> Thy saints have dwelt secure;
> Sufficient is Thine arm alone,
> And our defense is sure.
>
> Before the hills in order stood,
> Or earth received her frame,
> From everlasting, Thou art God,
> To endless years the same.

God is our hope; He is our shield. We can put our faith and trust in Him, and He will guide our steps and be our sure defense.

Pit Stop PROMISE

In this world where nothing is certain, you can be sure of this: God is your help, your hope, your home.

January 30

> Therefore, my dear brothers, stand firm. Let nothing move you. Always give yourselves fully to the work of the Lord, because you know that your labor in the Lord is not in vain.
>
> 1 CORINTHIANS 15:58

Stand firm. Let nothing move you. Stand strong in what you believe. To be steadfast and immovable in your faith, you must know what you believe and why you believe it.

As a follower of Christ, you cannot compromise on certain things. Jesus is the only way of salvation. There is no other way. The Bible is the inspired, infallible Word of God. God is Lord of all creation.

I'm immovable on those things. I believe with all my heart, and I've cast my lot. I will not compromise these beliefs, and I would die for them. Be steadfast, my friend.

Give yourself fully to the work of the Lord. Don't be discouraged in well-doing, because God will give a harvest if you are faithful. Know that "nothing you do for the Lord is ever useless" (1 Corinthians 15:58, *NLT*). God's going to honor your commitment; He's going to honor your steadfastness. There will be a harvest.

You are His. Stand strong for Him. Work done for Him is never done in vain.

Pit Stop
POWER

Jesus said that the world would hate those who followed Him and that His followers would be betrayed and some would even be killed. But He promised, "Not a hair of your head will perish. By standing firm you will gain life" (Luke 21:18-19). Jesus holds you in His hands, and nothing can separate you from His love. Stand strong and gain life!

January 31

> Count yourselves dead to sin but alive to God in Christ Jesus. Therefore do not let sin reign in your mortal body so that you obey its evil desires. Do not offer the parts of your body to sin, as instruments of wickedness, but rather offer yourselves to God, as those who have been brought from death to life; and offer the parts of your body to him as instruments of righteousness. For sin shall not be your master, because you are not under law, but under grace.
>
> ROMANS 6:11-14

Romans 6:11-14 is packed with all kinds of help for us in our walk with the Lord. In verse 11 we learn we are dead to sin and alive to God in Christ. My friend, that is a fact!

When Christ died, He died to break the power of sin. Our old sinful selves were crucified with Him, too, "so that sin might lose its power in our lives" (Romans 6:6, *NLT*). So why should we allow any sin to reign in our mortal bodies? Consider that question.

Christ paid for your sins. Why should you give your body as an instrument for unrighteousness? You belong to God; present yourself to God as His instrument, to be used to bring Him honor and glory.

Walk in that truth today, my friend, and sin will not be your master. Stand firm!

Pit Stop
POWER

You are no longer a slave to your human nature! "Because you belong to [Christ], the power of the life-giving Spirit has freed you from the power of sin that leads to death" (Romans 8:2, *NLT*). You are free to live in step with the Spirit, and His power will give you the strength to endure and stand strong.

FEBRUARY

Obeying the Call

Go . . . and tell the people the full message of this new life.

ACTS 5:20

February 1

February is the month of hearts and valentines and flowers and candy. And love. This season of the year, like no other time, gives us an opportunity to exhibit the love of Christ. John writes in 1 John 4:9 about God's love for us:

> This is how God showed his love among us: He sent his one and only Son into the world that we might live through him.

God loves us and became human so that we could know Him and have victory in this life. Because He first showed such great love toward us, we show His love to others. Our mission as His representatives is to show His love to the world He died for.

Choose somebody to show the love of Christ to. Maybe it will be a homeless person, maybe someone in your church who cannot find a job, maybe somebody who has physical issues right now and can't get yard or farm work done. Look for a way to give yourself away in the name of Christ's love.

You might think you're just too overwhelmed with your own list of things that need to be done, but I can guarantee that if you will intentionally be a conduit of God's love, you will be the recipient of blessing. It never fails. God works in *you* when you love others.

Today, ask God to show you somebody who needs to see the love of God.

Pit Stop
POINT TO PONDER

"I am giving you a new commandment: Love each other. Just as I have loved you, you should love each other" (John 13:34, *NLT*). Jesus commanded this of every one of His followers. How has He loved you? In what ways can you love others as He loves?

February 2

What would be the greatest compliment you could ever receive? What would you like people to say about you?

Even more important than what people think about you is what the Lord thinks about you. So what would be the greatest compliment the Lord could give you?

You may debate me on this one, but here's my answer: One of the greatest compliments anyone, including God, could pay me would be to say what was said of Jesus in Luke 15:2: "This man welcomes sinners and eats with them."

In its original context, this remark was an accusation, not a compliment! The Pharisees were criticizing Jesus for associating with such sinful people: "This guy hangs out with sinners and even eats with them. Can you imagine?"

Jesus answered the criticism with several stories: one about a lost sheep, one about a lost coin, and one about a lost son. In each story, once whatever had been lost was found, there was great rejoicing over it.

This is what Jesus came for, my friend: He came to find all of us who were lost. Now we, as His representatives here, are called to also seek those who are lost. One of the greatest things we can do, I believe, is have people in our homes and share the gift of hospitality as a way of reaching out and welcoming sinners both into our space and into Jesus' presence.

Someone might accuse you of welcoming and eating with sinners. Oh, what a great compliment that would be!

Pit Stop
POINT TO PONDER

Now that you know Christ, you are part of His mission on this earth. You have a part in God's plan to bring people back to Himself.

STEVE WINGFIELD

February 3

Did Christ o'er sinners weep, and shall our cheeks be dry?
Let floods of penitential grief burst forth from every eye.

BENJAMIN BEDDOME, "DID CHRIST O'ER SINNERS WEEP?"

The words from Benjamin Beddome's hymn should cause us to examine our hearts. How long has it been since you cried over somebody who doesn't know Jesus?

Jesus did. He cried over a city whose citizens would not open their hearts to Him: "As he approached Jerusalem and saw the city, he wept over it" (Luke 19:41).

Christ wept over Jerusalem. That picture tells me of the urgency of the matter. It's not His will that any should perish; He wants all to repent and come to Him. His desire is that all people would live in relationship with Him.

He asks us to partner with Him in His ministry of reconciliation. Although we do that through praying for those who don't know Him, I believe He also wants us to share His compassion for the lost, to express an emotional connection with people who do not know Christ.

How long has it been since your emotions were touched because somebody is without Christ?

Today, ask the One who weeps over the lost to give you more of His compassion for those who do not know Him.

Pit Stop
PRAYER

Lord, open my eyes to see those around me as You see them and open my heart to love them as You do.

February 4

Are you a channel of God's blessing? He wants to use us to show His love and goodness to the world around us, but sometimes our channels get blocked.

One of the best things we can do when we spend time reading the Word and praying is to ask God to speak to us and put His finger on whatever issue is blocking our channel of His blessing. Ask Him what is keeping you from being the person you should be. Be honest with Him, and He'll be honest with you.

This is really a wonderful way to live. Because, you see, we can trust Him: "Before I formed you in the womb I knew you, before you were born I set you apart; I appointed you as a prophet to the nations" (Jeremiah 1:5). "I know the plans I have for you, . . . plans to prosper you and not to harm you, plans to give you hope and a future" (Jeremiah 29:11).

David recognized that God has always known every one of His creations: "All the days ordained for me were written in [God's] book before one of them came to be" (Psalm 139:16).

Isn't that powerful? God knew you even before you were in the womb. He planned every day of your life. He has plans for you. He wants to work in you, but in order for Him to do that, you have to be in communion with Him.

Set aside a portion of quiet time when you're not distracted and say, "God, speak to me, and if my channel is blocked, help me to know where so that we can work together to clear it away. I want to be that channel of blessing that You want me to be."

Pit Stop
PRAYER

"Put me on trial, LORD, and cross-examine me. Test my motives and my heart" (Psalm 26:2, *NLT*).

February 5

You know, we have a story to tell to the nations. We do. In Revelation 15:4, John writes, "All nations will come and worship before you, for your righteous acts have been revealed."

In 1896, H. Ernest Nichol wrote the hymn "We've a Story to Tell to the Nations," and every line of that hymn is true today, too. We have a story to tell that carries a message of new life. How desperately the world needs these truths!

> We've a story to tell to the nations,
> That shall turn their hearts to the right,
> A story of truth and mercy,
> A story of peace and light,
> A story of peace and light.
>
> We've a Savior to show to the nations,
> Who the path of sorrow has trod,
> That all of the world's great peoples
> Might come to the truth of God,
> Might come to the truth of God.

Today, think about how the story you have to tell could change one person's life—that one person that God will bring into your life today.

Pit Stop
POINT TO PONDER

Who in your life needs unconditional love and mercy? Who needs to hear the truth that God wants all of us to come back to Him? Will you be the one who tells that person the story?

February 6

One day, Jesus and His disciples had been so busy with all the people who came to see and talk with them that they had not even had time to eat. So the Lord suggested they get in a boat and find a quiet place to rest. But when Jesus and His disciples reached the shore, the crowds had run ahead and were waiting for them. Jesus saw the people with all their many needs and was moved by love for them:

> When Jesus landed and saw a large crowd, he had compassion on them, because they were like sheep without a shepherd. So he began teaching them many things (Mark 6:34).

God wants you to be a person of compassion, and here you can see Jesus modeling that for you. Compassion is giving of yourself to someone in need. There are all kinds of need around you, but when you look around and see a great need, you may wonder what you can do about it. You can do something, my friend, even if it's just to reach out with an offer of a cup of cold water given in Jesus' name. We all have the ability to do *something*.

Martin Luther King Jr. once said, "Everybody can be great, because anybody can serve. You don't have to have a college degree to serve.... You only need a heart full of grace. A soul generated by love."

We can talk to the world about Christ's love, but things really are more caught than taught; and if we exhibit compassion in the way we live, then our words will take on greater meaning, because we are living out the love of Christ in what we do.

Pit Stop
POINT TO PONDER

In the Gospel of Mark, a man with leprosy came to Jesus begging to be healed. "Moved with compassion, Jesus reached out and touched him" (Mark 1:41, *NLT*). May the Spirit of Christ move you with compassion so you are willing to touch others who need God's healing.

February 7

Peter and the apostles were once locked up in jail for preaching the message about Jesus. "But during the night an angel of the Lord opened the doors of the jail and brought them out. 'Go, stand in the temple courts," he said, "and tell the people the full message of this new life'" (Acts 5:19-20). At daybreak, they were back in the Temple, delivering the message of new life in Jesus. Shortly thereafter, Peter and the apostles were given a strict order to be quiet and not preach in Jesus' name. But they replied, "We must obey God rather than men!" (Acts 5:29). Their enemies were furious and wanted to kill them.

When I first went to Romania, I got into some trouble with the secret police because I was preaching. My friend Peter pounded on the desk of the chief of police and said, "We will obey God!"

I admit that made me a little nervous, because I didn't want to get locked up in a Romanian jail. I wanted to be able to go home. Then I realized that this man who was representing me was someone who had been beaten and persecuted—physically mistreated and almost killed—because he was a follower of Christ. Yet he said, "I'm going to obey God regardless of the consequences." And you know, with someone like that standing at your side, you just have to follow.

Now, I'm not looking to be a martyr. But I do want to be faithful to the Lord, whatever He asks me to do; and if push comes to shove, I must obey God. I pray that we will never experience such persecution, but whatever does happen, remember that above all God calls us to tell the message of new life in Christ, and we must obey Him.

Pit Stop
PROMISE

Jesus told His followers that every generation is to tell people everywhere about Him and make disciples. He knows there will be resistance, persecution and hatred toward this message. But He promised, "Be sure of this: I am with you always" (Matthew 28:20, *NLT*).

February 8

A woman who called herself Peace Pilgrim spent a good part of her life walking over 25,000 miles, talking, writing and encouraging people toward peace. She wrote this about obeying God:

> The purpose of problems is to push you toward obedience to God's laws, which are exact and cannot be changed. We have the free will to obey them or disobey them. Obedience will bring harmony, disobedience will bring you more problems.[4]

Did you ever think of problems as a way of pushing you toward obedience? We can choose to obey or disobey what God has asked us to do. But every choice we make has consequences. "Obedience will bring harmony, disobedience will bring you more problems."

What else does obedience bring to our lives? Take time to read Psalm 119, and listen to all the wonderful promises:

> I run in the path of your commands, for you have set my heart free (verse 32).

> Direct me in the path of your commands, for there I find delight (verse 35).

> I will never forget your precepts, for by them you have preserved my life (verse 93).

What a way to live! Run in the paths of obedience, my friend, with a free heart, delighting in God's commands.

Pit Stop PRAYER

Lord, You have set my heart free! I want to run in the path of Your commands, but I am so prone to wander. "Let thy goodness, like a fetter, bind my wandering heart to Thee" (Robert Robinson).

February 9

Sometimes you probably want to argue with God. He wants you to walk in obedience, but when He speaks, you might be tempted to have a mental argument with Him. "Did You really say this, Lord? Is that really what You meant?"

That reminds me of another discussion somebody got into a very long time ago. In the Garden, the enemy of God planted a seed of doubt in Eve's mind: "Did God really say . . . ?" (Genesis 3:1).

My friend, when God speaks, we need to obey. Do right and obey. Jesus said it again and again: "If anyone loves me, he will obey my teaching" (John 14:23). The refrain from one of my father's favorite songs sums this up: "Trust and obey, for there's no other way / To be happy in Jesus, but to trust and obey."

Dietrich Bonhoeffer wrote, "One act of obedience is better than one hundred sermons." Now, I like to preach, but obedience is better than sermons. When God speaks, we must obey.

So what is God asking you to do today? Are you resisting something He's called you to do? Are you arguing with Him?

Or will you trust God and obey?

Pit Stop
POINT TO PONDER

Think about these words from the song "Trust and Obey": "Then in fellowship sweet we will sit at His feet, or we'll walk by His side in the way." What a great way to live—in sweet friendship with the Lord! That fellowship comes from hearing Him, trusting Him, and obeying Him.

Your obedience is a measure of how much you trust Him.

February 10

Are you called?

Jesus said, "Therefore go and make disciples of all nations, baptizing them in the name of the Father and of the Son and of the Holy Spirit" (Matthew 28:19). This verse is known as the Great Commission.

There's a Great Commission text in each of the Gospels and also one in the book of Acts. Just prior to the Lord's ascension, Jesus told His disciples, "But ye shall receive power, after that the Holy Ghost is come upon you: and ye shall be witnesses unto me both in Jerusalem, and in all Judea, and in Samaria, and unto the uttermost part of the earth" (Acts 1:8, *KJV*).

You might be thinking those instructions were for the first disciples and not meant for anyone today. But if you know Christ in a personal way, you have been called by God to represent Him. You may not be a gifted teacher or a preacher or an evangelist, but if you believe in the name of Christ, you *are* called by God to be an effective witness for Him.

Many years ago, Dr. Bill Bright from Campus Crusade for Christ shared with me the definition of an effective witness: Someone who takes the initiative to present the claims of Christ in the power of the Holy Spirit and leaves the results to God.

You are called to be God's witness, an *effective* witness. Follow hard after Him, and represent Him well in all that you do.

Pit Stop
POINT TO PONDER

If you know Christ as your Lord, you bear His name. What witness will your life present to the world today?

February 11

> My word that goes out from my mouth: It will not return to me empty, but will accomplish what I desire and achieve the purpose for which I sent it.
>
> ISAIAH 55:11

God's Word is powerful. It is "sharper than any double-edged sword" (Hebrews 4:12). David knew that hiding God's Word in his heart was a guard against sin (see Psalm 119:11).

God's Word is powerful. His Word, my friend, will not return void. That means it will not be fruitless; it will accomplish its purpose. Think about His words, and then think about the words you use.

Our words are powerful, too. We can't put them back in once they go out. Each of us knows that. Each of us has learned that from painful experiences—times when we've said something we should have stifled, and our words wounded and distressed another person.

God says His Word will always accomplish His purpose. He has called you to be one of those who send forth His Word. His Word will work with power, and you have been given the privilege of letting it work through you.

Today, think about being a conduit of God's Word. Let the power of His Word work in you as you reach out to the world around you.

Pit Stop
POINT TO PONDER

Some followers decided that Jesus' teaching was too hard for them and turned away, but Peter declared his loyalty. He recognized that Jesus alone had "the words that give eternal life" (John 6:68, *NLT*). Christ has not only saved you, but He has also called you to be His partner in spreading those words that give eternal life.

February 12

Years ago, I did a crusade in Kansas. One morning, I woke up and looked out the window and saw at least eight combines crawling across an immense wheat field, harvesting the heavy heads of grain. The scene reminded me of what Jesus said about fields being ready for harvest, so I picked up the *King James* Bible left by the Gideons in my motel room and read John 4:35: "Look on the fields; for they are white already to harvest."

I looked out the window again, and those combines were still going through the *golden*—not white—field. I went to my own *NIV* Bible, and John 4:35 read, "Open your eyes and look at the fields! They are ripe for harvest." That made sense.

But later that day, I was in a pastor's office, and together we looked up John 4:35 in the original Greek. The original Greek word means "white." So I was back to square one. Why did Jesus say the fields were white? That night at the crusade, I was talking to a retired Kansas wheat farmer, and I asked him what "white already to harvest" meant. Why would a wheat field be described as white?

I've never forgotten his response. "Well, that's easy, son," he said. "That means it's almost too late."

"What do you mean?"

"Maybe because of weather, because of sickness, or for whatever reason, the farmer was not able to get in and harvest his crop at the peak of harvest. Then it loses that golden luster and takes on a dullish white color. You can still go out and get a harvest, but a lot of it is going to fall out and be trampled underfoot."

The old farmer nodded his head and said, "The Lord was trying to get our attention and say, 'Get busy.'"

Pit Stop PRAYER

Lord, wake me up. Pull me out of the trap of a busy schedule and open my eyes to see the harvest that is ready for You. Then give me a little shove to get busy.

February 13

Tomorrow is Valentine's Day, so let's prepare ourselves by looking at what John had to say about love. Actually, he said quite a bit in his three little books toward the end of the New Testament. For instance, in 1 John 3:18 he wrote:

> Dear children, let's not merely say that we love each other; let us show the truth by our actions.

So here's my suggestion. This Valentine's Day, do not love with only words or flowers or candy or some other special gift. Those things are okay, but also think of ways you can show real love by your actions. Think about it. Be creative and do something very, very special that will communicate your love.

You know, in 1 Corinthians 13—that chapter we've come to call the "Love Chapter"—Paul talked about what love is; and everything he listed there is an action: what we *do* and how we *act* toward others. Love is patient, kind, not rude or selfish or irritable; it does not hold a grudge, is happy when truth wins, always hopes, and endures through everything.

This may be the greatest gift we can give: a love that *acts out* 1 Corinthians 13.

Pit Stop
PRACTICE

Think of 1 Corinthians 13 as a workout regimen for your heart. Practice the actions you find there. Practice patience and kindness; practice letting go of grudges; practice hope and truth and endurance. Practice love, and it will grow stronger.

February 14

I love the story in Acts 8 about Philip and the Ethiopian eunuch. An angel came to Philip and told him, "Go south to the desert road that goes to Gaza." So Philip "started out." He didn't debate or argue or ask why. He did what he was told to do.

On the road, he saw a man riding in a chariot, a person who was evidently wealthy and of some importance. The Spirit said to Philip, "Go to that chariot and stay near it." When Philip approached, he heard the man reading from Isaiah, and he asked, "Do you understand what you're reading?"

"How can I, unless somebody explains it?" The stranger invited Philip to ride in the chariot with him, and Philip had the opportunity to explain the message of the cross.

One of the keys of being an effective witness is listening and asking good questions. Philip listened first of all to the message from God. He must have been tuned in to listening for the Spirit's voice. He did what he was told, and God used Him to bring someone to Christ. He also listened and then asked a simple question of the person who was seeking truth. Learn to ask good questions. Listen and be observant.

I've been sharing my faith as a way of life for almost 40 years, and I've never had anybody get mad at me. I've had people say they don't want to talk about it, and then I have to respect that. But my goal is to leave a sweet taste in their mouths as a result of our encounters. That's what an effective witness is. If we take the initiative to present the claims of Christ by the power of the Holy Spirit, He will give us results.

Today, listen, ask good questions, and be prepared to give an answer.

Pit Stop
PROMISE

God told the shepherd Moses to lead His people out of Egypt, but Moses was unwilling. God's response? "Go! I'll be with you, and I'll tell you what to say." That is God's promise to you today. His Spirit will teach you what to say and when to say it, and His command is still "Go!"

February 15

Jesus says, "You did not choose me, but I chose you and appointed you to go and bear fruit—fruit that will last" (John 15:16). God wants to use you to bear much fruit.

Are you saying, "But I'm just an usher" or "I'm just a Sunday School teacher" or "I'm just on the hospitality committee"? Remember that if your branch is connected to the Vine, the Vine uses your branch to bear much fruit (see John 15:1-17).

Charles Richard Kimble was "just a Sunday School teacher" who was burdened for one of the students in his class, so he went by the young man's place of work to talk with him. Later that day, that young man went back into the stockroom and knelt down and gave his life to Christ. That young man was D. L. Moody, and God used him to proclaim Christ all over the world.

Most people don't know who Charles Richard Kimble was, but God used him to reach someone who would become a giant in the faith.

God wants to use you, too. Do not say, "I'm just a . . ." No, you're not "just a . . ." You are a child of God. You are called to be His representative, and He wants to use you for His honor and His glory and the advancement of His kingdom.

Whatever God has given you to do today, be faithful. That's all He asks you to do. He will produce the fruit, if you are faithful.

Pit Stop
POWER

Hear Jesus' words to you today: "I am the vine, and you are the branches. If you stay connected to me, you'll bear the fruit I desire. But without me, you can't do anything" (see John 15:5).

February 16

D. L. Moody once said that he saw people with a big *L* on their foreheads until he knew whether they were lost or saved.

A few years ago, I went into a place that was surely one of the darkest places I've ever been. Meeting the people there made me sad. Many of them were addicted and locked in bondage, with no hope. I felt the heart of Jesus for these people, a heart of compassion; and I prayed that God would release them from their captivity.

> When [Jesus] saw the crowds, he had compassion on them, because they were harassed and helpless, like sheep without a shepherd. Then he said to his disciples, "The harvest is plentiful but the workers are few. Ask the Lord of the harvest, therefore, to send out workers into his harvest field" (Matthew 9:36-38).

Are you praying the prayer Jesus commanded? How do you look at this world around you? God wants us to see the world as He sees it. He wants us to pray for the harvest.

Today, pray that He will give you eyes to see the world as He does and a heart to feel the compassion of Jesus for harassed and helpless sheep without a shepherd.

Pit Stop PRAYER

Lord Jesus, give me Your heart of compassion. Forgive me for ignoring the needs around me, and make me a more willing and courageous partner in Your work here in this world.

February 17

A personal question today: Do you believe there is a hell, a place of eternal separation from God?

If we really, truly believe that hell is a place of eternal punishment, outer darkness and unquenchable fire, how can we not weep over those who will enter that Christ-less place?

Remember the story in Luke 16 about Lazarus and the rich man? From a place of torment in the flames, the rich man could see Abraham and Lazarus, far away; and he called out, "Father Abraham, have pity on me and send Lazarus to dip the tip of his finger in water and cool my tongue, because I am in agony in this fire" (verse 24). But Abraham told him the chasm between them was too wide, and there was no longer any hope for the rich man.

And there in hell the rich man became an evangelist. He was concerned about his father and his brothers who were still living. "Go tell them," he pleaded, "so that they won't come to this place" (see verses 27-28). But Abraham knew they would not listen; they had not listened to Moses and the prophets, and they would not listen even to someone who rose from the dead with a warning message for them.

Jesus rose from the dead, and the lost world is still not listening. But Jesus has called you to use every available means to reach every available person. You are called. Go in Jesus' name.

Pit Stop
PRACTICE

Maybe you are timid about speaking to lost loved oneabout Jesus. You may wonder what to say, or you may be afraid of their reactions, or you may not want to be thought of as a religious nut. Ask the Lord to teach you what to say and how to say it. Ask Him for just one small opening today to tell someone what a difference Jesus has made in your life. Then be faithful, and when He gives you that opening, speak up! Tell someone how God has changed your life.

February 18

Elton Trueblood, a great theologian and author, once wrote, "Evangelism is not a professional job for a few trained men, but is, instead, the unrelenting responsibility of every person who belongs to the company of Jesus."

Do you belong to the company of Jesus? Have you invited Him to come into your life and asked Him to forgive your sins? If that is the case, my friend, it is your responsibility to tell others of His love and forgiveness. It is the *unrelenting* responsibility of all who know Christ—a responsibility we can't get away from, a responsibility that should motivate us, challenge us and call us to do everything we can to tell others about the importance of inviting Christ into their lives, too.

Jesus said, "You will be my witnesses" (Acts 1:8). Wherever we are, we're to tell people about Jesus.

If you have neighbors or family or friends or work associates who do not know Jesus, pray for them. Pray that God will begin to speak into their lives. Pray that God would use you as His representative to touch their hearts. Pray that they might come to know this Christ who loves us—and who put upon us an unrelenting responsibility to proclaim Him until He comes again.

Pit Stop
POINT TO PONDER

If you belong to the company of Jesus, He has made you a new person, given you a new life and brought you back to God. All of that was a gift of His love and grace; He provided a way for the world to come back to Him. Now He also gives you a part in His plan: You are a partner in Jesus' ministry of reconciliation.

STEVE WINGFIELD

February 19

Two thousand years ago, Jesus went to the cross for a purpose. That purpose was to pay the price for the sins of all of humanity. God loved the world so much that He gave His Son to die so that everyone might have everlasting life. Now He wants the nations to know about His salvation:

> May your ways be known throughout the earth, your saving power among people everywhere (Ps. 67:2, *NLT*).

That's the heart of God, my friend; and He has given us the responsibility of proclaiming Christ till He returns.

Not everybody has a gift of evangelism, but all of us are called to be an effective witness and to hasten the spread of the gospel. I want to challenge you today to think of ways you can be used by God to make known His power to save. As you do that, you will be fulfilling His heart, which is spreading salvation among all nations.

In your walk today, use every available means to reach every available person. Some opportunities are big, some are small; but God has placed you where you are today for a purpose—for His purpose. He wants people everywhere to know Him, and you are called to make His ways known.

Pit Stop
POINT TO PONDER

"So we are Christ's ambassadors; God is making his appeal through us. We speak for Christ when we plead, 'Come back to God!'" (2 Corinthians 5:20, *NLT*).

February 20

In the book of Acts, you can read stories of the early Christians who were inflamed with the desire and urgency to tell the good news about Jesus: "All the believers were one in heart and mind. No one claimed that any of his possessions was his own, but they shared everything they had. With great power the apostles continued to testify to the resurrection of the Lord Jesus, and much grace was upon them all" (Acts 4:32-33).

In another Bible translation, verse 32 says that they were "all together in one accord." They were unified in heart and mind for the purpose of spreading the gospel of Jesus Christ. They testified with great power, and much grace was on them all. What an exciting time that must have been!

We live during a time when the news about Jesus Christ is just as urgently needed. The world does not know Jesus; oh, that we would unite our hearts with fellow believers to partner with the Lord and be channels of His blessing to a world in desperate need!

That's your calling, my friend. God wants to use you to be that channel. His power and grace will work in and through you as you work to expand the kingdom.

Spend time with God today so that you will have the resources you need to expand the Kingdom exponentially using every available means to reach every available person.

Pit Stop
PRAYER

Father, open my eyes to see opportunities for action in the ministry You've given me, the ministry of bringing those in darkness to You, the Light who gives life. May it be Your words that come out of my mouth and Your love that motivates what I do.

February 21

Margaret Clarkson, a teacher in a Canadian mining camp, longed to serve on the mission field but could not because of a physical disability. God taught her, instead, that her mission field was right where she was. One of her more famous hymns is "So Send I You":

> So send I you to labor unrewarded,
> To serve unpaid, unloved, unsought, unknown,
> To bear rebuke, to suffer scorn and scoffing,
> So send I you to toil for Me alone.
>
> So send I you to bind the bruised and broken,
> O'er wandering souls to work, to weep, to wake,
> To bear the burdens of a world aweary—
> So send I you to suffer for My sake.

Jesus said, "As my Father hath sent me, even so send I you" (John 20:21, *KJV*). He sends each one of us to our mission field, to hard hearts and blind eyes we meet every day.

Pit Stop
POINT TO PONDER

Read the song again. Are you willing to endure the things described in order to spread the message of reconciliation? Would you work unrewarded, alone, scorned? Could you give up your life's ambition? Are you willing to go to hate-filled hearts and speak to blind eyes and stubborn minds? Will you spend time, energy, even blood? Christ did. That was His mission. He is sending you on the same mission.

February 22

John recorded a very significant statement made by Jesus: "I am the way and the truth and the life. No one comes to the Father except through me" (John 14:6).

I believe what Jesus said (Jesus *is* truth; Jesus cannot lie). I believe that He is the only way to heaven and to God.

Now that may not be politically correct in this day and age, but you know something? It's theologically correct. And one day, you, my friend, will stand before the living God and give an account of how you have either lived that truth out or rejected it.

I have staked my life on what Jesus said. That's why I do what I do. That's what drives me 24/7. God called me to be an evangelist and communicate His good news. But I'm not the only one who is called to do that. God has called all believers to represent Him to this world.

There's a world that really does need to hear Christ's message. Ask the Lord today for an opportunity and the courage to tell someone about the only way.

Pit Stop PRAYER

Lord, You are the only One who gives life. Give me courage to point people to You.

February 23

Several years ago, I read an article about an epidemic of teenage suicides that had swept through an affluent Houston suburb. One of the stories grabbed my heart, and I just grieved over this boy. He had hung himself in a tree in the backyard and pinned a note to his clothes that read, "This is the only thing around here with roots."

Not only young people but also people of every age in this world are looking for hope. We live in a desperate hour and a dangerous world of despair and frustration and very little hope. Jesus came "to proclaim freedom for the prisoners and recovery of sight for the blind, to release the oppressed" (Luke 4:18). He said, "I love you, and I want you to live in relationship with Me. I want to forgive your sins and heal your diseases. I want you to come to know Me."

Jesus will develop a relationship with whoever comes to Him, and He has asked us to introduce people to Him. What would happen if you picked out one person to begin to pray over and then prayed also for an opportunity to let that person know about Jesus' love and forgiveness?

Do that. Pray for one person, and ask God for opportunities to speak into that one life. The followers of Christ have a message of hope for this world.

Pit Stop — PRACTICE

Fill in the following line with the name of someone you know who needs to know about Jesus' love: "I determine to pray for _____." Now look for opportunities to represent Jesus to that person.

February 24

> Live in harmony with one another. Do not be proud,
> but be willing to associate with people of low position.
> Do not be conceited.
>
> ROMANS 12:16

A challenge for some people within the Church is that they don't know people outside the Church. And even if they know them, they choose not to hang out with them. But God wants believers to hang out with people who are not like them.

It's good to have friends I can relate to, friends I enjoy being with, friends who are believers; but it's also important that I have friends who are outside the Body of Christ. Otherwise, how are they going to see and hear and know the truth?

Think of some people who you see on a regular basis but don't yet have a relationship with, and then start befriending them. Just look for ways to be friendly: maybe a cup of cold water or simple things that extend friendship. Pray for opportunities and ideas, and then pray for those people you're befriending.

I believe God will use those friendships in a major way as you build relationships and look for ways to show Jesus to your friends.

Pit Stop
PRACTICE

Peter encourages you to "worship Christ as Lord of your life. And if someone asks about your Christian hope, always be ready to explain it" (1 Peter 3:15, *NLT*). Think about the rich inheritance of hope you have in Christ. Let praise to your Savior spill into your conversations.

February 25

More than 2,000 years ago, Jesus Christ left the glory of heaven to come to this earth. He lived in this world, identifying with humanity, for the purpose of going to the cross to give His life so that we can have life. And He wants all of us to be His effective witnesses.

Charles Spurgeon said, "You may be certain that whatever God has made prominent in His Word, He intended to be conspicuous in our lives." Jesus told His disciples to "go and make disciples of all nations" (Matthew 28:19). We are to be His witnesses in every part of the earth. This is the whole story of the gospel; it is why He came—to draw all people to Himself. And He chose you to now be one of His representatives in this world.

What a mission you've been given! Jesus gave His life for this world. I hope your heart's desire is to answer His call with all of your life.

Remember Dr. Bill Bright's definition of an effective witness: Someone who takes the initiative to present the claims of Christ in the power of the Holy Spirit and leaves the results to God. I like that because it lets you and me off the hook. We're called by God to be His effective witnesses, but we're not asked to do any of this on our own. The power of the Spirit works in us to present Christ, and God takes care of the results. He's in the saving business. He's made that desire prominent in His Word.

So here's the question: Is being a witness and telling the story of Christ conspicuous in your life?

Pit Stop
PRACTICE

Take some time today to think of one small change you can make in your daily life that will step up your witness to the world around you. Take one small step to the next level in being an effective witness.

February 26

It's possible that you know John 3:16 by heart. It's often one of the first Scriptures people memorize. Today, read it aloud, filling in each blank with your name:

> For God so loved _____ that he gave his one and only Son, that if _____ believes in him _____ shall not perish but have eternal life.

The song "The Love of God" tries to describe how boundless and immeasurable God's love for us is. If every stalk on earth were a quill and every person were a scribe—if the oceans were filled with ink and the skies were paper—we could never describe the full love of God.

There's no limit to His love, my friend. He has poured out His love on you, even before you knew Him, even while you were His enemy. That's the love that died for you. That's the love that is available to every person who will receive it.

"The LORD, the LORD, the compassionate and gracious God, slow to anger, abounding in love and faithfulness, maintaining love to thousands, and forgiving wickedness, rebellion and sin" (Exodus 34:6-7). That was Moses describing the Lord. God forgives wickedness, rebellion and sin. That's really what God's love is all about.

I can guarantee that you have friends, neighbors, co-workers and even family members who have never experienced this great love of God, His forgiveness and compassion. Now read John 3:16 above—aloud—and fill in each blank with the name of one of those people. God loves them. Jesus died for them. They *must* hear the story!

Pit Stop
PRAISE & PRAYER

"Your unfailing love is better than life itself; how I praise you!" (Psalm 63:3, *NLT*). O Lord, let my life be a gift of praise to You for all my days.

February 27

The children of Israel were at the Jordan River, ready to cross into Canaan, the land God had promised them. The river was high, overflowing its banks. But as the priests went into the water carrying the Ark of the Covenant, the waters began backing up, and soon the people hurried across on dry land.

They camped that night at Gilgal, and God told Joshua to have a representative from each of the 12 tribes get a stone from the place in the riverbed where the priests had held the Ark of the Lord while the people crossed into the Promised Land. With the stones, they built a memorial. Those stones were to be a sign. Whenever the Israelites' children and their children's children asked what the stones meant, the people were to tell the story of how God had powerfully dried up the river until they had all crossed into the Promised Land.

It's good to record the mighty things God has done in your life so you don't forget them and you can share them with your children and your children's children. So look for opportunities to tell about your stones at Gilgal. If you've been walking with Jesus, you have stories to tell! Don't hold back, my friend. Let the next generation—every generation—know the mighty things God has done for you.

Pit Stop
POINT TO PONDER

Today, think about your Gilgal stones. Remember what God has done in your life that only He can do—healing, peace, forgiveness, freedom, guidance, miracles. These are the stories to share, my friend. Give the Lord thanks and praise by telling others what He has done for you.

February 28

We are called by God to tell every person we can about the importance of knowing Christ. The following challenge from William Booth, founder of the Salvation Army, moves my heart and intensifies my concern about those people who do not know Christ. It's a bit long, but read it as though he is speaking to you—because he is!

> "Not called!" did you say? "Not heard the call," I think you should say. Put your ear down to the Bible, and hear him bid you go and pull sinners out of the fire of sin. Put your ear down to the burdened, agonized heart of humanity, and listen to its pitiful wail for help. Go stand by the gates of hell, and hear the damned entreat you to go to their father's house and bid their brothers and sisters, and servants and masters not to come there. And then look Christ in the face, whose mercy you have professed to obey, and tell him whether you will join heart and soul and body and circumstances in the march to publish his mercy to the world.

My prayer for you is that your heart will be so burdened for those in this world who do not know Christ that you cannot help but tell them about His mercy. You are called. Tell the story.

Pit Stop
POINT TO PONDER

God has put the friend or neighbor or work associate or loved one you are praying for in your path so that you can share the message of new life. Ask God to give you the opportunity and words to tell that person the story of what God's love has done in your life.

MARCH

Being the Doxology

Blessed are those who have learned to acclaim you.

PSALM 89:15

March 1

> Praise be to the God and Father of our Lord Jesus Christ! In his great mercy he has given us new birth into a living hope through the resurrection of Jesus Christ from the dead.
>
> 1 PETER 1:3

Francis Schaeffer, a great man of God, wrote:

> One day all Christians will join in a doxology and sing God's praises with perfection. But even today, individually and corporately, we are not only to *sing* the doxology, we are to *be* the doxology.[5]

Whether you know it or not, if you proclaim Christ and profess to know Him, people are watching how you walk and how you live. Is your life a doxology, a hymn of praise and worship to your God?

We've been called to represent Jesus in all that we do. Answering the call does not mean we live in bondage; instead, we find joy and freedom as we learn to be more like our Master and reflect His image in the way we talk, the way we think and the way we act.

Are you singing the doxology of God's perfection? Are you being the doxology? Are you living out a doxology of praise to God as you live the new life He's given you?

Today, ask the Holy Spirit to teach you how to live out a life of praise to Him.

Pit Stop
POINT TO PONDER

Want to truly worship God? Then offer yourself to Him,
a living sacrifice of praise and thankfulness for all He has done for you
(see Romans 12:1).

March 2

One of the most powerful verses in the Bible tells us that we "are being built together to become a dwelling in which God lives by his Spirit" (Ephesians 2:22).

Say that thought aloud, making it personal: "*I am the dwelling place of God.*"

If you know Christ, then God—the God who spoke this world into existence, the God who knit you together inside your mother's womb and scheduled every day of your life—has taken up residence in you. How awesome is that!

If you've asked Christ to forgive your sins and to come into your life, you have been forgiven; and by the power of His Spirit, Christ dwells within you. The God of all creation resides in you!

God lives in us to equip us and strengthen us. He wants to use us to introduce people to Him, as His representative in a ministry of healing and reconciliation.

Take some time today to think about the relationships God has brought into your life. Maybe you'll think of work associates, neighbors or a clerk at a store. Maybe you'll think of your family. I don't know who the Spirit will bring to your mind, but God lives in you so that you can be the presence of Christ in the lives of all the people around you.

You are to represent Jesus in every relationship you have. When you go about your day remembering that this is your call, it will change the way you relate to people.

Pit Stop
POINT TO PONDER

The Spirit of Christ living in you will change how you interact with others. Galatians 5:22 lists fruits of the Spirit: "love, joy, peace, patience, kindness, goodness, faithfulness, gentleness and self-control." When you allow the Spirit to grow these things in your life, God touches and transforms your relationships.

March 3

Christ began a good work in you when you put your faith and trust in Him. He took up residence in you, and He now desires to shape you into the image of who He wants you to be.

You may have sung this verse when you were a child: "He's still working on me, to make me what I ought to be. It took Him just a week to make the moon and stars, The sun and the earth and Jupiter and Mars. How loving and patient He must be, He's still working on me."

God wants us to grow day by day. He wants us to cooperate with Him and allow Him to work in us. He asks us to say again and again throughout our day, *Yes, Lord. Yes, Lord. Yes, Lord.* The new life He's given us is a life of growth, a life of maturing into what He wants us to be.

If you've put your faith in Jesus and asked Him to dwell in you, I claim for you Philippians 1:6:

> Being confident of this, that he who began a good work in you will carry it on to completion until the day of Christ Jesus.

I pray that He will continue the good work that He has begun in you. When will that work be completed? When you go to be with Him in glory!

Walk today in the awareness that He is working in you.

Pit Stop PROMISE

"May you always be filled with the fruit of your salvation— the righteous character produced in your life by Jesus Christ—for this will bring much glory and praise to God" (Philippians 1:11, *NLT*).

March 4

David opens Psalm 34 with the declaration, "I will extol the LORD at all times; his praise will always be on my lips."

What a way to live!

I don't know what you'll face today at work, at home, in traffic, in conversations with other people and even in your own thoughts. But I promise you, if you keep this one goal in mind, your day is going to be a good day: *Lord, I want to extol Your name. My desire is to extol You at all times today. Your praise will continually be on my lips.*

When you put Jesus first, when you extol His name and let His praise be on your lips continually, you bite that tongue and praise the Lord. If you do say something you shouldn't have said or you have those bad thoughts, pray, *Oh, Lord, forgive me. I'm going to praise You instead.*

It might sound impossible to praise the Lord always, in every circumstance. But here's something to think about: How would that change your day? Deciding that you want to live continually praising God can have a profound effect on your life. And I'm really quite sure that the Lord approves that desire.

Pit Stop
PRACTICE

We've all had the experience of blurting out something that we immediately regretted. Look again at the fruits of the Spirit listed in Galatians 5:22-23; the last one is *self-control*. If you want your lips to be praising God, ask the Spirit to help you choose your words.

March 5

What stirs your heart to compassion?

Images of the Gulf Coast after Hurricane Katrina, the flood devastation in Pakistan or starving children in Kenya may raise compassion in your heart. Things close to home may also touch your heart, like the co-worker who has a terminally ill child or the family down the street whose father lost his job or the elderly man standing by his car with a flat tire.

Whether our hearts warm with compassion toward those caught by great disaster or toward those who struggle with daily problems, it's important to not just see and have our hearts stirred; we also need to put our compassion into action. The Lord wants us to get involved in people's lives. It's important to act on our words.

Psalm 145:9 tells us that God Himself has great compassion over this earth: "The LORD is good to all; he has compassion on all he has made." That's a great word about God's love for this world. He made all of creation. He spoke it into existence, and He has compassion over this earth and the people of this earth. It's not His will that any should perish but that all should come to repentance.

He calls you to be His representative of compassion, to be His hands and His feet and His love in action.

Show compassion to someone today; show His love in action.

Pit Stop
POINT TO PONDER

Jesus taught that you're to love your enemies and do good to them without expecting anything in return. Then, Jesus said, "you will truly be acting as children of the Most High, for he is kind to those who are unthankful and wicked. You must be compassionate, just as your Father is compassionate" (Luke 6:35-36, *NLT*). Yes, even toward those who are wicked! That's the Father's compassion.

March 6

> Blessed are those who have learned to acclaim you, who walk in the light of your presence, O Lord. They rejoice in your name all day long; they exult in your righteousness.
>
> PSALM 89:15-16

"Acclaim" and "exult"—now those are two words we don't hear very much in daily conversations. I'll save you the trouble of going to your dictionary. "Acclaim" means to praise enthusiastically and publicly. "Exult" means to be very happy and joyful.

Are you exulting in the name of the Lord all day long? Yes, I know, you have responsibilities and you have to go to the office or take care of the kids or be at the hospital or the fire station or the shop. We must all deal with daily concerns and affairs. But whatever we do, I believe God wants us to exult in His name, to express a happiness and joy that just flow out of us because of our relationship with Him. Exulting in Him should be our way of life, for we are blessed.

As exulting in God becomes a way of life, words of praise and adoration because of what He's done will just naturally come into our speech. I don't think we should be obnoxious about it, but as we experience the joy of the Lord as we go about our day, praising Him should be automatic.

We can rejoice in God's righteousness. Our God is a righteous God, and He's made us righteous, not because we deserved it, but because He loves us. That's something to keep us joyful all day long!

Pit Stop
PRAISE

"What can I offer the Lord for all He has done for me? I will lift up the cup of salvation and praise the Lord's name for saving me" (Psalm 116:12-13, *NLT*).

March 7

Be real, real honest with me. Does any of this sound familiar?

> I shouldn't have to worry about evangelism. I'm not called to be a missionary. I'm a good person, and even if I don't talk about Jesus, that's a good enough witness. People will see my life and know I'm a Christian, right? I don't want to offend anyone. People can lose their jobs talking about their faith. If I talk about Jesus, I could get into trouble. And besides, evangelism isn't my gift. I'm just plain scared.

Instead of telling others about Christ, are you giving excuses? You may choose to believe what the world tells you about evangelism—that you shouldn't witness out of respect for the beliefs of others, or there are things you cannot say in certain places because the government has ruled you cannot.

But, my friend, Jesus didn't give us the option of making excuses. He said, "You will be my witnesses" (Acts 1:8). Jesus could have said, "If it's convenient or if it comes up in a casual conversation or if someone asks you a direct question, then I'd like you to be My witness. If you think you won't get into trouble or if you feel like it, then you can be My witness." But did He say that?

No. Jesus gave His followers absolutely no option. He said, "You will be my witnesses, at home, in your city and your state and in all parts of the earth." We don't have a choice. Our only choice is whether we will be effective witnesses or ineffective witnesses. So today, ask Jesus to open your eyes to opportunities to be His witness.

Pit Stop
POINT TO PONDER

Fill in the blank with your name as you read what Jesus says to you: "I chose you, _____, and you are mine. You will be My witness today. Wherever you go, whatever you do, whenever you speak, you will be representing Me to the world around you."

March 8

Paul and Silas had ruffled some feathers with their teaching in Philippi, and an angry mob brought them to city officials who had them severely beaten and then thrown in jail. Sitting in the inner dungeon with their feet in stocks, they were praying and singing hymns. Acts 16 tells us that the other prisoners listened to them.

At midnight, an earthquake shook the jail, and all the doors flew open and the shackles fell off the prisoners' legs. The jailer, who had been ordered to make certain no one escaped, feared that all the prisoners were gone. He was about to kill himself when Paul shouted to him that everyone was still there.

The jailor must have been listening to Paul and Silas earlier, too, because of what happened next: "[The jailer] then brought them out [of the dungeon] and asked, 'Sirs, what must I do to be saved?' They replied, 'Believe in the Lord Jesus, and you will be saved—you and your household.' Then they spoke the word of the Lord to him and to all the others in his house" (Acts 16:30-32).

We have no indication that Paul and Silas were bemoaning the fact that they were in jail. Instead, they prayed and sang—and their witness continued to reach others! Thank God for the freedoms we have in this country; others are not so fortunate. However, if someday I am arrested for preaching the gospel or for talking about Jesus, I hope I will represent Him well—even in prison.

Today, remember that no matter where you are or what situation you find yourself in, you have a message of hope for the world.

Pit Stop PRAYER

Father, I know I cannot carry the message of hope by complaining or being critical or pessimistic, yet all too often that is what comes out of my mouth. Teach me to be thankful in all circumstances and to praise You for all You have done in my life.

March 9

Would you describe yourself as a reservoir or a channel? I really believe that God intends to use you as a channel of His blessing.

You may go to church and Sunday School or do a Bible study—and those are all good things to do—but God's plan is not that you just *take in*. God's plan is that you receive in order to give. Jesus said, "From everyone who has been given much, much will be demanded; and from the one who has been entrusted with much, much more will be asked" (Luke 12:48).

To be a giver takes strength—strength you may not always have. When you spend time with God, though, He gives you the endurance and power to be His channel. Then you're able to run and not grow weary, to walk and not faint, and to soar on wings like an eagle (see Isaiah 40:31). His promise is not that you'll just somehow muddle through but that you'll soar!

Everything in God's creation gives, and His plan is that you will be a channel of what He wants to give to this world. He will give you the strength to do it.

Spend time with God today. Ask Him to renew your strength so that you can give His blessing to others.

Pit Stop PRAYER

Lord, You have given me so much! My heart's desire is to be more like You, but You know I need the power of Your Spirit to help me give to others—to love unconditionally, forgive as You forgive, and live my life for others. Help me!

March 10

> Everything comes from him and exists by his power and is intended for his glory. All glory to him forever! Amen.
>
> ROMANS 11:36, *NLT*

Read Romans 11:36 again, with the thought that it is referring to *you*. You came from God. You exist because of His power.

Each of us is just one breath away from being in God's presence. You are here now because of His grace, His mercy and His power in your life. He holds your time in His hands, and if He withdrew His hand from you—and this applies to every person, even those who don't know Him—then you're done.

The whole purpose for your existence is that you are "intended for his glory." Are you living out His intended purpose for you? Does your life sing the doxology? Does the light shining from you bring Him praise and glory?

Live in this awareness today: Whatever you do and wherever you go, you are representing the One who created you and calls you His own.

Pit Stop PRAYER

"Teach me your ways, O LORD, that I may live according to your truth! Grant me purity of heart, so that I may honor you. With all my heart I will praise you, O Lord my God. I will give glory to your name forever" (Psalm 86:11-12, *NLT*).

March 11

*Let every created thing give praise to the Lord,
for he issued his command, and they came into being.*

PSALM 148:5, *NLT*

We read in Colossians 1:17 that Christ is the essence that literally holds all of creation together. Everything revolves around the lordship of Jesus Christ. The heavens declare His glory and every created thing gives Him praise.

As Jesus' followers sang His praises when He entered Jerusalem, some of the religious leaders tried to quiet them. Jesus said, "If they keep quiet, the stones will cry out" (Luke 19:40). Can you think of anything more silent, more lifeless, than a stone? Yet even rocks will praise God, if we do not. He is the Creator, the One in whom everything and all of us exist.

Are you giving God His due praise as you go about your day? We are to do that as a way of life.

In your office today, at your school, in your home—wherever you are—give God praise. Don't be afraid to let people know that you are thankful for the Lord's blessing and His goodness. Testify to the fact that He has radically changed your life. In doing so, you will give God the glory and praise due Him.

Pit Stop
POINT TO PONDER

First Peter 1:18 reminds us that Jesus Christ's blood was the ransom paid to save us from empty lives. You have been given a new life. Is that life bringing God glory and praise?

March 12

David's heart was overflowing when he prayed the prayer in 1 Chronicles 29:10-11: "Praise be to you, O LORD, God of our father Israel, from everlasting to everlasting. Yours, O LORD, is the greatness and the power and the glory and the majesty and the splendor, for everything in heaven and earth is yours."

Do you feel the passion with which David was praying and communicating with the God of all creation? His God is the great and powerful and glorious and majestic God! I think David was so overcome with the love of God that he just had to express what was in his heart, and this prayer is what came out.

When computers first arrived on the scene, "Garbage in, garbage out" became a popular saying. You may not hear that much anymore, but it is true. If garbage is fed into the computer, garbage comes out.

That's really true of our lives, too. Whatever we put in is what's going to come out. If we spend time alone with the Lord on a regular basis and focus on an intimate relationship with God, that relationship will express itself in our lives, shaping what we say and what we do. Giving God thanks and praise, as David did, is a wonderful way to spend a portion of our days; and it will affect the rest of our days, too.

Take some time today just to praise God and thank Him. Thank Him for His love. Thank Him for what He's done. Thank Him for what He is doing. Thank Him for what He's going to do.

Pit Stop
POWER

"Let your roots grow down into [Christ], and let your lives be built on him. Then your faith will grow strong in the truth you were taught, and you will overflow with thankfulness" (Colossians 2:7, *NLT*).
Spend time building your relationship with Christ.

March 13

Here's a great prayer from Nehemiah 9:5-6 that we would each do well to adopt as our very own:

> Blessed be your glorious name, and may it be exalted above all blessing and praise. You alone are the LORD. You made the heavens, even the highest heavens, and all their starry host, the earth and all that is on it, the seas and all that is in them. You give life to everything, and the multitudes of heaven worship you.

The stars of heaven, all of heaven, worship God. Should we do any less? Why don't you take some time right now and offer praise to God. We have so many things to thank and praise Him for.

Not long ago, I came across "Drinking from My Saucer," a poem that has been set to music and sung by many artists. Its repeating line is, "I'm drinking from my saucer, 'cause my cup has overflowed."

You probably have received so many blessings from God that you can't even begin to count them. So no matter what's going on in your life right now, take time to thank Him and worship Him. Don't let this day go by without spending some time worshiping the Lord and letting Him know that you are deeply appreciative of His love, His mercy and His grace.

Pit Stop PRACTICE

The three-part plan for peace suggested on January 1 was this: (1) Pray; (2) tell God what you need; (3) thank Him for what He's done. Have you been praying and telling and thanking? The peace of God invades a life filled with these things.

March 14

> I will extol the LORD at all times; his praise will always be on my lips. My soul will boast in the LORD; let the afflicted hear and rejoice. Glorify the LORD with me; let us exalt his name together.
>
> PSALM 34:1-3

A friend of mine had been going through a time of intense pressure at work. He was part of a team that was working toward a deadline, and my friend told me that he "was really in the groove, knocking it out, doing a great job." He was having a good time and getting the job done.

Then one morning during my friend's devotions, the Lord said, "What about Me? I'm the One enabling you to do this." My friend was convicted; he had not been giving the Lord the praise for what He had done. So on his way to work, he committed to giving God all the praise for what he had accomplished.

God gave him an opportunity to do just that in a staff meeting that very morning. The team was brainstorming about what they could do to stay on target and get the project done on time. When the leader wrote "Prayer" on the board, the person beside my friend said, "Aw, that's crazy. Don't bring that stuff into the workplace."

My friend spoke up and said, "Wait a minute, wait a minute. I gotta tell you, prayer works." And he began to tell how the Lord had been helping him to do such a good job.

God will give you such opportunities if you'll make yourself available. Tell Him you're available today, and then give Him praise for all He does.

Pit Stop
POINT TO PONDER

When you give God glory and praise for what He is doing in your life, you light a beacon of witness. That light not only points a dark world to the Lord, but it also encourages other believers in their own walks with Christ.

March 15

I once read a quote by Robert Moffat, a missionary to Africa in the 1800s, that stopped me in my tracks:

> Oh, that I had a thousand lives and a thousand bodies! All of them should be devoted to no other employment but to preach Christ.

The passage reminded me of the first line of a great old hymn of the Church by Charles Wesley: "Oh, for a thousand tongues to sing my great Redeemer's praise."

Are you using the one life and body and tongue that you have to preach and praise? Or do you let opportunities slide by and not give God praise and glory so that others might see Christ in you? How many words do you think slide out of your mouth every day, and how many of those sing God's glory?

If you know Him, if you've experienced His love, if you've experienced His forgiveness, don't drift away from that first-love experience. Let yourself be overwhelmed by what Christ has done for you. Let a passionate love for Him declare, "My mouth will speak in praise of the LORD. Let every creature praise his holy name for ever and ever" (Psalm 145:21).

Oh, for a thousand lives to live and a thousand bodies! All of them should be devoted to singing the doxology of God's salvation and perfection!

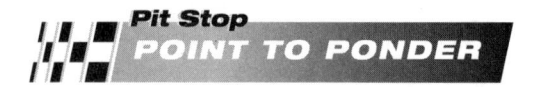

Pit Stop
POINT TO PONDER

Answer this question honestly: Is your life devoted to preaching Christ?

March 16

Let all who take refuge in you be glad; let them ever sing for joy.

PSALM 5:11

A number of years ago, I read about a survey of unchurched Americans. The survey found that people who did not attend church had preconceived ideas of who and what the church is. They described the church as boring, judgmental and hypocritical.

Now that's very, very sad. I'm out to change those perceptions! Will you join me?

The first three fruits of the Spirit are love, joy and peace (see Galatians 5:22-23). We should be known for those fruits, not for being boring, judgmental and hypocritical. Can we open our arms to the lost, pagan world that does not know Jesus, and say, "God loves you. I am His representative, and I love you. And I want you to experience the love, joy and peace He gives."

That's what God has called us to do, my friend. I know we all make mistakes. Sometimes we get angry and say things we shouldn't say. We have days when everything seems to go wrong and we don't feel very peaceful. But the bottom line is that Jesus wants us to represent Him to the world. He is love; He is joy; He is peace. He is longsuffering and patient. He is gentle and compassionate. All those fruits of the Spirit are what should be our calling card.

Today, focus on just one of those fruits—joy, for instance—and say, "I'm going to be joyful today. I choose joy." Then ask the Spirit to help you, strengthen you and remind you.

Pit Stop
POINT TO PONDER

David wrote, "Because You are my helper, I sing for joy in the shadow of your wings" (Psalm 63:7, *NLT*). Jesus sent the Spirit to be your Helper, and if you walk in step with Him, He will produce the love, joy and peace that come only from God. That's a reason to sing for joy!

March 17

God intends for our lives to be filled with joy.

Every life sees some hard times and difficulties; it rains on the just and the unjust alike. These are especially anxious times, and many people are going through a lot of difficulties right now.

But our hope is in the Lord, and He intends for us to be filled with joy and not be controlled by the affairs of this world. Joy, the second fruit of the Spirit, is an important part of who we need to be. And it is possible to have joy in the midst of harsh circumstances.

Many of Paul's letters in the New Testament were written while he was in jail. He was in prison, but he still wrote about having great joy. Regardless of our circumstance, regardless of what life dishes out, the Spirit can produce joy in our lives. If you are a believer, let your heart cry out with joy. Praise God! That's what you're called to do. Be of the same mind as David: "I will praise you, O LORD, with all my heart; I will tell of all your wonders. I will be glad and rejoice in you; I will sing praise to your name, O Most High" (Psalm 9:1-2).

There is a difference between happiness and joy. Happiness is temporary; it fades away. But true joy is eternal. Knowing Christ and all that He's done produces joy.

In your daily conversations, acknowledge God and tell of all His wonders. Praise Him. And let the joy of the Lord be your strength.

Pit Stop
PROMISE

"Good tidings of great joy!" (Luke 2:10, *KJV*). That's how the angels announced the coming of Christ. Prophecies said He would bring the oil of gladness to replace despair. On His last night on earth, Christ told His disciples, "I have told you these things so that . . . your joy will overflow" (John 15:11, *NLT*). When Christ comes into a life, He brings joy.

March 18

> Shouts of joy and victory resound in the tents of the righteous: "The LORD's right hand has done mighty things!"
>
> PSALM 118:15

I have a really personal question for you today: Do shouts of joy resound from your dwelling?

Your dwelling, your home, is one of the best places where those who know Christ can be the doxology.

I'll be flat-out honest with you: My home is one of the most difficult places to live under the control of the Holy Spirit. (It seems the enemy delights in attacking us in our homes.) I would never get on a stage or behind a pulpit and speak in a hurtful way or use a tone of voice that would be damaging to you; but at times, I'm tempted to speak to Barb, my wife, in a way that I would never think of speaking elsewhere. That is an attack of the enemy to bring division into my home.

God wants our dwelling to be a place of joy, where the fruit of the Spirit rules with abundance. One of the ways we can invite the Spirit to rule in our home is to get into the habit of repeating these words when we push the button to open the garage door or put the key in the door: "Be controlled by the Holy Spirit."

I want to be under the control of the Holy Spirit in my home. I want joy to reside there; I want shouts of joy to ring from my dwelling. You, too, are called to be a doxology, especially in your home.

Pit Stop
POINT TO PONDER

The believers in Thessalonica suffered severe persecution; but the Holy Spirit gave them great joy, and they became examples to all believers throughout Greece. Paul told them, "Now the word of the Lord is ringing out from you to people everywhere" (1 Thessalonians 1:8, *NLT*). May a message of great joy ring out from your life and from your home!

March 19

Octavius Winslow, a nineteenth-century preacher, once wrote that "the religion of Christ is the religion of JOY."[6] Winslow then went on to describe everything a believer has to be joyful about (it's long, but that's because there is so *much* to be joyful about). See if you don't come to the same conclusion as he does—that with such a Savior, such a God, such a hope, we cannot help but be joyful:

> The believer in Jesus is essentially a happy man. The child of God is, from necessity, a joyful man. His sins are forgiven, his soul is justified, his person is adopted, his trials are blessings, his conflicts are victories, his death is immortality, his future is a heaven of inconceivable, unthought-of, untold, and endless blessedness—with such a God, such a Saviour, and such a hope, is he not, ought he not, to be a *joyful* man?[7]

Joy is so important in world evangelism. If we are going to win this world, we must show the joy Christ can bring to those who are in desperate need of it. I'm convicted at times that I don't represent it well. But with such a God, such a Savior and such a hope, how can we not be joyful? "The LORD has done great things for us, and we are filled with joy" (Psalm 126:3).

Today, when you go to work, to the grocery store, to school—wherever you go—meditate on the great things the Lord has done for you, and let joy be a part of who you are.

Pit Stop
PROMISE

No matter what happens in the world around you, you can rejoice in your relationship with your Creator. Scriptures often talk about joy in the midst of sorrow and rejoicing in spite of trouble. You have that joy because its source is the God of all hope and comfort, and when His Spirit lives in you, He'll bring joy beyond any this world can give or imagine, even in the most unlikely circumstances.

March 20

> Sing to the Lord, praise His name; proclaim his salvation day after day.
>
> PSALM 96:2

Sing to the Lord! Praise His name! Proclaim His salvation day after day! Declare His glory and marvelous deeds among all the people! That's what He's asked us to do. As Priscilla Jane Owens wrote in her hymn "Jesus Saves":

> We have heard the joyful sound: Jesus saves! Jesus saves!
> Spread the tidings all around: Jesus saves! Jesus saves!
> Bear the news to ev'ry land, climb the steeps and cross the waves;
> Onward! 'tis our Lord's command; Jesus saves! Jesus saves!
>
> Waft it on the rolling tide: Jesus saves! Jesus saves!
> Tell to sinners far and wide: Jesus saves! Jesus saves!
> Sing, ye islands of the sea; echo back, ye ocean caves;
> Earth shall keep her jubilee: Jesus saves! Jesus saves!

Our song is a song of victory! Speak to someone today about trusting Jesus. Proclaim His salvation, and explain that victory comes by putting faith and trust in Jesus alone.

Pit Stop PRAYER

Father, help me spread the news everywhere, far and wide, in the midst of battles and through days of gloom, even in the face of death itself. I want to sing Your glory, shout Your victory and rejoice in Your salvation wherever I go.

March 21

One of my friends often reminds me that God gives us weekday pulpits so that we can proclaim Him. In the relationships God brings into our lives, He wants us to acclaim Him and represent Him well. People are watching what we do and listening to what we say.

> For you were once darkness, but now you are light in the Lord. Live as children of light ... and find out what pleases the Lord (Ephesians 5:8-10).

> Let your light shine before men, that they may see your good deeds and praise your Father in heaven (Matthew 5:16).

God has called you to let the light He's given you shine to His glory. Look at Psalm 89:15: "Blessed are those who have *learned* to acclaim [God]" (emphasis added). Acclaiming is a learned activity and takes time and practice to perfect. So think about how you can *practice* effectively proclaiming Him in all that you do. If you're in the grocery line, at the office or on the golf course, how can you let the light of His presence in you shine for others to see?

In all your daily activities today, look for ways to acclaim the Lord. Just look for them. I pray that you will find opportunities everywhere you look and that you will be filled with great joy and will rejoice in His name.

Pit Stop
PRACTICE

Shine for Christ! Those who live in Christ's light are to shine "like bright lights in a world full of crooked and perverse people" (Philippians 2:15, *NLT*).

March 22

> No one has ever seen God; but if we love one another, God lives in us and his love is made complete in us.
>
> 1 JOHN 4:12

Is God's love being made complete in you? Oh, what a privilege, what an honor, what *joy* it is to show God's love to those around you.

I am mechanically challenged. I just don't get it. My dad could take anything apart and put it all back together—and the item worked. I can take something apart; but when I put it back together, I almost always have parts left over and it usually doesn't work. My son, David, has my dad's talent, but somehow it skipped my generation.

So even a string of Christmas lights is a challenge for me. Several years ago, I had a string of lights that would not work. It was one of those strings that when one bulb burns out, all of them go out. I knew one bulb was good, so I kept taking one out and putting the good one in, taking one out and putting the good one in, taking one out . . . you get the idea. After one particular switch, the lights all suddenly came on.

Sometimes we can be like that bulb that keeps a whole string of lights from shining. When my light goes out, it doesn't affect only me; it affects all those around me. Keeping our lights shining brightly *does* affect those around us. God's love working through us *does* flow out and make a difference in others' lives.

Maintain that spiritual filament so that your light will shine brightly. When it breaks, when you blow it, ask God to forgive you so that you can move on and get reconnected. But keep that light shining, because it's touching the lives of all those around you.

Pit Stop
POINT TO PONDER

Jesus taught His disciples, "You are the light of the world. . . . Let your life shine brightly so that everyone will praise your heavenly Father" (see Matthew 5:14-16). You are part of Christ's mission on earth, and your light is also necessary to show people the way back to God.

March 23

It is light that makes everything visible. This is why it is said: "Wake up, O sleeper, rise from the dead, and Christ will shine on you."

EPHESIANS 5:14

John Wesley often preached and wrote about self-deceivers. "Wake up!" he told them. "The body of Christ needs you!"

It's good for us sometimes to rub the sleep out of our eyes, come into the light of God's Word and see where we are spiritually. Are we living in victory? Are we living out the inheritance of power available to each child of God? Or are we so weighed down by the affairs of this world that we're ineffective in our walk with the Lord? The Lord wants His power to work in and shine through our lives.

So wake up, look at your spiritual life, take an honest inventory of where you are and then do what needs to be done to get where you need to be. If you don't know God, come to know Him. If you do know Him and you have slipped in your devotional time or you're not praying the way you should and you're not maintaining that relationship with Him, stop! Stop living every day in this powerless way!

Start spending more time with God, and be all that He wants you to be!

Pit Stop
POINT TO PONDER

"Let the message about Christ, in all its richness, fill your lives" (Colossians 3:16, *NLT*). If you do an honest inventory of your life, what fills your days? Worry? Ambition? Scrambling to stay ahead of bills? Looking for fun? Trying to find the right spouse? Draw closer to Christ, and find out what richness He has planned for you.

March 24

All you have made will praise you, O LORD; your saints will extol you. They will tell of the glory of your kingdom and speak of your might.

PSALM 145:10-11

All of creation praises the Creator. You are one of His works! If you know Jesus, go about your day as a part of the creation that sings His praises. Speak of the glory of His kingdom. Point people to Jesus, and talk about His power.

Several weeks ago, a friend of mine decided to do exactly that. She was visiting a lady who was facing surgery, and at first their conversation was casual and friendly.

Then my friend asked, "Can I ask you a personal question?"

The lady said, "Sure."

"Do you know for sure that if you die, you'll go to heaven?"

The lady teared up and said, "No, I don't. But I'd like to know."

You know, there are people all around you in that same position. They need you to love them enough to confront them with the gospel of Christ. Be a part of the Lord's creation that shows His glory and power and points people to Him.

Pit Stop Prayer

Father, make me sensitive to the needs of people around me, needs that only You can fill. Give me Your compassion and courage to point people to You.

March 25

> Land that drinks in the rain often falling on it and that produces a crop useful to those for whom it is farmed receives the blessing of God.
>
> HEBREWS 6:7

Do you realize you're blessed of God? Maybe you're facing physical problems or are in a severe financial crisis. Maybe you've lost a loved one. Perhaps you think it's impossible to rejoice and be thankful at this time in your life, but just stop for a moment and count your many blessings. As that old song says, "Count your many blessings, Name them one by one. And it will surprise you What the Lord hath done."

When you're burdened with a load of care, when you're beaten by the storm, when you're drained by discouragement, count your blessings. And even better—spread the blessings of God around.

Think creatively about how you can be a blessing to others. I'm not talking about monetary blessings right now (although I do think we should use those to bless others, too). One of the most meaningful gifts I've ever received was a coupon to go to a particular event with my son. To me, that was far better than anything he could have bought me, because it was time with him.

Look for ways that you can spread the joy of God all around. You can be His instrument of blessing by simply doing something small or speaking a word of encouragement to people He brings into your life.

Today, count your blessings, and then look for ways to spread His blessings to others.

Pit Stop PROMISE

"The generous will prosper; those who refresh others will themselves be refreshed" (Proverbs 11:25, *NLT*).

March 26

Jesus and two criminals were taken to a place called the Skull, a hill of execution. There, nails were driven through Jesus' hands and feet. He had been beaten beyond recognition, and as He hung on the cross, His life ebbed away. But He looked at the very people who had hung Him there and said, "Father, forgive them, for they do not know what they are doing" (Luke 23:34).

We represent Jesus in this world where all kinds of people still crucify Him daily. They don't know Him; they reject Him; they deny Him. Yet He still longs to forgive them. He still longs to live in relationship with them. That's the message of the cross.

That's what the Easter season is all about. And even people who don't know Christ are often sensitive to the Spirit of God during this season. Think about who you might invite to go to church with you this Sunday as you celebrate the resurrection. Use this Easter as an evangelistic outreach opportunity, and see what God might do.

Because He still longs for people to know Him.

Pit Stop
POINT TO PONDER

Jesus said to those who believe in Him, "As [the Father] sent me into the world, I have sent [you] into the world" (John 17:19). Jesus was sent to show the way back to God, and now He sends you into the world on that same mission.

March 27

In Ephesians 2:10, Paul says that "we are God's workmanship." In the original Greek, the verb "are" is a present continuous action verb. It shows action right here and now, but the action doesn't stop—it goes on and on into the future. We are God's workmanship, in present continuous action! God keeps working on us, and He isn't finished yet.

The purpose of God's work in you is to bring you to a mature walk with Him, to shape you into the image of Christ. He does not want you to stagnate. Whatever your age, 100 or 10, He wants you to continue to grow in your life in Christ.

A scene at a nursing facility I once visited blessed my heart. A lady who must have been 90 was sitting in the lobby in her wheelchair, next to a lamp, reading her Bible. She also had a devotional guide, and she wasn't just reading—she was marking, too.

That picture spoke to my heart. This lady still wanted to mature in her walk with the Lord. She was still crying out for nourishment so that she could grow more like her Master.

Today, take time to be with God, to listen to Him, to read His Word and commune with Him in prayer. Tell Him that you want to cooperate with His work in you; and if there be anything in your heart or mind that is hindering that work, ask Him to show that to you.

Then be willing to let Him prune you, remove hindrances and continue His workmanship.

Pit Stop
PRAYER

Pray or sing these words from "O Jesus Christ, Grow Thou in Me," a hymn by Johann Lavater: "Oh, Jesus Christ, grow Thou in me, and all things else recede! My heart be daily nearer Thee, from sin be daily freed. Make this poor self grow less and less, be Thou my life and aim; Oh, make me daily through Thy grace more meet to bear Thy name."

March 28

> God does not have to come and tell me what I must
> do for Him, he brings me into a relationship with Himself where
> I hear His call and understand what He wants me to do,
> and I do it out of sheer love to Him.
>
> OSWALD CHAMBERS

Do you do what you do out of sheer love to God? When people say they've been called to foreign service or some other particular sphere of work, they mean that their relationship to God has enabled them to realize that they can do this for God. They do what they do out of love for God.

God did what He did for you out of His great love for you. Don't ever get over the wondrous fact that God loves you with an everlasting love and that He left the glory of heaven and came to this earth to go to the cross because He loves you. Because of what He did, your life has been transformed.

> When He died, he died once to break the power of sin.... Give yourselves completely to God, for you were dead, but now you have new life.... Sin is no longer your master, for you no longer live under the requirements of the law. Instead, you live under the freedom of God's grace (Romans 6:10-14, *NLT*).

Hallelujah! God loved you and did this for you before you even knew Him. Does your love for Him motivate you to do anything for Him?

Assess your love for Christ. Choose to love Him more and more. Desire to serve Him better and be what He wants you to be—all because you love Him.

Pit Stop
POINT TO PONDER

"Those who obey God's word truly show how completely they love him" (1 John 2:5, *NLT*).

March 29

If you belong to Christ, you are part of a great communion of souls throughout the whole earth who praise His name! William A. Dunkerley made this clear in his hymn "In Christ There Is No East or West":

> In Christ there is no East or West,
> In Him no South or North;
> But one great fellowship of love
> Throughout the whole wide earth.
>
> In Him shall true hearts everywhere
> Their high communion find;
> His service is the golden cord,
> Close binding humankind.

His service is the golden cord that binds all believers together, no matter what part of the state or country or world they inhabit.

Spend some time today praying for your brothers and sisters in other parts of the world. You may not know any of them personally, but just pick out a part of the world—Asia, China, Africa, the United States—and pray for those who are being persecuted because they are singing the doxology of God's perfection. Pray that God will give them strength and courage to stand strong for Him.

Pit Stop
POINT TO PONDER

All believers have been adopted as children of God and given life by the same Spirit. You might look different from me and your worship might be different from mine, but the same Spirit lives in both of us and we share one mission: to point people to Christ as the way back to God.

March 30

> Grow in the grace and knowledge of our Lord and Savior Jesus Christ. To him be glory both now and forever! Amen.
>
> 2 PETER 3:18

Are you growing in your walk with the Lord? Are you growing in His grace? As you look back on where you were a year ago today, are you closer to God than you were a year ago? Has your relationship with Him grown? Are you saying "Yes, Lord" on a daily basis as He changes and shapes you?

Growth requires some effort on your part. It requires proper nourishment. Daily, spend time in prayer and in God's Word. Even if you read only one verse a day, meditate on that verse and ask the Spirit to teach you. In other words, make the effort each day to grow to become more like the person who God created you to be. Don't ever slack off. Don't ever slow down. Keep your eyes on Him.

Don't be discouraged, either; you are going to mess up sometimes. You aren't going to do everything you wish you would do, and sometimes you'll do things you wish you hadn't done. (Sound like the apostle Paul?) You're human. The question is, Are you making progress?

Spend time with God. That's the only way to make progress from one day to the next. That's how you learn to know Him, how you learn what pleases Him, and how He transforms your thinking and your heart into what He wants you to be.

Say yes to God today.

Pit Stop
PROMISE

As you grow in spiritual wisdom and understanding, "the way you live will always honor and please the Lord, and your [life] will produce every kind of good fruit. All the while, you will grow as you learn to know God better and better" (Colossians 1:10, *NLT*). Learn to know Him better!

March 31

My prayer for all who read this book:

> *Lord God, I pray for all who answer the call to acclaim Your name here in this world.*
> *I pray that You will watch over them.*
> *I pray that You will keep them.*
> *I pray that You will keep Your hand strong upon them.*
> *I pray that You will protect them from evil and harm.*
> *I pray that You will continue to expand their opportunities to serve You.*
>
> *God, I ask that You would bless them indeed.*
> *As they go about their day, may they be instruments of peace.*
> *Where there is hatred, may they love.*
> *Where there is injury, may they pardon.*
> *Where there is discord, may they bring about unity.*
> *Lord, may they represent You in all of life, wherever they go.*
>
> *In Jesus' name, amen.*

Pit Stop PRAYER

Lord, I answer the call to acclaim You here in this world!
I want my mouth and life to sing the doxology of Your praise.
Teach me how to do that more effectively.

APRIL

Representing Christ Well

You will be my *witnesses*.
ACTS 1:8

April 1

We are living in exciting days. Yes, these are turbulent days and days of desperate need, but God has allowed you and me to live during this portion of human history for a reason. We are here for such a time as this, just as Esther was made queen for a crucial time in Jewish history.

What a thought! You have been placed where you are by the living God for each day you are now living!

Jesus told His disciples, "As long as it is day, we must do the work of him who sent me. Night is coming, when no one can work" (John 9:4). There will be a day when you'll no longer be able to work, when you'll no longer be able to do what you can do today. Night will come when you cannot work. "Night" may refer to death, when you go home to be with the Lord, or it may refer to something else that will prevent you from having the opportunity to do the work God has asked you to do.

God has given you this moment. He has given you life at this time and wants to use you to do His work in whatever situations you find yourself in today.

Wherever you go today, take every opportunity—while you have it—to do His work.

Pit Stop
PRAYER

Father, open my eyes to opportunities. I can get so caught up in the busyness of the day and my own agenda that I do not hear an opening in a conversation when I could witness to Your love and goodness, or see the moment when I could show someone kindness and mercy. Slow me down and wake me up so that I do not miss those opportunities.

April 2

In the first chapter of the book of Acts, we find the account of Jesus' ascension into heaven. Before He left His disciples on the Mount of Olives, He told them, "You will receive power when the Holy Spirit comes on you; and you will be my witnesses in Jerusalem, and in all Judea and Samaria, and to the ends of the earth" (Acts 1:8).

"You will be my witnesses." That's an emphatic statement. Disciples of Jesus do not have an option to be a witness or not to be a witness. We bear His name, and we *are* His witnesses. Our only choice is whether we will be an effective witness or an ineffective one.

My friend, we have our marching orders. Because of what Christ has done in us, we are to represent Him both in Jerusalem, Judea, Samaria and all the earth—in other words, wherever we live and in our entire sphere of influence. He has strategically located each one of us as His representative. We are to declare His glory to those around us.

As you serve Him, God will use you to expand His kingdom. You have an opportunity in this day and age to represent Him to people who do not know Him. They're all around you. Use your life to point people to Jesus.

Pit Stop
POINT TO PONDER

Does the word "witness" scare you? A witness doesn't have to be a preacher or an evangelist. A witness is simply a person who tells what he or she has seen. Talk about the difference Jesus has made in your life. Show your new nature by your actions. Tell others the good news about your new life.

April 3

> To this you were called, because Christ suffered for you, leaving you an example, that you should follow in his steps. "He committed no sin, and no deceit was found in his mouth."
>
> 1 PETER 2:21-22

God gives us guidelines on how to live, following the example of Jesus Christ. We are to follow in the steps of our Lord and become more like Him.

Every now and then when I'm in an airport or I'm sitting beside somebody at an event, the person often asks, "Are you a preacher?" or "Are you a Christian?" The question comes even when I have not bowed my head in prayer or opened my Bible. I always wonder what brought that question about. I wish it would happen more often!

I believe that as we walk with the Lord, something about us attracts others to God. Not to ourselves, but to the character of Christ in us.

Now, you might be thinking, *I've got a long way to go, because Christ committed no sin.* I've got a long way to go, too; my wife and children can tell you that. I know I'll never get there on this side of heaven, but my heart's desire is to grow more like Him every day. That's where I want to live.

Do you want to be more like the Master? The only way that happens is by spending time with Him. The more time you spend with Him, the more He can mold you into His image.

Spend some time with Him today; become more like Him.

Pit Stop
POINT TO PONDER

When you turned to Jesus, you turned to Truth. And the more you get to know the One who is truth, the more His Spirit works to make you like Him. Make it a daily priority to spend time with Him.

April 4

How do you leave a lasting legacy? I was reading something from Dr. D. James Kennedy, senior pastor of Coral Ridge Presbyterian Church, who once talked about several massive structures, like the great pyramid of Giza, the Taj Mahal and the Great Wall of China. Did you know that the astronauts can even see that wall from outer space?

Now, you might have recognized the names of those structures and you might even have an image of each one in your mind, but do you remember who built them? They're impressive building projects and people still travel to see them, but do you remember why they were built? I don't. The answers to those questions have pretty much faded away as time has gone by.

Scripture says that we can leave a legacy that is not fleeting and does not pass away quickly:

> Those who lead many to righteousness [shall shine] like the stars for ever and ever (Daniel 12:3).

What a great word! We shine like a star when we show Jesus to the world and bring people to meet Him. And that is something that will not fade away. Those results will last forever and ever.

Pit Stop PRAYER

Lord Jesus, take my eyes off the things that will fade away and fix my gaze on Your unseen kingdom, on the things that will last forever.

April 5

Jim Elliot was one of the five missionaries killed by the Auca Indians in Ecuador. The missionaries had spent months attempting to contact and gain the trust of the fierce tribe in order to learn their language and translate God's Word into words the tribe could understand.

One day when a large group of spear-wielding Aucas approached, the missionaries hoped for a friendly meeting; but there, on the beach, these five young men—husbands and fathers—were killed by the Aucas.

Even before he went to Ecuador, Jim Elliot had written in his journal, "He is no fool to give what he cannot keep to gain that which he cannot lose." His life exemplified that belief. He gave his life for the mission of Christ. Jesus said, "Whoever loses his life for me and for the gospel will save it" (Mark 8:35).

Another journal entry from Jim Elliot is not as well known, but it is just as powerful: "Lord, make me a crisis man. Let me not be a milepost on a single road, but make me a fork that men and women must turn one way or another in facing Christ in me."

In other words, Elliot's desire was for anyone he met to see and hear Jesus in him and be forced to make a decision to accept or reject the Lord. That's what we need to be if we want to see a renewal and awakening come to this land. We need to be lightning rods for Jesus, pointing people to Him. Devoting our lives to His mission, we must give what we cannot keep to gain what we cannot lose.

Pit Stop
POINT TO PONDER

You may not have to die as a witness of Christ, but you will have to put to death your own wishes and wants and ambitions. You'll have to give up living for yourself and live for one thing: Christ's mission to bring people to Himself. Every day you must make the choice: Are you going to live for yourself or for the One who paid the ransom to save you?

April 6

Henry Ward Beecher gave us a good picture of forgiveness:

> Forgiveness ought to be like a canceled note—torn in two, and burned up, so it can never be shown against one.

Have you ever been to one of those ceremonies where a mortgage is torn up and burned, because it's paid in full? The loan has been paid, and the creditor no longer has any power. This is the forgiveness we need to practice as a way of life.

That's how Jesus forgives our sin. He said He'd remove our sin "as far as the east is from the west" and remember it no more (Psalm 103:12; see also Hebrews 10:17).

So why keep accounts against others? When we do not forgive, we harbor bitterness. But Jesus came to set us free from that way of life, and He was pretty clear about how often we must forgive: "Seventy times seven!" (Matthew 18:22, *NLT*). "Make allowance for each other's faults, and forgive anyone who offends you. Remember, the Lord forgave you, so you must forgive others" (Colossians 3:13, *NLT*).

The world can learn about God's forgiveness by watching how we forgive those who wrong us. Forgive, my friend, even seventy times seven times.

Is there someone you need to forgive today? Tear up that note you've been holding, burn it, and follow God's example.

Pit Stop
PRAYER

Lord Jesus, test my heart today. Show me if I'm harboring bitterness or anger. Help me to forgive and let go of those attitudes and instead be kind and merciful.

April 7

> The Spirit of the Sovereign LORD is on me, because the LORD has anointed me to preach good news to the poor. He has sent me to bind up the brokenhearted, to proclaim freedom for the captives, and release from darkness for the prisoners.
>
> ISAIAH 61:1

One day in the synagogue in Nazareth, Jesus stood up and read the first two verses from chapter 61 of the prophecies of Isaiah. Then He added, "The Scripture you've just heard has been fulfilled this very day!" (Luke 4:21, *NLT*).

Can you imagine what the Jewish people must have felt and thought when Jesus made this claim? That passage of Scripture makes some pretty significant statements.

Jesus was sent to bind up the brokenhearted and proclaim freedom. All of the people in Jesus' audience that day were in captivity to the Roman Empire. He was sent to release prisoners from darkness. They understood this terminology because a prison in that day was not like the ones we have today; it was basically a hole in the ground where a prisoner either died from disease or simply awaited execution. Jesus said, "I'm sent to release prisoners from punishment and death."

What a calling! Do you know people who need the good news? Do you know anyone who is brokenhearted, who is a captive or who is a prisoner in darkness?

You are Jesus' representative now on this earth, and you are called to present His claims and the good news He has for this world!

Pit Stop
POINT TO PONDER

Paul wrote in 2 Corinthians that God has anointed us (see 2 Corinthians 1:21)—the same word used to refer to Jesus being anointed (see Acts 4:26-27; 10:38). We have been commissioned to do the same work that brought Jesus to earth: Spread the good news to the brokenhearted, the captives and those who sit in darkness.

April 8

Life is not always easy. Are you discouraged today?

I'm continually amazed that God would choose to use me, but I figured out a long time ago that if He could use a donkey to talk for Him, He could use me (see Numbers 22:21-41). Still, we all have days when we fight discouragement; we focus on our shortcomings, failures and weaknesses; and we doubt whether God can really use us.

Paul struggled with a weakness of some kind and begged God to take it away. God answered, "My power is made perfect in weakness" (2 Corinthians 12:9). The *New Living Translation* reads, "My power works best in weakness." What a statement! The times when we are weak and think we're too flawed or imperfect to be used by God are the precise times His power can best work in us. That's contrary to what society says today, for it commends and praises self-sufficiency and human strength.

None of the people listed in the Bible were free from weaknesses, but God used all of them. He had a plan and a purpose for each one to fulfill.

If He could use these people, my friend, He can use you, too. Let Him use all your weakness and imperfection to bring Him glory.

Pit Stop
POINT TO PONDER

Scriptures say that you have the light of God shining in your heart, like a great treasure in a fragile jar of clay (see 2 Corinthians 4:6-7). Have you felt like a cracked, flawed and inadequate jar? That makes it easier for God to use you! When you feel like a perfect pot—strong, flawless, self-sufficient—your self-importance gets in the way of God's work in your life. When He uses a fragile jar of clay in great ways, it is clear that the power and glory belong to Him alone.

April 9

Mario was a young man who did not know Christ. He was invited into a home and offered a bowl of soup. That simple invitation had a major impact on his life.

Later, Mario shared his testimony, the story of how he came to Christ. He recalled that first time he was invited into his co-worker's home. The two had planned to go somewhere, but when Mario arrived at his co-worker's house, the family first invited him to have a bowl of soup with them. They prayed and then ate; and he sat there observing the family, especially how the man and his wife related to each other.

"I asked myself when I would have that kind of relationship with my fiancée," said Mario. "When I realized the answer was never, I concluded that I had to become a Christian for the sake of my own survival." What a powerful testimony! The invitation to have a bowl of soup and join a family for a short time had such an impact that he thought he would not survive without having a similar relationship. That's how God can use a simple gesture of kindness to advance His kingdom.

"Live wisely among those who are not believers, and make the most of every opportunity. Let your conversation be gracious and attractive so that you will have the right response for everyone (Colossians 4:5-6, *NLT*). "In very simple, everyday ways, you can represent Jesus. You don't have to preach a sermon—just live a sermon.

I hope what you are today will speak so loudly that people cannot help but hear what you say.

Pit Stop
PRAYER

Lord, make my life so attractive that others will see the difference and know it is only because I belong to You.

April 10

> Praise the LORD, my soul. Lord my God, you are
> very great; you are clothed with splendor and majesty.
> He wraps himself in light as with a garment; he stretches
> out the heavens like a tent.
>
> PSALM 104:1-2

Today, as you go about all your activities, whatever they might be, look for ways to praise the Lord. You are the representative and ambassador of the almighty God, Creator of heaven and earth.

Imagine that you get a call from the White House, and the president of the United States is on the line asking you to serve as ambassador to England. That might be one of the highest honors you as an American citizen could ever get.

Well, my friend, because you know Christ, you have received a personal call from God, asking you to be His representative. You are now His ambassador to a needy world that He loves.

Christ gave you a new life. Live it to bring glory to the very great God who has saved you.

Pit Stop PROMISE

"For once you were full of darkness, but now you have light from the Lord. So live as people of light! For this light within you produces only what is good and right and true" (Ephesians 5:8-9, *NLT*). What a promise! Your life *can* give glory to God because the Light within you produces right living—it's not up to you, in your own human power. Walk in the light, and watch how He changes you!

April 11

Here's what Jesus said about loving others: "Greater love has no one than this, that he lay down his life for his friends" (John 15:13).

If you are a recipient of the love of God, give it away!

Giving God's love away is really your primary responsibility here in this world. I know you have all these other responsibilities at your job, in your family and in your church; but as a child of God, as someone who has been showered with His great love, you're now asked to show that love to the world by giving it away.

How do you do that? Scripture says that every act of unselfishness is an act done for Jesus (see Matthew 10:42). As you go about your day, look for ways you can extend grace and mercy and love to others.

You can even do that in places like rush-hour traffic. You can extend love and mercy in your driving. That's a challenge to me; I admit I can be an aggressive driver sometimes, and I have to pray over that one. Yes, I have places to go and a schedule to keep. But more than anything, I want to represent Jesus well wherever I am and whatever I'm doing.

If you were arrested for being a Christian, would there be enough evidence to convict you? Based on what you do and how you live your life, could your accusers prove you were a follower of Christ? I hope so.

Today, think about ways you can extend God's love to those around you.

Pit Stop Prayer

**Lord, I want to live a life filled with love.
Teach me how to love like You do.**

April 12

Isaiah had stepped into the audience chamber of the God of all creation. He saw the Lord, high and lifted up, and the seraphim were crying one to another, "Holy, holy, holy is the LORD Almighty" (Isaiah 6:3).

And what did Isaiah do when he saw all this? He tried to get out of the presence of God because, he said, "I'm a man of unclean lips, and I live among a people of unclean lips, and my eyes have seen the King, the LORD Almighty" (Isaiah 6:5). But the Lord touched those lips with a hot coal and cleansed him.

> Then [Isaiah] heard the voice of the Lord saying, "Whom shall I send? And who will go for us?" And I said, "Here am I. Send me!" (Isaiah 6:8).

If you know Christ in a personal way, you too have been cleansed for the purpose of being sent. So wherever you go today—your job, your home, your shopping—whatever you do, God is sending you into the world. That is His plan, His purpose. That's why you have been redeemed. He did not pay the price for your sins and adopt you into His family just to take you off to heaven but to continue His mission on earth.

As you go about your day, think about the fact that you are being sent. I hope you respond, "I am here! Send me!"

Pit Stop Prayer

Holy Spirit, remind me today in the midst of all my actions and all my words that Christ has sent me as His representative. Just as God sent His Son to the world, so too the Son sent His followers. I bear His name and have been entrusted with His mission and message. Remind me.

April 13

> If anyone gives a cup of cold water to one of these
> little ones because he is my disciple, I tell you the truth,
> he will certainly not lose his reward.
>
> MATTHEW 10:42

In Matthew 10:42, Jesus states that by serving others, we also serve Him. Another time, Jesus said that if we see someone hungry and feed that person, then in effect we will be giving food to Jesus. If we visit the lonely or those in prison, then we'll be doing it as unto Him (see Matthew 25:35-40).

Think about how you might serve Jesus today. Look at places you might ordinarily overlook. Look for people others usually ignore—the lonely person, the person who needs help but won't ask for it, the person who has a wall up and never wants to talk about Christ, the person who feels forgotten and unloved. Look in the forgotten, ignored and lonely places.

Then be Jesus' hands, His feet, His listening ears and His caring heart. Yes, you will be rewarded in heaven for what you do, but do this just because you love Jesus and want to show His love to those who need Him.

Today, look for ways to serve Jesus by serving others. Look for someone you can bless in Jesus' name. I promise you, if you do it, your day will be much better. And you'll end up being the recipient of blessing. You can't out-give God.

Choose to bless people in Jesus' name, and make it a way of life.

Pit Stop — POINT TO PONDER

Do you ever think of your life as being the fragrance of Christ? God does! As you serve in Jesus' name and spread the message of Christ, your life is "a Christ-like fragrance rising up to God" (2 Corinthians 2:15, *NLT*).

April 14

> Light is shed upon the righteous and joy on the upright in heart. Rejoice in the Lord, you who are righteous, and praise his holy name.
>
> PSALM 97:11-12

The psalms are so wonderful. A good practice is to read five psalms every day for one month. By the end of the month, you'll have read through the entire book, and the Scriptures will have spoken to you and deepened your communion with the Father.

In those wonderful, wonderful passages, we find the heart of God—His goodness and love and care. We find all the struggles and trials humans deal with—all the battles, confessions, joys and victories.

Psalm 97:11-12, the two verses for today, speak of the light and joy in our lives that result in praise and rejoicing. That's one of the ways we show to the world that Jesus Christ makes a difference in our life. We are always going to meet difficulties in life. But if we carry the joy of the Lord as a part of who we are, His presence in us will shine wherever we go. While driving, in stressful situations at home, or during conflicts at work, if the joy of the Lord is our strength, it will be evident to all those around us.

Jesus said He came "to bestow . . . the oil of gladness instead of mourning, and a garment of praise instead of a spirit of despair" (Isaiah 61:3). If you don't have that joy, ask Him for it! He will pour out the oil of joy upon you.

Pit Stop
POINT TO PONDER

After Moses had spent time with God on Mount Sinai, his face glowed so brightly that the people could not look at him, so he wore a veil over his face until the glow subsided (see Exodus 34:29-35). Do your face and your life glow with God's presence?

April 15

God has called us to represent Him to those around us. Do you feel inadequate? Do you feel as though He's asking something of you that is just "not you"? Are you thinking, *I just don't even know where to begin?*

That's part of the reason for these daily meditations—so you can think about *how* you can better represent your Master in this world.

We need to remind ourselves every day that we bear Jesus' name. We belong to Him, so we are a witness of what it means to be redeemed by Christ, to have a new life in the Spirit and to have our lives controlled by Jesus.

But when we feel inadequate or timid, Scripture reminds us that He "equips us with every good for doing His will," and He works in us to produce what is pleasing to Him (Hebrews 13:21).

God will do that, my friend! His plan is to work in you, to equip you to do everything He's asked and to become everything He's created you to be. There are things you will do that I'll never be able to do; I'll do things you won't be able to do. He equips each of us for the specific work He's given us.

It pleases God when we allow Him to work in us. I like to visualize God just looking over us and smiling because we are allowing Him to work, allowing Him to make us what He planned for us to be.

When you're feeling weak or unable or afraid, go to Him and ask for assurance. He will equip and empower you, but sometimes you just need His reassurance. He'll meet that need.

Pit Stop
POINT TO PONDER

"It is God who enables us, along with you, to stand firm for Christ. . . . And He has identified us as His own by placing the Holy Spirit in our hearts" (2 Corinthians 1:21-22, *NLT*). How reassuring! God's power keeps you firm; and the Spirit within you changes and empowers you and tells you that you belong to Him. Hold tight to that promise.

April 16

> Whatever you do, whether in word or deed, do it all in the name of the Lord Jesus, giving thanks to God the Father through him.
>
> COLOSSIANS 3:17

There's no name like the name of Jesus. It truly is the sweetest name I know—our comfort and the only hope for this world. We wear His name, and when we take it everywhere we go, we represent Christ to the world. As Lydia O. Baxter states in her hymn "Precious Name":

> Take the name of Jesus with you,
> Child of sorrow and of woe,
> It will joy and comfort give you;
> Take it then, where'er you go.
>
> Precious name, oh, how sweet!
> Hope of earth and joy of heav'n.
> Precious name, oh, how sweet!
> Hope of earth and joy of heav'n.
>
> Take the name of Jesus ever,
> As a shield from every snare;
> If temptations round you gather,
> Breathe that holy name in prayer.

Take the name of Jesus with you. Breathe that name wherever you go.

Pit Stop Promise

God promises that someday every knee will bow at Jesus' name, in heaven and on earth and under the earth, and every mouth will acknowledge that Jesus is Lord (see Philippians 2:10-11). What a day that will be!

April 17

> The LORD does not look at the things man looks at. Man looks at the outward appearance, but the LORD looks at the heart.
>
> 1 SAMUEL 16:7

A lot of people speak today about dressing for success and looking the part. All kinds of articles for job seekers give advice on how to dress to impress a prospective employer in an interview. Certainly there's nothing wrong with looking good and dressing well. And I admit that as humans our perceptions of a person's character are often affected by outward appearance.

But no one can impress God with outward appearance. He looks at our hearts. And a key point is that from our hearts flow the words we speak and the actions we live out (see Matthew 12:34; Luke 6:45).

As followers of Christ, we want to magnify the person of Jesus Christ in the way that we live. If we spend time with Him—in His Word, and in prayer and communion with Him—He shapes us into what He wants us to be. And that changes our heart and the way we live.

So my question to you today is this: Is your heart in communion and fellowship with the One you call Master and Lord?

Pit Stop
PRAYER

Lord Jesus, dress my heart today in love, joy, peace, patience, kindness, goodness and faithfulness. I cannot do it on my own; only the power of Your Spirit will grow these things in my heart. I am willing, Lord, and desiring to be molded into what You want me to be.

April 18

> Next time you catch yourself absorbed in you-know-who, stop and think about what you can do for someone around you. Remember your freedom in Christ and spend it on others.
>
> JOHN FISCHER

Have any free time today? Is there an hour or two when you will have the freedom to choose what you'll do? Why don't you bless somebody?

I was traveling one day and noticed an elderly African-American lady sitting on the bus that took us from one terminal to another. I just thought she looked like she needed some help, and I wanted to be the person who offered it to her.

It turned out she did need help. She had not traveled in a long time, and she was confused. I took the time to help her off the bus and to get her to her gate. I had about an hour layover myself, so I was not rushed and I could give her this assistance.

I cannot tell you the joy that brought me, and I believe it brought joy to her, too. She thanked me and said I was an angel. I don't profess to be that, but I do believe God used me in that situation.

Here's my point: I chose to help her. I could have walked by. Everybody else on the bus ignored her and went their various ways. But because I chose to do what I did, God used me to bless both of us.

"Do you have the gift of helping others? Do it with all the strength and energy that God supplies" (1 Peter 4:11, *NLT*). Today, find someone to spend your freedom on. And do it with all the strength and energy God gives you.

Pit Stop
POINT TO PONDER

Jesus said that He came to serve and give His life for others. He set you free from all the things that held you prisoner so that you could give yourself fully to His mission on this earth—serving others in love and showing the way to God.

April 19

Paul wrote in 1 Corinthians 15:14, "And if Christ has not been raised, our preaching is useless and so is your faith." You are alive in Christ only because of the resurrection. Own that truth; you have the life you now have only because Christ rose from the dead.

A former Archbishop of Canterbury, Michael Ramsey, once said, "No resurrection, no Christianity." Those four words sum it up well, my friend.

> Don't you know that all of us who were baptized into Christ Jesus were baptized into his death? We were therefore buried with him through baptism into death in order that, just as Christ was raised from the dead through the glory of the Father, we too may live a new life (Romans 6:3-4).

If you know Christ in a personal way, the old you is buried and gone; you have been raised to a new life! You no longer live, but now Christ lives in you. You represent the new life that Christ gives. He gave you that life, and now He's strategically placed you to share the good news with those around you.

Isn't there someone you know who is longing for a new life?

Pit Stop
POINT TO PONDER

Daniel T. Niles wrote, "Evangelism is witness. It is one beggar telling another beggar where to get food. The Christian does not offer out of his bounty. He has no bounty. He is simply a guest at his Master's table and, as evangelist, he calls others too." If the old you has died and you've been born into a new life, tell others where they can also find new life.

April 20

In John 13:35, Jesus says, "All men will know that you are my disciples, if you love one another."

Jesus commands us to love one another, and this love will be our witness. It's through our display of this divine love, this *agape* love, that the world will see Jesus in us. Are you exhibiting that? Or have you allowed disunity or grudges or other differences to separate you from someone else who is a follower of Christ?

All too often we may find ourselves arguing and bickering and tearing down our brothers and sisters who disagree with us over one little area of theology or practice. But God wants us to focus on Him and love people as He has loved us.

If the world sees this example, I think they'll want what we have. But until they can see that Christ makes a difference in our lives, they're going to question everything we do. What the world needs is Jesus' love, made real in us.

Jesus says, "Love people. Speak love into their lives." Today, look for opportunities to live out His command to love others.

Pit Stop
PRAYER

Lord Jesus, You've commanded me to love others as You love me. I can only do that through the power of Your Spirit. Teach me. In everything I say and do today, show me how to love as You do.

April 21

The following prayer, written by Saint Francis of Assisi, is also a good prayer for those who want to represent Jesus in this world:

> *Lord, make me an instrument of Your peace.*
> *Where there is hatred, let me sow love;*
> *Where there is injury, pardon;*
> *Where there is doubt, faith;*
> *Where there is despair, hope;*
> *Where there is darkness, light;*
> *Where there is sadness, joy.*
>
> *O Divine Master, grant that I may not so much seek to be consoled as to console;*
> *to be understood as to understand;*
> *to be loved, as to love.*
> *For it is in giving that we receive.*
> *It is in pardoning that we are pardoned,*
> *and it is in dying that we are born to eternal life.*
>
> *Amen.*

Pit Stop — POINT TO PONDER

Jesus said, "If you refuse to take up your cross and follow me, you are not worthy of being mine. If you cling to your life, you will lose it; but if you give up your life for me, you will find it" (Matthew 10:38-39, *NLT*).

April 22

> What is the price of two sparrows—one copper coin? But not a single sparrow can fall to the ground without your Father knowing it. And the very hairs on your head are all numbered. So don't be afraid; you are more valuable to God than a whole flock of sparrows.
>
> MATTHEW 10:29-31, *NLT*

If God provides for the sparrows, if He gave such beauty to the lilies of the field without a bit of toiling or spinning on their part, how much more will He care for you, His beloved child? He even knows the number of hairs on your head!

Know that His eye is on you. He created you and loves you so much; He knit you together inside your mother's womb and scheduled every day of your life. He has plans to prosper you, plans of hope for your future. You can rest secure in His hands.

God's plan is also that you'll be His representative in this world. So as He cares for you and guides your day, wherever you go—the grocery store, your office, your school, your home—realize that He has a purpose for you. He's watching over You, and He will empower you and strengthen you so that you can carry out the work He has for you.

Pit Stop
PROMISE

By His divine power, God has given you everything you need for living a godly life (see 2 Peter 1:3). Remember that the power that works in you is the same power that raised Jesus from the dead. God provides that power for you every moment of every day! Ask Him. Rely on Him.

April 23

Our Teacher and Master said, "Bless those who curse you" (Luke 6:28). That's a tough instruction. Sometimes it's really difficult to live out a walk of faith, and this one challenge is especially hard for me. But it's really important.

Do you bless even those who curse you? If somebody curses me, the old Steve in me wants to rise up and strike back. When I'm mistreated, I want to demand my right for revenge and say, "You're not going to treat me like that."

But Jesus said, "Bless those who curse you."

What would this world be like if all of us who call Jesus Lord would live out His teachings? What would your life be like at work? At home? What would your response be when someone insults you? Jesus said, "Bless them." That's not a normal response!

The world lives with the normal, but Jesus wants you to live above normal. It's not normal to bless somebody who curses you. It's not normal to forgive seventy times seven. It's not normal to give away your coat. It's not normal to walk an extra mile. Those are just not normal things to do.

My friend, Jesus saves you from normal. It's normal to sin. It's normal to get angry. It's normal to seek revenge. But Jesus saved you so that you will not be normal and so that you will display His character to the world around you.

Live above normal today.

Pit Stop
POWER

Scripture says that your old human nature will always be fighting against your Spirit-given desire to live as Jesus wants you to live. But Jesus died to break the hold sin has on your life, and the power of His Spirit within you can free you from the prison of your human nature.

April 24

One of the persons we learn from in Scripture is Job. He was in the depths of despair when he asked, "Where is God my Maker, who gives songs in the night?" (Job 35:10).

That's a good question. Maybe you have struggled with the question of where God is when you are suffering or in trouble. When you have no songs in the night, does He care? C. F. Weigle addressed this question in his hymn "No One Ever Cared for Me Like Jesus":

> I would love to tell you what I think of Jesus
> Since I found in Him a friend so strong and true;
> I would tell you how He changed my life completely,
> He did something that no other friend could do.
>
> No one ever cared for me like Jesus,
> There's no other friend so kind as He;
> No one else could take the sin and darkness from me
> O how much He cares for me.

My friend, I hope you've discovered that nobody can love you like Jesus. And if you have experienced His assurance and His strong and loving arms around you through your own dark or lonely days, then introduce someone else to the Friend who cares like no one else.

Pit Stop
POINT TO PONDER

David wrote, "Unfailing love surrounds those who trust in the LORD" (Psalm 32:10, *NLT*). God's love does not depend on your being worthy; He loved you even before you knew Him, and He sent Jesus to bring you back to Himself. When you meet those today who do not know Christ, ask the Spirit to remind you how much He loves them too.

April 25

In Romans 12, Paul wrote that our lives and minds are to be transformed and that our actions show sincere love. Here's one command that spoke to me: "Honor one another above yourselves" (verse 10).

Now, what does that verse mean to you? In this day and age, we don't talk much about honoring others, unless we're honoring a hero or veterans or people who have given all the years of their lives to some kind of service. We do honor those people.

But I think Paul was talking about something most people do not do on a daily basis. Here are some other ways that statement has been translated: "Give preference to one another in honor" (*NASB*); "excel at showing respect for each other: (*ISV*); "outdo one another in showing honor" (*ESV*); "take delight in honoring each other (*NLT*).

I especially like, "Outdo one another in showing honor." What a goal! What would happen if you went about your days trying to outdo others in showing respect and in treating others with dignity? I'll guarantee that it would make everyone's day a whole lot better.

Go through life looking for opportunities to show respect to others. Show a love that loves unconditionally, that doesn't keep score of wrongs, that is patient and kind and rejoices in what is right. Bless the people you come into contact with. That's really what your mission is all about.

Outdo others in showing honor. As you do that, you will be a sweet aroma as you present Jesus Christ to the world around you.

Pit Stop
POINT TO PONDER

Jesus said, "You know that the rulers in this world lord it over their people, and officials flaunt their authority over those under them. But among you it will be different. Whoever wants to be a leader among you must be your servant, and whoever wants to be first among you must become your slave" (Matthew 20:25-27, *NLT*).

April 26

In Matthew 27, we have the story of the crucifixion of our Lord Jesus Christ. People watched Him on the cross, hanging there, dying for you and for me. And some of them said, "He saved others, . . . but he can't save himself!" (Matthew 27:42).

Jesus chose to stay on the cross and die. What held Him on that cross? It wasn't the nails. It was His love for you.

As you go through your day today, think about the fact that God loves you unconditionally. He knew you before you were in your mother's womb, and He loved you before you even knew Him. He loves you with an everlasting love.

Scripture is very clear: Jesus is God of all creation, and He came to this earth for the very purpose of dying for you. He could have saved Himself at any time, but He chose to stay on that cross so that He could have a relationship with you.

Jesus did not save Himself so that He could save you. Live in the sweetness of relationship with Him! Why not tell Him today how much you love Him?

Pit Stop
PRAISE

Jesus said that He came to seek and to save those who were lost. That was you, my friend. He came on a mission to save you! He sought you out, and He paid the ransom to give you life and a new relationship with God. Say with the psalmist David, "With every bone in my body I will praise him: 'Lord, who can compare to You?'" (Psalm 35:10, *NLT*).

April 27

We hear a lot today about the concept of servant-leadership. That might be a new term to you, but the idea isn't new. Jesus Himself talked about it. He said, "If someone forces you to go one mile, go with him two miles" (Matthew 5:41). A servant-leader goes above and beyond the call of duty.

Jesus taught at the time of Roman occupation of His country. A Roman soldier could force a Jewish person to carry things for him as he traveled along the road, and the Jew was required to comply. But Jesus said, "If someone forces you to go one mile, go ahead and go two."

Can you imagine the conversation during the second mile? The first mile is required, but if someone said, "I want to go ahead and carry this another mile for you," what do you think that soldier's reaction would have been? I think he might have been a little more open to whatever that second-mile person had to say.

I believe the same is true today. The best way to win people is to love them to Jesus. Show the gift of hospitality; exercise servanthood. Let people know you are there to serve them.

Be a second-mile person today. Look for people who need help, and invest in them by going that second mile. You'll make a significant difference in their lives.

Pit Stop
POINT TO PONDER

Think about this simple formula for ordering your actions today: "Don't let evil conquer you, but conquer evil by doing good" (Romans 12:21).

April 28

I was once a guest speaker at a church, and the man who introduced me was a friend of mine. Forty years ago, we had worked together at an ambulance business. He had given his life to Christ since, and he's been a good friend for all these years.

When he introduced me, he said that my life way back then had influenced him so much that he *had* to give his life to Christ. That remark was humbling for me, because I know I don't measure up in so many ways. "May the words of my mouth and the meditation of my heart be pleasing in your sight, O Lord, my Rock and my Redeemer" (Psalm 19:14).

Be mindful of your influence every day, wherever you are and whatever you do. People are watching your life, and if you make it your first priority that your words and thoughts are acceptable to the Lord, then how you live will reflect Jesus to those around you.

When I was about 12, our postmaster knocked on our door one day. I went to the door and invited him in, and he asked if my dad was there. Dad came into the room, and our guest broke down and cried. "Preacher Wingfield," he said, "I've been watching you and your family . . ."

No one is perfect. I know that. But we want people to see Jesus when they look at our lives. A prayer for today and every day: *May the words of my mouth and the meditation of my heart be pleasing in Your sight, O Lord, my Rock and my Redeemer.*

Pit Stop PRAYER

Jesus, thank You for the light You brought to my life! Let Your light shine through me so that others may come to know who You are.

April 29

> If we claim to have fellowship with him yet walk in the darkness, we lie and do not live by the truth. But if we walk in the light, as he is in the light, we have fellowship with one another, and the blood of Jesus, his Son, purifies us from all sin. If we claim to be without sin, we deceive ourselves and the truth is not in us. If we confess our sins, he is faithful and just and will forgive us our sins and purify us from all unrighteousness.
>
> 1 JOHN 1:6-9

It's good to examine ourselves every now and then and ask Jesus, "Lord, is everything straight?"

We want to walk in the light as He is in the light. The only way we can do that is to put all known sins behind us. When we confess our sins, He'll forgive us and cleanse us and we can move forward with a clean account.

So take just a moment and pray, *Lord, speak to me and see if there be any wicked way in me.*

Then listen. And if God reveals something to you, confess it, ask Him to forgive you, and then go forward and walk in the light this day.

Pit Stop PRAYER

"Create in me a clean heart, O God. Renew a loyal spirit within me" (Psalm 51:10, *NLT*).

April 30

Dear friends, let us love one another, for love comes from God. Everyone who loves has been born of God and knows God. Whoever does not love does not know God, because God is love. This is how God showed his love among us: He sent his one and only Son into the world that we might live through him. This is love: not that we loved God, but that he loved us and sent his Son as an atoning sacrifice for our sins. Dear friends, since God so loved us, we also ought to love one another.

1 JOHN 4:7-11

A prayer for all of us as we represent God's great, great love:

Lord God, continue to speak into our lives,
Continue to draw each of us to Yourself,
That we might be recipients of everything You have for us.
Thank You, Lord, that You have strengthened us in our inner beings.

Thank You for equipping us so that we can be Your representatives in this world.
Help us to be faithful.
Help us to walk in humility.
Help us to serve You well, that others might know You.
In Jesus' name.

Amen.

Pit Stop
PRAYER & PRAISE

Today, consider these lyrics from Laurie Klein: "I love you, Lord, and I lift my voice to worship You, oh, my soul, rejoice! Take joy my King in what You hear, let it be a sweet, sweet sound in Your ear."

MAY

Communing with God

I ***wait quietly*** before God, for my victory comes from him.

PSALM 62:1, *NLT*

May 1

*In the morning, O LORD, You hear my voice; in the morning,
I lay my requests before you and wait in expectation.*

PSALM 5:3

If you want to grow in your walk with the Lord, if you want God to speak into your life, you have to spend time with Him.

You might say that God is first in your life and you've committed your life to Him; but if you're not spending time with Him, then that's probably not the truth.

So how is your quiet time?

What is a quiet time? It's a time you set aside every day to commune with the Lord. It's a time for you to be together with Him and no one else, shutting out distractions and all the other things that clamor for your attention.

Morning is best for my own quiet time. I'm a morning person; I get out of bed, and I'm ready to go. That may not be true for you. You may be more of an evening person, with your most productive time coming later in the day. I have a friend who spends his lunch hour with the Lord. Whatever is the best time for you to let the Lord speak into your life, commit that time to Him on a daily basis.

God does hear your voice, and you will hear His voice, if you give Him this time. Today, give Him the best part of your day.

Pit Stop PRAYER

This month, use this prayer to begin your quiet time with the Lord: "My heart has heard you say, 'Come and talk with me.' And my heart responds, 'LORD, I am coming'" (Psalm 27:8, *NLT*).

May 2

There's something very special about the mornings. Not everyone is a morning person, but I do believe the morning can set the pace for the rest of your day. Listen to what the psalmist says about mornings:

> I rise before dawn and cry for help; I have put my hope in your word (Psalm 119:147).

> How precious to me are your thoughts, O God! . . . When I awake, I am still with you (Psalm 139:17-18).

> Let the morning bring me word of your unfailing love, for I have put my trust in you. Show me the way I should go, for to you I lift up my soul (Psalm 143:8).

God is thinking about you. Are you thinking about Him? Does He hear your voice in the morning? Do you come to Him in expectation?

Whether or not you're a morning person, get into the habit of beginning your day with thoughts of Him. Live in the awareness that the moment you wake up in the morning, He is thinking about you. He has watched over you through the night, and He's going to direct you through the day ahead.

Begin your day by saying, "Good morning, Lord." Or thank Him for a night's rest and ask Him to direct your steps. He said He will never leave you; be aware of His presence and have a grateful, thankful heart full of praise and adoration as you begin your day.

I promise you, this will change your day.

Pit Stop PRACTICE

Each night this month, as you close your eyes, determine that your first thought in the morning will be a prayer. When you awake in the morning, offer a prayer of thanks or praise and ask God to guide your steps that day.

May 3

In the poem "Columbus," the famous American poet James Russell Lowell wrote, "The nurse of full-grown souls is solitude."

We're living in such a hectic and busy world that solitude is difficult to practice. I remember the day when there were no cell phones and no email. In many ways, that was a really good place to be. Now there's instant and constant contact with the whole world. We are bombarded. There's an instant awareness of what's going on around the world. If there's an earthquake in China, we know about it today.

Because of that constant connection to the world, it's sometimes difficult to maintain solitude and quietness. For the sake of your own soul, for the sake of your relationship with the Lord, you need to shut off your phone, shut off your computer, turn off the TV, and get alone with the Lord on a daily basis. Let Him speak to you.

> I wait quietly before God, for my victory comes from him (Psalm 62:1, *NLT*).

Are you waiting quietly before the Lord? I challenge you to take this month to establish a new habit. Summer is usually a busy time for most people, and that means you'll need the blessing of His peace and joy even more in the next few months. Begin now to seek Him every day and your summer, your year, will see victory after victory.

Pit Stop
PRACTICE

"Search for the LORD and for His strength; continually seek him" (Psalm 105:4, *NLT*).

May 4

Hear God saying to you today, "Be still, and know that I am God; I will be exalted among the nations, I will be exalted in the earth" (Psalm 46:10).

We live in a rat-race world. Every day seems filled with pressure, pressure, pressure. You probably don't need me to remind you of that. Maybe you've got a whole list of things you need to get done today.

"Be still," God says. Know that He is God.

My son, David, and I spent a week hiking the Appalachian Trail. It was a wonderful time for me to have a walk in the woods and be still. Yes, we were walking and sometimes talking; but we were away from the world in which we normally live, with its noise and commotion. In that week on the trail, I had a chance to quiet my mind and my soul and think about my God. There were no cell phones, computers or televisions, just the beauty of His creation and the privilege of uninterrupted time with my son. It was really, really special.

Now, I know not everybody can or even wants to hike the Appalachian Trail, but I encourage you to find the time and a place to be still. When God met Elijah on the mountain, God was not in the windstorm, He was not in the earthquake, and He was not in the fire. God came to Elijah with a still, small voice (see 1 Kings 19:9-18). In order for you to hear that gentle whisper, you need to be still.

Be still, and listen for your God today.

Pit Stop PROMISE

Hear God's invitation and promise: "Come to me with your ears wide open. Listen, and you will find life" (Isaiah 55:3, *NLT*).

May 5

> When your words came, I ate them; they were my joy and my heart's delight, for I bear your name, O LORD God Almighty.
>
> JEREMIAH 15:16

You probably eat three times a day, maybe occasionally less and maybe often more! You will seldom go through an entire day without eating some kind of food; after all, your body craves the nourishment.

Do you think of words from God as food? Does your soul crave nourishment from Him?

If you want to know God better, you have to spend time with Him. It's like any friendship. If I don't spend time with my wife, Barbara, we're not going to be connected. If I don't spend time with my friends, we're not going to be connected. If I don't spend time with the Lord—specifically set-aside time to get to know Him better—then I'm not going to grow and mature in my walk with Him.

When we strengthen our human friendships and bonds, we have more joy in those relationships. The verse from Jeremiah says that same joy is found when God speaks into our life. We bear His name; we are His children. And communing with Him will nourish our souls.

Make sure you get the nourishment of God's words today. Set aside some time to spend with Him only, and ask God to speak to you during that time. Read His Word. Pray about your day. Make this time together a habit, and you'll get to know Him better, you'll walk more closely with Him, and you will have more joy in your life.

Pit Stop PROMISE

God says, "Why spend money on what is not bread, and your labor on what does not satisfy? Listen, listen to me, and eat what is good, and your soul will delight in the richest of fare" (Isaiah 55:2). What are you feeding on today? Choose what satisfies, and feed on God's rich fare.

May 6

In the book of Mark, we read that, "very early in the morning, while it was still dark, Jesus got up, left the house and went off to a solitary place, where He prayed" (Mark 1:35). If Jesus needed to get alone in a solitary place so that He could commune with His Father, how much more do you and I need to get alone and spend quiet time communicating with Him?

The Bible will be self-authenticating as you spend time in it. If you haven't been spending time in God's Word, I recommend that you start in the Gospel of John. Just set aside time to read a few verses or read a chapter each day.

Before you start reading, pray, *Lord, speak to me.* And as He speaks to you, talk to Him. If you don't understand something, tell Him you don't understand and ask, *What are You trying to say to me through Your Word?* That is really how we get to know Him. We have to spend time with Him.

You may not have a solitary place where you can go to be with the Lord, but you can find a way to shut out the rest of the world while you talk with and listen to Him. Set aside the time, and then turn off everything else as you meet with the Master.

And if you're not a believer but a seeker and searcher, you can be honest with God. Say, *God, I want to know—is this stuff true? Would You speak to me? Would You help me to know?*

Spend some time with Him; and if you do that, He will speak to you.

Pit Stop PRACTICE

God is with you every moment of your day, and finding a special place to pray where you can shut out the noisy world is just as important to you as it was to Jesus. Conrad Hoover writes, "We need someplace to go in order to more fully enter into the Presence who enables us to pray. . . . We go apart to be quiet and expectant in the Lord's presence."

May 7

In him our hearts rejoice, for we trust in his holy name.

PSALM 33:21

Are you relaxed before God?

That might seem like a strange question, but I frequently meet people who get all uptight about a Bible; they don't even want to touch it. I've left my Bible on the bed in a hotel room and come back to find a note saying, "I didn't want to make your bed because your Bible was there." People still do have a reverent fear of God and His Word.

But you don't have to *fear* God. He is not out to get you. Fear, as it's used in the Bible, means respect. Respect God, but relax in His presence. Relax toward His will and plan, because you can trust Him. He created you and knows you and loves you, and He wants what's best for you. Be relaxed in His presence.

If you spend time with Him, He will direct your path. He will strategically place you where He wants you to serve Him. He will empower you to be that channel of blessing that you were created to be. As you work in unison with Him, you can trust Him to do all things well for you.

That's the purpose of spending time with God, my friend. When you learn to know Him, you learn that you can relax and trust Him and His plan for your life.

Today, intentionally give Him your best time of the day.

Pit Stop
PROMISE

Now is a good time to review your plan for peace. Remember the words from Philippians 4:7: "The peace of God, which transcends all understanding, will guard your hearts and your minds in Christ Jesus." God is present with you and cares about the details of your daily life! You can trust His love.

May 8

One of the things that often troubles me during my time with the Lord is an active mind. When I try to read or pray, I think about all the things that I need to do. Do those thoughts bother you? How do you combat that?

> We demolish arguments and every pretension that sets itself up against the knowledge of God, and we take captive every thought to make it obedient to Christ (2 Corinthians 10:5).

Invading our thought life to interrupt our communion with our Father is one way the enemy comes against us in our quiet time. But in this verse from 2 Corinthians, Paul challenges us to take captive every thought.

My dad used to say, "You can't keep the birds from flying over your head, but you can keep them from building nests in your hair." You can't keep the thoughts from coming, but you can take them captive. I keep a notepad with me, and when a distracting thought comes, I write it down. Then I can get back to my time with God and deal with the other issue later.

The battle is real, my friend. The enemy of your soul uses everyday thoughts to work against your getting to know God. Satan doesn't want you to know your Father. But if your heart's passion is to know Him, love Him, and serve Him, then take those thoughts captive and don't let the enemy interrupt your time with the Lord.

Pit Stop PROMISE

"You will keep in perfect peace all who trust in you, all whose thoughts are fixed on you! Trust in the Lord always, for the Lord God is the eternal Rock" (Isaiah 26:3-4, *NLT*). He is the only solid Rock, the only hope, the only One in whom you will find safe refuge. Keep your thoughts fixed on Him, and His peace will flow into your life.

May 9

> Out of the depths I cry to you, O Lord.
> PSALM 130:1

As we spend time with the Lord and get to know Him better, we get to know ourselves better, too. When I examine my own soul, my own needs, my own person and I'm with Him in communion, I can cry to Him from the very depth of my soul.

I love the way Psalm 130 begins: "Out of the depths I cry to you, O Lord." That could be interpreted several different ways. It could be a cry out of deep despair. Maybe it comes out of deep thought. Or perhaps it's from the depth of need.

Wherever we are, we can look to God. He is our resource, our strength, our shield. He is our "ever-present help" in times of trouble (see Psalm 46:1). He is a friend who sticks closer than a brother. Scripture promises all of those things, and God invites us to turn to Him.

Wherever you are today, whatever your need is today, cry out to Him: "Lord, I have nowhere else to go! I turn to You, God. Help me! I want to know Your presence and power."

Be honest with Him. Talk to Him just as you would talk to your best friend. You will find there is no friend like Jesus.

Pit Stop
POWER

"Trust in him at all times, O people; pour out your hearts to him, for God is our refuge" (Psalm 62:8).

May 10

> Thou, O Lord, art a God full of compassion, and gracious, longsuffering, and plenteous in mercy and truth.
>
> PSALM 86:15, *KJV*

How do you describe God? He is who He is, and there's no way to get Him in a box. But several of His attributes are described in Psalm 86:15.

The Lord is a God "full of compassion." I have moments of compassion. I think I'm a fairly compassionate person. But the Bible says God is "full of compassion." That says to me that He is just oozing all over with compassion. And He wants to show compassion to all people. My compassion falls far short of the fullness of His.

God is "gracious." You don't weary Him by coming to Him. He has your best interests at heart.

He is also "longsuffering." That means He's patient; He's willing to hang in there with you. And some of us need a very patient God!

He is also "plenteous in mercy." (I love the way the Bible is written!) He doesn't have just a little bit of mercy, but His mercy is overflowing, abundant and more than sufficient.

He is truth. And the truth is, this compassionate, gracious, longsuffering and abundantly merciful God loves you and wants you to know Him.

Spend time with God today, and let His love surround and hold you.

Pit Stop
POINT TO PONDER

Scripture also speaks of God's "*tender* mercy" (Luke 1:78, emphasis added). When you come to Him, think of these words: "compassion," "patience," "tender mercy," "truth" and "gracious." He says to His beloved child, "Come to me, and know me. I am always with you; I will hold you and help you and keep you secure." How He loves you!

May 11

How do you deal with the anxieties of life? In Matthew 6:34, Jesus told His followers, "Do not worry about tomorrow, for tomorrow will worry about itself. Each day has enough trouble of its own."

Worry really is a sin, because Jesus told us that we're to cast all our anxiety upon Him. He cares for us! Why do we worry?

What are you worried about? Stop reading for just a moment and answer that question. Then I've got another question: Is your worry going to help that situation? I don't even know what your worry is, but I can answer this last question—no!

Your only hope, your only refuge, is to look to Jesus Christ. Let Him meet that need. Cast all your anxiety upon Him. If you have to do it 10 times, 20 times, 100 times in one day, keep giving it to Him. He has promised that He will work for your good in everything.

Here's another reason it's so important to spend time with Him: If you don't, then you begin to carry all the anxiety and worry on your own. The enemy comes to you and plants the thought that you have so much to do that you can't spend time with your Lord. That's a thought to take captive! Martin Luther said that on days he had so much to do, rather than spending one hour with the Lord, he had to spend two hours; because he knew that if he didn't have extra time with the Lord, then he would never get everything done.

Take time to be alone with God today. And if you're carrying worry and anxiety, ask Him to carry it for you.

Pit Stop
PRACTICE

Practice giving your worries to God. Trust Him enough to say, "Lord, I'm worried about this thing, but I'm going to let You take care of it, because my worry doesn't accomplish anything." Then hand over your burden to the One who has promised to always be working for your good. Let Him have it, because He cares.

May 12

I think the importance of spending time with the Lord is obvious. If you don't spend time with Him, then there's no way you can know Him. But not everybody is convinced of that.

People are looking for light and truth and guidance in all kinds of places and are asking all kinds of questions: *What shall I do? Where shall I go?* Listen to what Isaiah says:

> Someone may say to you, "Let's ask the mediums and those who consult the spirits of the dead. With their whisperings and mutterings, they will tell us what to do." But shouldn't people ask God for guidance? Should the living seek guidance from the dead? Look to God's instructions and teachings! People who contradict his word are completely in the dark (Isaiah 8:19-20, *NLT*).

You can take this to the bank, my friend: If you are not looking to the living Word of God, then you are following a blind guide, and you are a blind follower.

You must look to Jesus Christ. He is your hope. He is your answer. He is your shield. He is your help. He loves you with an everlasting love.

What shall you do? Where shall you go? Go to the living God and Him alone.

Pit Stop
PRAYER

Lord Jesus, by Your Spirit, help me measure everything against Your Word and Your truth. Let me look to You alone to guide my steps and lead me along the path of life.

May 13

In Deuteronomy, Moses commanded the priests and elders of Israel to "assemble the people—men, women and children, and the aliens living in your towns—so they can listen and learn to fear the LORD your God and follow carefully all the words of this law" (Deuteronomy 31:12).

Now, I know we're living in New Testament times, and I know that Jesus said He came not to abolish the law but to fulfill it, but there are some key things that I want you to hear in what Moses said.

What was the purpose of bringing all the people together? So they could listen to the words of God's law and learn to fear the Lord. Did you see the word "learn"? There's a process you must go through if you're to grow and become the channel of blessing that God wants you to be. Your growth requires time—time spent with Him. You didn't grow up instantaneously. It took some tender loving care for you to mature physically. Similarly, spiritual growth takes time and care.

The Navigators use the five fingers on one hand to illustrate the ways in which a person learns from God's Word, with each finger representing something we must do: (1) hear the Word, (2) read the Word, (3) study the Word, (4) memorize the Word, and (5) meditate on the Word.

Listen and learn, that you might become the channel of blessing that God wants you to be.

Pit Stop
POWER

Psalm 119 begins, "Joyful are people of integrity, who follow the instructions of the LORD. Joyful are those who obey his laws and search for him with all their hearts" (verses 1-2, *NLT*). This long psalm goes on to tell of the importance of the Word of God: It encourages and teaches, keeps us from sin and gives hope, makes us wise, guides our steps, leads to joy and freedom. Spend time reading and meditating on God's Word. It will change your day.

---

156   Winning the Race Every Day   STEVE WINGFIELD

May 14

God and Moses had an amazing relationship. Read some of the stories about Moses in the Bible and try to imagine yourself in his shoes. What do you suppose it was like to spend time on Mount Sinai, alone with God, receiving God's words for His people?

In Exodus 25, we read all God's instructions on how to set up the tabernacle and everything in it. God spoke these words to Moses:

> Be sure that you make everything according to the pattern I have shown you here on the mountain (verse 40, *NLT*).

Moses spent time with God, receiving all these instructions. "Be sure to follow the plan," said God. He and Moses had been in communion with each other on the mountain.

Now, I know that God called Moses for a special mission. He set Moses apart for the work He wanted him to do. That is a special relationship, but the point is this: They spent time together. And look at what God did through Moses.

God wants to use you as well. He does! He has a purpose for every one of us. But for Him to be able to use you, you must spend time with Him, listening to His voice. Psalm 119:105 says that His Word is a light for your path. If you're going to have that light shine on your way, you must spend time in the Word.

Make your relationship with your Father a special, treasured, amazing relationship. Spend time with Him daily.

Pit Stop
POINT TO PONDER

"The LORD your God is with you. He is mighty to save. He will take great delight in you, he will quiet you with his love, he will rejoice over you with singing" (Zephaniah 3:17).

STEVE WINGFIELD

May 15

"Jesus, Savior, Pilot Me," a hymn written by Edward Hopper, is sometimes called "The Sailor's Hymn," but it is also a prayer for every one of us who must sail through stormy seas. It's a prayer for those times when we cry out, "I'm drowning, Lord! Save me!"

> Jesus, Savior, pilot me
> Over life's tempestuous sea;
> Unknown waves before me roll,
> Hiding rock and treacherous shoal.
> Chart and compass come from Thee;
> Jesus, Savior, pilot me.
>
> As a mother stills her child,
> Thou canst hush the ocean wild;
> Boisterous waves obey Thy will,
> When Thou sayest to them, "Be still!"
> Wondrous Sovereign of the sea,
> Jesus, Savior, pilot me.

I don't know what you're facing today, my friend, but maybe this song was just for you. Storms blow through every life. The storm may be sickness, it may be financial trouble, it may be the loss of a loved one, or it may be the loss of a job. I don't know what storm is raging through your life today; but whatever it is, ask Jesus to pilot you through. He will.

Pit Stop PROMISE

In 2 Corinthians 1:3, Paul wrote that our Lord is "the Father of compassion and the God of all comfort." Pour out your heart to Him and trust Him. He will be your solid Rock and will bring you through any storm.

May 16

Henri Nouwen wrote a great deal about Rembrandt's painting of the prodigal son's homecoming (see Luke 15:11-32). Nouwen says this about the depiction of the father embracing his wayward son:

> With his son safe within his outstretched arms, the father's expression seems to say to me: "I'm not going to ask you any questions. Wherever you have gone, whatever you have done, and whatever people say about you, you're my beloved child. I hold you safe in my embrace. I hug you. I gather you under my wings. You can come home to me."[8]

Nouwen goes on to say that we are all prodigals, kneeling before the heavenly Father in prayer. As we commune with God, He embraces us, holds us against His chest, and we listen to His heartbeat. Note Paul's words in Ephesians 6:23: "Peace be with you, dear brothers and sisters, and may God the Father and the Lord Jesus Christ give you love with faithfulness" (*NLT*).

You can count on God's welcoming embrace, my friend. No matter where you have been or what you've done, when you come home to the Father, He will hold you in His arms, forgive you and cleanse you. It doesn't matter what anybody else says; God says, "You are my child, and I love you."

Take time each day to enjoy an intimate relationship with your loving, forgiving, welcoming Father.

Pit Stop
POINT TO PONDER

Scripture says that you were bought with a price far greater than silver or gold (see 1 Peter 1:18). God desires an intimate relationship with you! Throughout your day, go to Him, talk to Him, listen to Him. He welcomes you with unconditional love.

May 17

Somebody once asked me, "Steve, do you ever get discouraged? You always seem so upbeat." I do enjoy being "up", and I hope I'm up all the time. I'm the proverbial optimist, and I think it's a great way to live.

But you know, that's probably more of a personality trait than a sign of great spirituality. Some of the greatest saints who have ever lived have struggled with depression. David was one of those. Sometimes when we feel discouraged, the book of Psalms is a great place to go, because David often expressed his feelings honestly, even when he was down and discouraged.

For example, read what David says in Psalm 31:7 (*NLT*):

> I will be glad and rejoice in your unfailing love, for you have seen my troubles, and you care about the anguish of my soul.

Evidently, David was in great distress. He was not having a doxology day, yet he turned to the Lord and expressed his feelings. In the same way, God wants you to be honest with Him, and if you're discouraged or frustrated over something, He wants you to "cast all your anxiety on him *because He cares for you*" (1 Peter 5:7, emphasis added).

God cares about you. Make that fact a part of your life. He wants you to tell Him how you feel. He wants you to live in that kind of intimate relationship with Him.

So if you're discouraged today, turn to God and be honest about it, because He cares for you.

Pit Stop PROMISE

Your Father says, "You are my precious child. I am always here to help you, revive you, guide you. My love surrounds you and I hold you in My hands. Nothing can separate you from My love."

May 18

The LORD turn his face toward you and give you peace.
NUMBERS 6:26

Close your eyes and imagine God turning His head and looking at you and calling your name. How does that make you feel?

Zacchaeus was this little guy who was hated by most people because he was a tax collector. Jesus came walking down the street one day. Zacchaeus wanted to get a look at Him, but he was too short to see over the crowd. So he crawled up into a tree.

Jesus came to the tree where Zacchaeus was sitting, looked up at the tax collector, and then called him by name! Can you imagine the thrill Zacchaeus would have felt? *He's talking to me! He knows my name! And He wants to come to my house!*

The Lord turned His face to Zacchaeus, and I think peace began to resonate in that man's life immediately. Jesus went to Zacchaeus's house, and I believe to his heart also, because we see that Zacchaeus changed his life completely.

Imagine Jesus turning His face toward you right now and speaking peace into your life. Does that flood your heart with joy? He knows your name! He loves you and will give you peace.

As He turns His face toward you, friend, I pray that His peace floods your heart.

Pit Stop
PROMISE

Hear Jesus' tender words: "Come to me, all of you who are weary and carry heavy burdens, and I will give you rest" (Matthew 11:28, *NLT*).

May 19

Someone once asked D. L. Moody why he prayed so often to be filled with the Holy Spirit. Moody, in his quick-witted way, said, "Because I leak."

I guess we all leak. We all do or say or think things that are not from the Spirit. But the Bible says that Jesus Christ, the righteous One, is our advocate with the Father; and that if we confess our sins, God is faithful and just and will forgive us and cleanse us from all unrighteousness.

I mentioned earlier that Bill Bright, the founder of Campus Crusade for Christ, called this process of confessing and cleansing spiritual breathing: You exhale, confessing that you've sinned and asking God's forgiveness; and then you breathe in God's Spirit, asking Him to fill you, control you and cleanse you.

When you've said or done or thought something you shouldn't have, exhale. Confess to the Lord that you blew it and ask Him to forgive you. Then inhale, and ask Him to fill you afresh with His Spirit and to take control of your life. Paul encourages us, "So I say, live by the Spirit, and you will not gratify the desires of the sinful nature" (Galatians 5:16).

When God's presence becomes as real in your life as your breathing, and when you give the Spirit His rightful place in control of your life, then you are able to represent Him well in all that you say and in all that you do.

Pit Stop
PROMISE

"So letting your sinful nature control your mind leads to death. But letting the Spirit control your mind leads to life and peace" (Romans 8:6, *NLT*). Breathe in God's Spirit, and He will bring life and peace.

May 20

> The fruit of righteousness will be peace; the effect of righteousness will be quietness and confidence forever.
>
> ISAIAH 32:17

One of the greatest stress-inducers we face daily is noise. We live in such a busy world that we rarely have times we can be still and quiet. But think about what it would mean for you—how it would minister to your soul—if you could step back for a time of quietness every day.

Scripture refers to quietness over and over again:

I have stilled and quieted my soul (Psalm 131:2).

In quietness and trust is your strength (Isaiah 30:15).

The LORD your God . . . will quiet you with his love (Zephaniah 3:17).

You have been made righteous if you know Christ in a personal way, and only He can bring stillness and quietness to your soul. The fruit of righteousness is peace, tranquility. That's what God wants to give you. He doesn't want you to be caught up in this turbulent world and be all stressed out. He wants you to be quiet before Him.

Today, find some time, even if it's just a few moments, to be quiet and say, *Lord, speak to me.*

Pit Stop PRACTICE

If you do not have a special place to meet God and pray, look for other ways to find quiet moments to talk with Him. Get up early before the rest of your family or take a walk and commune with God. Look for a place at work where you can go for a few minutes during your break. Find those solitary moments of quiet to spend with your God.

May 21

> Better one handful with tranquility than two handfuls with toil and chasing after the wind.
>
> ECCLESIASTES 4:6

Have you ever tried to chase after the wind? Where does it come from? Where does it go? We can't ever catch it, yet we can get so caught up in this rat-race world that we feel as if we're chasing after the wind.

People run hard, but whatever it is they're chasing is elusive. People chase after so many things but never seem to ever have enough. There's always one more thing to achieve, one more thing to buy, one more thing to own—always one more goal that must be attained.

If there's a storm raging in your life today, I pray that God will speak tranquility into your heart. Maybe you're anxious about a trip to the doctor; maybe you're dealing with a rebellious child; maybe you've had a lot of stress at your job. In the midst of storms, God can bring peace, a peace that only He can give.

That tranquility does not come from any earthly things you chase or accumulate; it comes only from resting in the refuge of the Rock.

Rest in Him today. Just rest.

Pit Stop
PROMISE

"May God give you more and more grace and peace as you grow in your knowledge of God and Jesus our Lord" (2 Peter 1:2, *NLT*). Peace is found in your God! Seek Him and His peace will grow in your life.

May 22

> A man can no more take in a supply of grace for the future than he can eat enough today to last him for the next six months; or take sufficient air into his lungs at one time to sustain him for a week to come. We must draw upon God's boundless stores of grace from day to day, as we need it.
>
> D. L. MOODY, *SOVEREIGN GRACE*

Are you daily drawing on God's endless grace? Are you living that out as a way of life? God has made a boundless supply of grace available to us, but it can't be stored up. We can't pack in enough for tomorrow or next week. We need to be in daily communion with the Lord.

There are two lions fighting for supremacy in my life, and I have to choose which one to feed. At one time, the lion of my old selfish and sinful nature enslaved me and dictated all my thoughts and actions. With Christ's help, I want to starve that lion. The other lion—the one I want to feed—is the power of the Holy Spirit living in me. I feed that power in my life through prayer, through fellowship with other believers, through reading and studying God's Word, and through communion with Him.

Oh, my friend, I want you to feed on the grace of God that is at work in your life. Feed the lion of His strength and power within you. "Seek the Lord and his strength; seek his presence continually!" (1 Chronicles 16:11, *ESV*). As you do that, He will strengthen you so that you can walk consistently for Him.

Pit Stop
POINT TO PONDER

"And he who thinks, in his great plenitude [self-sufficiency], to right himself, and set his spirit free, without the might of higher communings, is foolish also." —George MacDonald (*The Diary of an Old Soul*, 1880)

May 23

When Jesus went to the Garden of Gethsemane to pray the night before His crucifixion, He stepped apart from His disciples to pray alone, in agony as He faced what He knew was ahead. But when He returned to them, He found them sleeping. "Could you not tarry with me one hour?" He asked (see Matthew 26:40).

From that question was born "Sweet Hour of Prayer," a hymn by William W. Walford. Quiet yourself just for a moment, listen to the words of this beautiful hymn, and tarry with Jesus before entering the world of care.

> Sweet hour of prayer! sweet hour of prayer!
> That calls me from a world of care,
> And bids me at my Father's throne
> Make all my wants and wishes known.
> In seasons of distress and grief,
> My soul has often found relief
> And oft escaped the tempter's snare
> By thy return, sweet hour of prayer!

God bids you come to His throne and seek His face. Have a sweet moment—or hour—with God today.

Pit Stop
POINT TO PONDER

King David knew the sweetness of time spent with the Lord. He wrote, "The one thing I ask of the LORD—the thing I seek most—is to live in the house of the LORD all the days of my life, delighting in the LORD's perfections and meditating in his Temple" (Psalm 27:4, *NLT*). May you seek to live in His presence all the days of your life.

May 24

> The Lord is my shepherd; I shall not want.
> He makes me lie down in green pastures.
> He leads me beside still waters.
> He restores my soul.
> He leads me in paths of righteousness
> for his name's sake
> Even though I walk through the valley of the shadow of death,
> I will fear no evil,
> for you are with me;
> your rod and your staff,
> they comfort me.
> You prepare a table before me
> in the presence of my enemies;
> you anoint my head with oil;
> my cup overflows.
> Surely goodness and mercy shall follow me
> all the days of my life,
> and I shall dwell in the house of the Lord forever.
>
> PSALM 23, *ESV*

The Lord is a friend who sticks closer than a brother. He is your best friend. Don't forget to talk to Him. Do not let a busy schedule keep you from consulting with Him, and He'll guide you in the way you should go.

Pit Stop
PROMISE

Psalm 23 sums up all of the Christian's hope: God cares and provides, heals and guides, protects and gives victory. He is with you constantly and loves you and calls you His own. And your final and eternal home is with Him.

STEVE WINGFIELD

May 25

> What makes humility so desirable is the marvelous thing
> it does to us; it creates in us the capacity for the closest
> possible intimacy with God.
>
> MONICA BALDWIN

We cannot be truly intimate with God unless we humble ourselves before Him. Humility is a criteria for intimacy. As I look at the people who have intimacy with God, I see humility as a way of life for them. I cannot name one person of arrogance that I would say is intimate with the Lord.

Augustine of Hippo once wrote that "it was pride that changed angels into devils; it is humility that makes men as angels."

I long for intimacy with God. I want that for my life. In Psalm 25:9, David says that God "guides the humble in what is right and teaches them his way." I want that humility that makes me teachable.

Scripture says that we should seek the higher gifts, and humility is one of those higher gifts. So ask the Lord for humility. Walk humbly before your God and develop intimacy with Him.

Pit Stop
PROMISE

Pride, self-sufficiency and arrogance can keep you from building a relationship with your Creator. God says that He may live in the high and lofty places, but He also dwells with the humble and contrite of heart. What a promise!

May 26

> Worship the Lord in the splendor of his holiness;
> tremble before him, all the earth.
>
> PSALM 96:9

There are all kinds of worship wars going on in our churches. I can't really understand that, because I believe that when you're worshiping, you're caught up in adoration and praise of your Lord. People get sidetracked, I guess. Some like to worship with choruses and some prefer hymns. Still others like to worship in silence.

Today, think about the seriousness of worship. We come into the presence of this God who made Himself known to us in the person of Jesus Christ, the God who entered human history to reconcile us to Himself so that we could know Him and have a relationship with Him. We worship the almighty God who created the universe, who has a plan for this world and each one of us.

Take some time each day to focus on and be caught up in the Lord. One thing that helps me to do this is to be outside and enjoy His creation. As I look around and marvel at creation, the reality of God is undeniable. One person I know likes to take a kayak out on a local lake and just get caught up in worshiping Him.

Take some time today to go someplace where you can focus on your great God, your Creator, your Master, your Savior and your Redeemer. God spoke all creation into existence. Let yourself be caught up in worshiping Him.

Pit Stop
PRACTICE

"Come, let us worship and bow down. Let us kneel before the Lord our maker, for he is our God. We are the people he watches over, the flock under his care" (Psalm 95:6-7, *NLT*).

May 27

Imagine this scene in heaven: "The twenty-four elders fall down before him who sits on the throne, and worship him who lives forever and ever. They lay their crowns before the throne and say: 'You are worthy, our Lord and God, to receive glory and honor and power, for you created all things, and by your will they were created and have their being'" (Revelation 4:10-11).

If these 24 elders are caught up in worship, how much more should we be worshiping our Lord and God? It's going to be a great day when we bow before Him. But you know, we ought to get warmed up a little bit right now—for some people, the worshiping in heaven will be a huge transition!

I read through the book of Revelation and I read about the praise and the adoration and the celebration that's going on in heaven. He is worthy of it all.

Think about this quote from A. W. Tozer: "Sometimes I go to God and say, 'God, if Thou dost never answer another prayer while I live on this earth, I will still worship Thee as long as I live and in the ages to come for what Thou hast done already.' God's already put me so far in debt that if I were to live one million millenniums I couldn't pay Him for what He's done for me."

So take time to worship God and tell Him that you love Him and that you are thankful for all that He's done in your life. Get caught up in worship, my friend!

Pit Stop
POINT TO PONDER

God sits on the throne and rules forever and ever! He created the world and sustains everything in it. And He has called you to be His child and share in His glory. Worship Him for who He is and thank Him for all He's done for you.

May 28

One hot, hot summer day, my son and I were hiking on the Appalachian Trail and I ran out of water. I can tell you, it's not a good thing to run out of water on a hot day. I longed for something to drink. Thankfully, my son came to my rescue. But that day, I knew what it meant to be desperately thirsty.

In Psalm 63:1-4, David describes a soul thirsty for God, crying out to Him:

> O God, you are my God, earnestly I seek you; My soul thirsts for you, my body longs for you, in a dry and weary land where there is no water. I have seen you in the sanctuary and beheld your power and your glory. Because your love is better than life, my lips will glorify you. I will praise you as long as I live, and in your name I will lift up my hands.

Are you caught up in a love relationship with Jesus Christ that you could express as David did? Does your soul thirst for Him? Do you long for Him?

Spend some time today seeking Jesus. You can do it wherever you are; meditate on His power and glory, lift up your hands to Him, sing with joy in the shadow of His wings.

Pit Stop PROMISE

Here's God's wonderful promise: When you are thirsty for Him, He satisfies your thirst! Use Psalm 63:1-7 often as a prayer of adoration and praise and thankfulness.

May 29

Make some time today to meditate on the love of God. Meditate on how much He loves you. Because of His great love, He sent His one and only Son to die for you. I think it's important just to spend time thinking about that.

Through your meditation, show your appreciation for what God did for you. Let Psalm 96:1-6 be your guide as you think about His love and what He's done for you:

> Sing to the LORD a new song; sing to the LORD, all the earth. Sing to the LORD, praise his name; proclaim his salvation day after day. Declare his glory among the nations, his marvelous deeds among all peoples. For great is the LORD and most worthy of praise; he is to be feared above all gods. For all the gods of the nations are idols, but the LORD made the heavens. Splendor and majesty are before him; strength and glory are in his sanctuary.

It's impossible to overstate or overvalue what Christ did for us when He gave His life. When He said, "It is finished" (John 19:30), the price was paid. All else pales in comparison when we focus on His salvation.

Today, focus on His great love.

Pit Stop PRAYER

Lord, Your great love and mercy have saved me from prisons that held me and from death that awaited me. You opened your arms and invited me to walk in Your presence as I live here on this earth. What can I offer You for all You have done for me? I will always praise Your name and give You the thanks and the glory. Amen (see Psalm 116).

May 30

In Exodus 34:6-7, God describes Himself this way to Moses: "The LORD, the compassionate and gracious God, slow to anger, abounding in love and faithfulness, maintaining love to thousands, and forgiving wickedness, rebellion and sin."

What a God we have! He is the rule of graciousness and the measuring line of compassion. That's our God. Slow to anger. Yes, He gets angry at times. He is angry when people turn their backs on Him, but He longs to forgive wickedness, rebellion and sin. Maintaining love to thousands, that is our God.

Throughout Scripture, we read stories of many people who did not deserve forgiveness and who did not deserve to live in relationship with God. Yet God stepped into their lives and forgave them. He took what had been wreckage and made something special out of it. No one deserves that love. All of us—*all* the Bible says: you, me, everyone who has ever lived—have sinned and come short of the glory of God. No one is righteous. But He is a compassionate, loving God who longs to live in relationship with us.

I pray that you have that relationship with God. And if you do, I pray that you will maintain it and grow in His love. He wants that love relationship to deepen. He wants it to be high and wide. He wants His love to go down deep into your life.

This will happen as you spend time with God. So continue to take time each day to focus only on Him and His love for you.

Pit Stop
POWER

"Your roots will grow down deep into God's love and keep you strong" (Ephesians 3:17, *NLT*). Roots give a plant stability, and through its roots a plant gains nourishment. Think about what it means to have your roots deep in God's love. Build your relationship on the foundation of His love.

May 31

Start out this new day in a wonderful, glorious way—by reflecting on the love of God.

F. B. Meyer once wrote, "The love of God toward you is like the Amazon River flowing down to water a single daisy." This is such a good picture of how much God loves you. Yes, you mess up and you don't do everything right, but He still loves you. He created you; He knew you even before He laid the foundations of the earth.

In Psalm 139, David says that God knit you together inside your mother's womb and scheduled every day of your life. He has plans for you, plans to prosper you even in these difficult and uncertain times. More than anything else, He wants you to live in relationship with Him. His plan for that is in John 3:16, that wonderful little Bible in one verse: "For God so loved the world that he gave his one and only Son, that whoever believes in him shall not perish but have eternal life."

God loves you so much that He gave His Son to die for you so that you could have everlasting life with Him.

Spend some time today just reflecting on the fact that God loves you. He loves you with an everlasting love. As you think about how much He loves you, ask Him to work in your life in such a way that you'll know Him more deeply, love Him more fully, and receive His everlasting love more completely.

Pit Stop
PROMISE

"May you experience the love of Christ, though it is too great to understand fully. Then you will be made complete with all the fullness of life and power that comes from God" (Ephesians 3:19, *NLT*). Living with roots deep in God's love promises a richness of life and power that can come only from Him.

JUNE

Trusting the Lord

Never will I **leave you**, never will I **forsake you**.

HEBREWS 13:5

June 1

Are you happy?

You might be thinking, *Happy? You don't know what I'm going through today.*

The Word of God says that people who give heed to the Word will prosper, and those who trust in the Lord will be happy (see Proverbs 16:20).

Happy is the person who trusts in the Lord. Proverbs 3:5-6 promises that when you trust in the Lord with all your heart instead of depending on your own understanding, He'll direct your path.

That's where happiness is found, my friend, no matter what you're going through. If you'll spend time in His Word and get to know Him and love Him, you will experience true happiness—a deep-seated happiness that the world cannot take away from you.

I like what Roy Goodman says: "Remember that happiness is a way of travel, not a destination."

As you travel along your way in life, trust the Lord, for this will make it much easier for you to sing a happy song or whistle a happy tune.

Pit Stop
POINT TO PONDER

Who or what are you trusting? Who or what are you depending on? Where have you placed your hopes? This month you're going to focus on putting your hope and confidence in the One who will never fail you—the Lord.

June 2

God has said, "Never will I leave you; never will I forsake you."
HEBREWS 13:5

What a promise God gives in this verse! He will never fail you or forsake you.

If you are anxious or worried about something today, Scripture is clear: Cast all your cares on God because He cares for you (see 1 Peter 5:7). At the end of his life, Joshua said that the Lord had kept every one of His promises. Not one did He renege on. In the same way, God has promised to supply your needs if you put your faith, your trust, and your hope in Him and Him alone.

Rest in Him. Lean on His promises. They cover all of life; and in them you'll find hope, security, comfort, strength and contentment. Above all, you have the huge promise that He will never leave you or fail you!

God's promises were written in His blood, my friend. You can trust Him, because He loves you that much.

Pit Stop
PROMISE

God says to His people, "Don't be afraid, for I am with you. Don't be discouraged, for I am your God. I will strengthen you and help you. I will hold you up with my victorious right hand" (Isaiah 41:10, *NLT*).

Jesus came to seek you out, to save you and to bring you back to Himself. He promises to bring His strength and power to your life and to never abandon you. What a hope you have!

June 3

Are you happy when you're insulted? Do you take delight in hardship or calamity or weakness? Do these sound like foolish questions?

I'll be real honest. When somebody insults me or when anything happens in my life that I see as a hardship, I'm tempted to mumble and groan and complain. To be contented and even delighted? Is that even possible?

The apostle Paul had more than his share of troubles. He was beaten and jailed and shipwrecked, and he endured all things for the cause of Christ. But there was apparently one personal thing that tormented him, and he consistently begged God to remove it from his life. I'm sure that God's answer, though, wasn't what Paul wanted to hear: "He said to me, 'My grace is sufficient for you, for my power is made perfect in weakness.' Therefore I will boast all the more gladly about my weaknesses" (2 Corinthians 12:9). Note Paul's reaction to God's answer. Other Bible versions say that Paul was "content with weakness" (*ESV*).

Contentment comes when we trust God—when we trust that He is working in our lives no matter what our outward circumstances. We trust that when we are weak, He will be strong and His power will work in us. In 1 Corinthians 1:27, Paul says that God chose the weak things of this world to confound the wise. It makes no logical sense, but I'll tell you what—it works spiritually, every time.

Today, think about those areas of your life where you feel weak or where you are having difficulty. Then trust your Father for His all-sufficient power that will rest on you.

Pit Stop
PRAYER

Say this prayer, filling in the blank with one area of weakness in your life: "Lord, today I ask for Your power in _____. You know my weakness; You know I cannot handle this part of my life on my own. I am going to trust You to work through my life in whatever way You want."

June 4

Our greatest cause for rejoicing tomorrow will not be that we have been spared from trial and suffering but that Christ has been present to sanctify the trials to us and comfort us in them.

T. J. BACH

So often, I want the easy road. Let me rephrase that: I *always* want the easy road. Who doesn't? But it's through difficulties and trials that God shapes us to become all He wants us to be.

My Romanian brothers and sisters have had a great impact on my life. When I first went to that country, the Christians I met there had been through unbelievable trials. Persecution brought some close to death; some even later died. But there was a radiance, a glow, about those brothers and sisters that I'm convinced came from knowing Christ's presence even through persecution.

In Romans 8:35, Paul says that nothing in this world can separate us from Christ's unfailing love. Trials and suffering sanctified by Christ's presence and power bring a quality of life that cannot be developed in any other way. Jesus promised never to leave us and to work for our good in all things, even though we might not be able to see that good right now. Clinging to His promises through everything deepens our trust in and love for Him.

Whatever you're going through today, my friend, I pray that you'll find your hope in the Lord and that you will allow Jesus to radiate through you, even in the midst of that pain.

Pit Stop
PROMISE

It may be hard for you to see how God can work in the troubles you face. But He has promised that He will! He has called you, He has a purpose for you in this world, and He is constantly working for your good. You can trust Him, no matter what your circumstances.

June 5

Several years ago in Romania, I watched as two large flocks of sheep came from two different directions and crossed the road in front of our car. The two flocks met and mingled, hundreds of sheep passing by each other. Yet the sheep never wavered. Each followed its shepherd, as one shepherd took his flock to the right and one took his flock to the left. The sheep knew the voice of their shepherd, and they followed him.

Jesus said, "My sheep listen to my voice; I know them, and they follow me. I give them eternal life, and they shall never perish; no one can snatch them out of my hand" (John 10:27-28). These words of Jesus came alive for me that day as I watched the two flocks following the voice of their particular shepherd.

What a great promise Jesus gave! We don't have to fear the devil, or his demons, or anything else if we listen to our Shepherd and fully trust and follow Him.

Do you know the voice of God? In order for you to know His voice, you have to spend time with Him—time in His Word, in prayer and in communion. When you spend quality time with Jesus, you learn to hear your Shepherd's voice.

Take time to be with your Shepherd today, listening to His voice.

Pit Stop
PRAYER

Lord Jesus, keep my ears tuned to Your voice. I want to hear Your promises and Your instructions clearly and follow only You through this life.

June 6

I once posted this Scripture on my Facebook page: "And the peace of God, which transcends all understanding, will guard your hearts and your minds in Christ Jesus" (Philippians 4:7).

In return, I received all kinds of thank-you notes. People are obviously yearning for peace. In today's world, where do you find peace? How can you have peace in your life?

Jesus said He would give us a peace that can never be found in anything of this world. God's peace goes beyond our ability to understand it. Even in situations where peace seems impossible, God can give His peace.

In Philippians 4:7, Paul says the peace of God will guard our heart and mind in Christ Jesus. Don't you feel sometimes as though your heart and mind need a guard around them, some protection from all that this world throws at you? The word picture that I see in this verse is that of an armed guard standing at attention and ready for action against any attack.

The peace of God is like that; it surrounds our heart and mind in Christ Jesus, no matter what's going on around us. It protects us from all the plots of the evil one, who likes to shoot darts of worry, anxiety, doubt and fear into our being.

May the peace of God, which is beyond anything you can comprehend, guard your heart and mind today. If you don't have that peace, get to know Him. Trust Him. Ask Him for peace.

Pit Stop
PRAISE

Praise God today with these verses from a hymn by Edward H. Bickersteth Jr.: "Peace, perfect peace, in this dark world of sin? The blood of Jesus whispers peace within. Peace, perfect peace, our future all unknown? Jesus we know, and He is on the throne."

June 7

The Lord is our protector. He is our shield and our strong tower. He encourages us to run to Him for protection. I know these things to be true, yet when I first read the following verse, I wondered, *Who can live like that? Who can have no fear of bad news?*

"He will have no fear of bad news; his heart is steadfast, trusting in the LORD" (Psalm 112:7). This verse really challenged me. It actually refers to the preceding verses, which talk about a person who fears God—one who lives rightly, is generous, lends freely and conducts his affairs with justice. He is a man of integrity, who is not trying to hide anything. The Lord is his protector, and he doesn't have to defend himself.

Now, the Lord doesn't want us to do dumb stuff or foolish things, but as we walk with Him, trust Him and release all things unto Him, we don't have to fear bad news. The devil and his demons cannot harm us! We belong to Jesus Christ and no one can snatch us away from Him.

This verse does not mean that bad things don't happen to good people. But if bad news does come, we can look beyond that bad news to Him, whose love always surrounds us.

I know that's a challenge. It's tempting to look at bad news and let that bad news overwhelm us. Instead, we must cling to our hope, our security, our protection in Jesus alone.

If you're anxious today, trust in the Lord and let your heart be steadfast.

Pit Stop
POINT TO PONDER

In Romans 8:31, Paul asks a question that begins, "If God is for us . . . " My friend, if God is for you, why be anxious or afraid? He gives us so many promises of His help, His power, His care, His protection—the almighty Lord of the universe is for you! Read His promises; keep your heart steadfast. Trust in Him.

June 8

How are you sleeping?

If you're a mom with a newborn, you might be sleep-deprived right now. If you work the night shift and you're trying to read this in the morning, you might have trouble keeping your eyes open. Maybe a sick child interrupted your sleep for the last few days, or maybe you're caring for a parent who requires attention during the night.

> When you lie down, you will not be afraid; when you lie down, your sleep will be sweet (Proverbs 3:24).

Does this verse make you long for sweet sleep? I thank the Lord that He made us so that we can sleep. Sleep is sweet for me. But if you're losing sleep because of anxiety and worry, hear the Lord saying that He wants to give you sweet, peaceful sleep.

God doesn't want you to live with anxiety. He doesn't want you to toss and turn because you are worrying about a need in your life. He invites you to give all your cares to Him and to let Him carry all those worries and concerns and fears so that your sleep will be sweet.

When you lie down, rest secure in His care because you have put your trust in the almighty God who has promised never to leave you or forsake you.

Pit Stop PRACTICE

When you can't sleep because you are worrying, turn to the One who sought you out to rescue you from darkness, and say, "Lord, I am so worried about this right now. I know You care about me and what's going on. Please take this cloud of anxiety away so I can rest. Help me trust You completely."

June 9

Why should we trust God? Why go to Him for help and hope and refuge? Let these thoughts from "There's a Wideness in God's Mercy," an old hymn by Frederick Faber, answer that question:

> There's a wideness in God's mercy,
> Like the wideness of the sea;
> There's a kindness in His justice,
> Which is more than liberty.

> There is welcome for the sinner,
> And more graces for the good;
> There is mercy with the Savior;
> There is healing in His blood.

These verses describe the God we can trust. He is a God of wide mercy, kind justice, welcome for the sinner, healing blood and a love greater than we can imagine. Why do we not take Him at His word?

Now, when Faber says that "our lives would be all sunshine in the sweetness of our Lord," he does not mean that we aren't going to have problems. But we will be recipients of God's mercy and grace and love, His forgiveness, His kindness, His compassion—all of that is there for us in our time of need. And yes, there will be sunshine in our hearts, even when the world around us is crumbling.

Whatever your situation today, have confidence in Jesus Christ, your eternal strength and refuge, your hope and your very present help.

Pit Stop
PRAYER

God of mercy, kindness and love, help my unbelief! Make my faith in You more simple. Let me take You at Your word, build my hope on You alone, and walk in the sweetness of the light of Your presence.

June 10

When you read the name *Job*, what do you think of? Trouble and suffering! Job's life story has come to symbolize an extreme amount of trouble. But there's much more to his story. Note these words from Job 11:18-19:

> You will be secure, because there is hope; you will look about you and take your rest in safety. You will lie down, with no one to make you afraid, and many will court your favor.

What great promises! Those two verses are jam-packed with hope, assurance and encouragement.

You will be secure. Now I don't know what's going on in your life right now and what difficulties are out there for you, but hear these words from Scripture: "You will be secure, because there is hope." Your hope is in Christ, the everlasting Rock.

You will look about you and take your rest in safety. You will lie down, with no one to make you afraid. God has promised that. Don't let the devil steal your joy, my friend. Hope and security are what you have in Jesus Christ. You can trust Him to be your protector.

Job trusted God. And even in the midst of all his trouble and suffering, Job said, "Though he slay me, yet will I trust in him" (Job 13:15, *KJV*).

You can trust Him, too. He wants to give you security, hope and peace.

Pit Stop PROMISE

"He who fears the LORD has a secure fortress, and for his children it will be a refuge" (Proverbs 14:26). That secure fortress the Lord offers cannot be shaken. No matter what enemy comes against it, it cannot be destroyed. Trust Him, and take refuge in Him.

June 11

> Why are you downcast, O my soul? . . . Put your hope in God,
> for I will yet praise him, my Savior and my God.
>
> PSALM 42:11

When we get our news from the newspaper, the television and other news sources, it's easy to feel sad or depressed. A daily dose of discouraging stories can easily make us feel downhearted. Or maybe we look at the Dow Jones Industrial Average and wonder what's happening to all that we worked so hard to save and invest. Just look at what's happening in the world—where's our security?

Our security and our hope should be in Jesus and Jesus alone. The psalmist says, "Don't be downcast. Put your hope in God. I'll praise Him, because He's my hope and my God."

My friend, God desires that we go through life praising Him, serving Him, putting our hope and our trust in Him, and living securely in Him. He is our only hope and our security.

Jesus said that the world could never give the peace He can give us. Through the prophet Jeremiah, the Lord warned that those who trust in mankind and the things of this world "will dwell in the parched places of the desert" (Jeremiah 17:6). Those who trust in God, though, will be like trees planted by the water, always refreshed, always green, always bearing fruit (see Jeremiah 17:7-8).

Choose to put your trust in God. When you feel downcast today, remind yourself that your hope lies in God. He alone is your security.

Pit Stop
POINT TO PONDER

Have you been looking around in the world for people or things you can count on? Have you been looking to the world to give you hope? Make the Lord your hope and confidence and you'll flourish like a tree planted by the water, not fearing heat or drought.

June 12

Dallas Willard is a great devotional writer. He lost his mother when he was just a child, and in his book *Hearing God,* he writes about another little boy whose mom also died. Every night the toddler would go into his dad's room and ask to sleep with him. But the little boy could only fall asleep when his father promised to sleep with his face turned toward his son. Willard writes:

> How lonely life is! Oh, we can get by in life with a God who does not speak. Many at least think they do. But it is not much of a life, and it is certainly not the life God intends for us or the *abundance* of life Jesus Christ came to make available.[9]

Do you feel like this little boy right now? Maybe you have so much turmoil going on in your life that you can't sleep. Just imagine the God of all creation turning His face toward you and speaking into your life today that He loves you and will care for you. He desires for you to be at peace.

> The eyes of the LORD are on those who fear him, on those whose hope is in his unfailing love (Psalm 33:18).

When you are fearful or anxious or overwhelmed, remember this: God is looking at you. He loves you so much that He can't take His eyes off of you.

Pit Stop PRACTICE

Scripture says that the Lord watches over all your steps and holds you by the hand. As you read the Word, keep a list of verses that promise His constant presence and care. Then, when you need His assurance, turn to that list and read His words to you, His beloved child.

June 13

Have you ever asked God, *Why?* Have you ever asked Him for understanding of what's going on but felt as if the heavens were sealed up? Have you ever wanted answers or explanations, but God did not give them to you?

"The secret things belong to the LORD our God, but those things which are revealed belong to us and to our children forever, that we may do all the words of this law" (Deuteronomy 29:29, *NKJV*). There are secret things that belong to the Lord, but there are also things that are revealed to us. When it comes to understanding things, we have some territory, but God has much more; and there are some things we are just not going to know on this side of heaven.

God has revealed some principles that will help you, especially when you cannot figure out and understand everything. Don't depend on your own understanding, but trust in the Lord with all your heart and He'll direct your path. We know that all things—not some things, but *all* things—work together for the good of those who love God (see Romans 8:28).

Those are powerful promises and you can hold on to them, especially when God does not give you an understanding of everything. God may explain some things, or He may not. But He has a plan, and He's working it out for your good and His glory. And He'll guide your steps along the right way, if you trust Him.

He wants us to trust Him, even though we don't understand everything. That's a tough place to be at times, but we can cling to His promises and know that He'll take care of us.

Pit Stop
PRAYER

Lord, expand my faith! When things are going well, it's easy to say I trust You and believe in Your love and care. But when circumstances are difficult, when I can't *understand* or *see* or *feel* Your hand, even then I want to trust You. By the power of Your Spirit, increase my trust, Lord.

June 14

> He guides the humble in what is right and teaches them His way. All the ways of the LORD are loving and faithful for those who keep the demands of his covenant.
>
> PSALM 25:9-10

There are some pretty big promises in Psalm 25:9-10. If you have ever wondered if God really works in His children's lives or if you've doubted that His hand is in your day, take a closer look at what God says.

He guides the humble in what is right and teaches them His way. He leads us. He teaches us. He directs our thoughts and our paths and shows us which way to go. He hears us when we bring our questions and problems to Him, and He takes us by the hand and leads us.

Did you notice *who* the Lord will guide? The humble. We've got to humble ourselves before Him and say, "Lord, I need You." We can't be going our own way and relying on our own strength and understanding. In all our ways we must acknowledge Him, and then He'll direct our paths.

We can trust God because all of His ways are loving and faithful if we "keep the demands of His covenant." There is a condition: We must know what His Word says if we want to be led by it. His Word is a lamp for our feet and a light for our path, but we have to obey what the lamp has shown us.

Trust and obey—that's the way to be happy in Jesus. If you trust and obey Him, then He will guide your steps and show you the way.

Pit Stop
POINT TO PONDER

Trust and guidance are based on relationship. Set your heart on learning to know God and determine to know what His Word says. Then He will guide and teach you as His beloved child.

June 15

*I will instruct you and teach you in the way you should go;
I will counsel you and watch over you.*

PSALM 32:8

How does God guide His people? I believe He guides us in five ways:

Through His Word—"I gain understanding from your precepts," says the psalmist (Psalm 119:104). God's Word is meant to guide us in the right path, to make us wise, and to keep us from the wrong path. He'll never ask us to do anything contrary to His Word.

By His Spirit—Jesus said He was sending the Spirit to live within us, remind us of everything He taught, and lead us into truth. Living by the Spirit of Christ transforms our thoughts and actions, to make us like Him. "Don't stifle the Spirit," said Paul (see 1 Thessalonians 5:13).

Through our prayers—We pray and seek His counsel. God says over and over again, "Call to Me. I'll answer you."

Through His peace—Romans 8:6 says that letting the Spirit control our minds leads to peace. Following His commands brings peace; walking uprightly leads to peace. We will feel that confirmation in our hearts when we are walking in the right way.

Through brothers and sisters—The persons who know us best can be used by God to counsel us. For me, that's Barb and our children and their spouses. We might also have accountability relationships that can help us hear God's words to us.

God directs the steps of His children. Today, listen for His guidance.

Pit Stop
PRAYER

Say this prayer from a hymn by Stella Kauffman: "Lord, as I walk with Thee from day to day, teach me to learn to love Thy blessed way; when I would wander, lead my erring feet, hold Thou my hand till journeys are complete."

June 16

*These are the words of Him who is holy and true. . . .
What he opens no one can shut, and what he shuts, no one can open. I know your deeds. See, I have placed before you an open door that no one can shut.*

REVELATION 3:7-8

Let's talk about providential guidance. Circumstance, in other words.

God opens doors for us, and He closes doors. He providentially works through circumstances to lead us in the way we should go; and if we're walking with the Lord, if we're spending time in communion with Him and asking for His guidance, He will open doors and He will close doors.

When we pray and seek the Lord, it's not just coincidence that brings us opportunities or cuts off choices. That's a part of His will and plan and purpose for us. Scripture says over and over again that He directs us. His Word is a lamp to our feet. The steps of the righteous are directed by the Lord.

Do you have faith to walk through the doors God has opened? Do you have the trust to say "Thank You, Lord" when He closes doors?

Spend time with Him, ask Him to direct your steps, and then trust Him to work through circumstance.

Pit Stop
POINT TO PONDER

When you walk through an open door, you cannot always know what is ahead. Likewise, when a door slams shut, you often do not know which way to turn. But God knows! He says He goes before you and follows behind and always places a hand of blessing on your life. You can trust Him because He promises, "I will guide you along the best pathway for your life" (Psalm 32:8, *NLT*).

June 17

Hope is one of the most powerful forces in all the world. I can't imagine living without hope. Hope helps someone persevere against the worst odds. No matter what, if I have hope, I can live.

> As for me, I will always have hope; I will praise you more and more. My mouth will tell of your righteousness, of your salvation all day long, though I know not its measure (Psalm 71:14-15).

Oh, my friend, I don't know what you're going through right now, but don't lose hope. Jesus is your hope; He wants you to put your hope in Him. He's promised to never leave you or forsake you.

After Moses died and Joshua was appointed to lead the children of Israel, the Lord told him, "Be strong and courageous. Do not be terrified; do not be discouraged, for the LORD your God will be with you wherever you go" (Joshua 1:9).

That's also His promise to you, to me and to everyone who serves Him. Trusting Him, we can live strong and courageous, because we know He will always be with us.

What a hope! Our God is the God of all hope. Spend some time today reading His Word, and look for His words of hope to you.

Pit Stop
PRAYER

If you're walking through a dark time right now, take Romans 15:13 and pray it as a prayer for yourself: "Lord, You are the source of all hope. Fill me completely with joy and peace as I trust in You. Fill me until I overflow with strong and confident hope."

June 18

The Bible tells us that several times David had to flee for his life. Saul was out to kill him, and David was on the run and in hiding. In Psalm 57:1-2, he cries out to God: "Have mercy on me, my God, have mercy on me, for in you my soul takes refuge. I will take refuge in the shadow of your wings until the disaster has passed. I cry out to God Most High."

"Help, Lord, I am in the midst of lions!" he says (see verse 4), referring to those who wanted to kill him. "They're setting traps for me; I am in great distress." Maintaining joy in the midst of trials can be a big challenge, but even in this life-threatening situation, David sang a song of joy and was determined to praise God. "Still, my heart is confident in God's love and faithfulness, and He will save me" (see verses 3,7).

Then David says in verses 9-11 "I will praise you, O Lord, among the nations; I will sing of you among the peoples. For great is your love, reaching to the heavens; your faithfulness reaches to the skies. Be exalted, O God, above the heavens; let your glory be over all the earth."

God promises the reward of joy to those who sow in tears, so when you suffer trials and difficulties, you can cry out to God. It's okay to show your emotion; it's okay to be heartbroken. God has promised to reward you with joy. Brokenness and heartache seasoned with heartfelt prayer will bring blessing and reward. God will revive and refresh you.

So don't be discouraged, my friend. In the midst of lions, cry out to God. His faithfulness reaches to the skies. Cast all your anxieties on Him, and He will give you joy in the midst of trouble.

Pit Stop
PROMISE

God promises, "When you go through rivers of difficulty, you will not drown. When you walk through the fire of oppression, you will not be burned up; the flames will not consume you. For I am the Lord, your God. . . . You are precious to me" (Isaiah 43:2-4, *NLT*). What comfort!

June 19

Be encouraged, my friend. God is for you!

He loves you and He believes in you. Paul made this point in Romans 8:31: "If God is for us, who can be against us?" He is our hope, He is our strength, He is our shield, and we can rest in Him.

Just call upon Him. Call Him today. I don't know what you're facing, I don't know what needs you have, but He says, "Call, and come." Accept that invitation and let Him speak encouragement into your life and meet your needs for this day.

I have a friend who lost a child. I can't imagine the pain of that loss. Barb and I have never had to walk through that experience. But I have met people who have gone through such a loss and other trials far beyond anything I've ever known, and they testify to me that our God, in His grace, His mercy and His provision, has stood with them during those difficult times and they have sensed His love and His peace that passes all comprehension.

God loves you more than you can ever comprehend. Romans 8:38 says that nothing—*nothing*—will separate you from His love. Cast your cares upon Him today. Trust Him to always be your hope, strength and shield.

Pit Stop
POINT TO PONDER

How amazing that the Lord of the universe, the Creator of everything we know, has promised to hold your hand and walk with you through everything. "I am here to help you," He says.

June 20

When I was growing up, a disc jockey on the radio who went by the nickname Little Jody Rainwater would sign off in the morning by saying, "Don't worry about nothin', 'cause ain't nothin' gonna come out right noway."

Rainwater's theology might not have been good, but I think it is true that it's useless to worry, because most things don't turn out the way you thought they would anyway. Listen to what Jesus had to say about worry: "For the pagans run after all these things [food and clothes], and your heavenly Father knows that you need them. But seek first his kingdom and his righteousness, and all these things will be given to you as well. Therefore do not worry about tomorrow, for tomorrow will worry about itself. Each day has enough trouble of its own" (Matthew 6:32-34).

Can I hear an "amen" to that? Each day has enough trouble of its own; that's just life. But Jesus said that we are to put our hope and trust in Him. The Lord knows what we need, and He's promised to provide for us. If we'll seek first His kingdom and His righteousness, He will provide all that we need.

I don't know what things you need today, but here's the key: Focus on His kingdom, His righteousness, and being in right relationship with Him. Seek those things first. If you do, He will provide for you. That's a great promise to hold on to. Tell God about your needs, and ask Him to take care of those worries.

Pit Stop
POINT TO PONDER

Studying nature will open your eyes to the fascinating ways God makes provision for every living thing. Jesus said that you are far more important to Him than birds or wildflowers, and He will certainly provide for you. Ask the Spirit to help you believe and live out that promise.

June 21

Do you know the joy of resting in the Lord's protection?

Somebody once asked Dr. Jerry Falwell if he had bodyguards. He had a lot of people who traveled with him to help in all kinds of ways, but he did not have people specifically hired for security. What was his answer to the question? "No. Nobody can touch me when God's hand is upon me."

That's a powerful way to live, trusting Jesus and knowing that the devil and all of his demons can't touch you because you're in the will of God.

Now, the Lord may remove His hand of protection to a degree. He did that with Job, and we'll have to wait until we get to heaven to discuss with Him the reasons for that; but He would not allow the devil to take Job's life. And Job stood the test.

Paul wrote, "The Lord is faithful, and he will strengthen and protect you from the evil one" (2 Thessalonians 3:3). Remember that your hope and security are always in the Lord. God has promised to be your shield and protector and to give you strength for whatever tests you must weather.

Ask Him to give you peace in the midst of whatever you're facing right now. Run to Jesus, that strong tower of refuge, and ask for strength and protection.

Pit Stop
PRAYER

"Even though I walk through the valley of the shadow of death, I will fear no evil, for you are with me" (Psalm 23:4).

June 22

Listen to the words from "Be Still, My Soul," a hymn written by Katharina Von Schlegel way back in the 1700s. The words of this hymn still ring true today, because our God's love and faithfulness do not change!

> Be still, my soul: the Lord is on thy side.
> Bear patiently the cross of grief or pain.
> Leave to thy God to order and provide;
> In every change, He faithful will remain.
> Be still, my soul: thy best, thy heavenly Friend
> Through thorny ways leads to a joyful end.
>
> Be still, my soul: thy God doth undertake
> To guide the future, as He has the past.
> Thy hope, thy confidence let nothing shake;
> All now mysterious shall be bright at last.
> Be still, my soul: the waves and winds still know
> His voice Who ruled them while He dwelt below.

Being still and trusting God doesn't mean we should become fatalists. I believe He wants us to exercise not only our faith but also the ability to do whatever we can do. But there comes a time when we just have to be still and say, "I don't know what to do and I don't know where to turn, but I'm going to just trust you."

That's what He's asking you to do. Be still, and trust Him. He is God. He will be exalted, and He will never leave you. He'll take you through whatever is before you.

Pit Stop
POINT TO PONDER

Corrie ten Boom once said, "There is no panic in heaven! God has no problems, only plans."

June 23

Here's a personal question for you today: Are you worried about anything? If, so, listen to the words of Jesus: "Do not be afraid, little flock, for your Father has been pleased to give you the kingdom" (Luke 12:32).

Jesus went on to say that we're not to worry about earthly things but to store up treasures in heaven. It is our Father's good pleasure to give us His kingdom! Will He not certainly then provide what we need for life?

The apostle Paul wrote in Philippians 4:6, "Do not be anxious about anything, but in everything, by prayer and petition, with thanksgiving, present your requests to God." I wonder what would happen if we started living this out every day, letting all our requests be known to God.

Whatever your need is, are you giving God the opportunity to meet that need? Or are you turning to other people or trying to figure things out through your own ingenuity and creativity? Don't get so wrapped up in the affairs of this world that you fail to remember who you are and what inheritance awaits you.

Go to God! He wants to give you His kingdom. Everything you need! He asks you to put your trust completely in Him for this day. Trust in Him and Him alone.

Pit Stop
POINT TO PONDER

Imagine the tenderness in Jesus' voice when He said, "Do not be afraid, little flock." He knows how you can worry and how little you can sometimes see of the glorious kingdom of God. But you are a child of God, and He gives you all the blessings He has for His children. Ask the Spirit to give you understanding of the inheritance that is yours.

June 24

When we ask Christ to come into our lives, Scripture says that He takes up residence in us and we become the dwelling place of God: "When you believed in Christ, he identified you as his own by giving you the Holy Spirit, whom he promised long ago. The Spirit is God's guarantee that he will give us the inheritance he promised and that he has purchased us to be His own people" (Ephesians 1:13-14, *NLT*).

That Scripture just amazes me, no matter how many times I read it. By the power of His Spirit, the God of all creation now lives in me and in you! His presence in us gives us assurance that we have been bought with a price—that we *do* belong to the Lord.

When Jesus went back to heaven, He said that He was going to prepare a place for us, but He also said that He would not leave us alone to carry on by our own strength. He gave us a Comforter, the Counselor who would be in us and teach us and guide us.

> Lord Jesus! May everyone who prepares his or her heart to seek Your face receive that spirit of adoption and be enabled to cry out, "Abba, Father." Let them now have power so to believe in Your name as to become children of God and know and sense redemption through Your blood and the forgiveness of sins.[10]

God has identified you as His own, my friend. I pray that His Spirit will help you know that you belong to Him.

Pit Stop
POINT TO PONDER

"To all who believed [Christ] and accepted him, he gave the right to become children of God" (John 1:12, *NLT*). How amazing! You were one of God's enemies, but now He has adopted you as His child.

June 25

> O praise God for all you have and trust Him for all you want!
> JOHN WESLEY

Praising God and trusting Him—that's a great way to live. Meditate on that thought today, and then spend some time in prayer.

You can find all kinds of times and places in your day to pray. More and more frequently, I spend my driving time in prayer and praise. I turn off the radio, and my car becomes a sanctuary for prayer as I drive. Find some of those times in your day, maybe while you drive or as you wait in line at the grocery store or even as you sit in the dentist's chair. Focus on praising God for what you have and trusting Him for all you want.

Wherever you are, just begin to praise God for everything He's done in your life. You may be facing all kinds of difficulties, but focus on what you *do* have, and thank Him for all of that. "O LORD my God, you have performed many wonders for us. Your plans for us are too numerous to list. You have no equal. If I tried to recite all Your wonderful deeds, I would never come to the end of them" (Psalm 40:5, *NLT*).

Remembering and recounting all that God has done for you will help you, then, to determine that you are going to trust Him for everything you want and need today.

Today, find those times when you can praise Him and tell Him that you trust Him.

Pit Stop
POINT TO PONDER

Psalm 40:16 reads, "May all who search for you be filled with joy and gladness in you" (*NLT*). Don't miss God in your life today. He is there! He is walking with you and has plans for you. Ask Him to make you more aware of His presence and His work in your life.

June 26

> For to us a child is born, to us a son is given, and the government will be on his shoulders. And he will be called Wonderful Counselor, Mighty God, Everlasting Father, Prince of Peace.
>
> ISAIAH 9:6

I know we're just about as far from Christmas as we can get on the calendar, but this verse in Isaiah 9:6 is for all of our lives, not just for the Christmas season.

What does it mean to have the God of creation as your counselor? Think about that. The almighty God—the all-knowing, all-powerful God who created all that is—has said He will be *your* counselor.

If you've invited Him to come into your life, He has taken up residence in you. That's also amazing. You are the dwelling place of God. Maybe you're like me and have just never gotten over the fact that the God of all creation lives in you!

God lives in you to equip you and strengthen you in your inner being so that you can be all that He wants you to be. He lives in you so that He can direct your steps. He's given you His Word as a lamp for your feet and a light for your path so that you do not wander in darkness. He has plans for your future, plans to prosper you. He lives in you to work in you and through you to declare His glory.

He will be your Counselor. He speaks to you through His Word, through His Spirit, through prayer. He gives you peace. He opens doors and closes doors. He hears all those who cry to Him for help and direction. Will you let Him speak into your life?

Pit Stop PRAYER

O Lord Jesus, You are truth, You have the words of life, You are the light that brings abundant life. Too often I run to other people for advice, instead of coming to You first. Give me a nudge; remind me that You are here to be my Wonderful Counselor.

June 27

The Sovereign LORD is my strength; he makes my feet like the feet of a deer, he enables me to go on the heights.

HABAKKUK 3:19

Your God is mighty, and He lives in you to help you with all the demands of life.

I don't need to tell you that life is filled with all kinds of demands. The pressures of this world seem to increase more and more. Maybe you're a single parent; maybe you're a full-time caretaker for a family member; maybe you have to hold down two jobs to make ends meet and you just have too much on your plate.

With all the pressures and demands of life, you need a mighty God to come along and say, "I'm here. I will give you the strength you need for the day. I will equip you for everything you will face today. I am everything that you need."

Your God is that mighty God. He is there to help you in your time of need, to give you strength and courage and hope. He's told you how much He cares for you and asked you to give Him all your cares and anxieties and let Him deal with them. He is there, and He wants you to rely on Him.

Turn to Him. Let your mighty God give you the strength you need for this day.

Pit Stop
POWER

The incredible power that raised Jesus from the dead is working in you, child of God! "Be strong in the Lord and in his mighty power" (Ephesians 6:10).

June 28

> Trust in the LORD and do good; dwell in the land and enjoy safe pasture. Delight yourself in the LORD and he will give you the desires of your heart. Commit your way to the LORD; trust in him and he will do this.
>
> PSALM 37:3-5

These very powerful verses are from one of my favorite psalms. What a beautiful picture of a life resting in Jesus!

When we trust in Jesus and delight in Him and commit everything to Him, He provides for us, protects us, guides us, gives us strength and grants the desires of our hearts. Do you hear the contentment, the satisfaction and the peace of such a life? This is the song of one resting in the care of the Shepherd.

Whatever you're facing, God has promised to be your refuge and strength. In other portions of this psalm, David says, "Do not fret because of evil men" (verse 1). God will see that they are cut off; your enemies will vanish like smoke. "But those who hope in the LORD will inherit the land" (verse 9). The entire psalm describes promises for those who rest in their trust of the Lord.

Trust in Jesus every day and for everything. That sounds so simplistic, doesn't it? But I tell you this—it works. Just put your trust in Him and give your life to Him, because the Lord "will not forsake his faithful ones" (verse 28).

Tell Him the desires of your heart. Delight in your relationship with Him. Trust Him with your life. He will never forsake you.

Pit Stop
POINT TO PONDER

If the Lord is your shepherd, you will have all that you need. Reread Psalm 23, and savor the richness of the life your Shepherd gives you.

June 29

Paul writes in 2 Corinthians 13:5, "Examine yourselves to see whether you are in the faith." It's important for us to examine where we stand so that we know we are in right relationship with the Lord.

This month we've been thinking about trusting Jesus for everything in our lives. The most important thing we trust Him for is our righteousness, a right standing with God. It's not infrequent that I talk with people who are putting their trust in good things, but not in the Lord. They are members of a church and attend it faithfully. Some even have certificates of baptism. They try to do good works and live the best lives they can.

But Scripture is really clear: Our best is not good enough. We have all sinned. We have sinful natures that make it impossible for us to meet God's standards of righteousness.

The only righteousness we can possess is in the person of Jesus Christ. That's what the cross is all about. When Jesus died on the cross, He paid the price for your sin and mine; He took my sin and yours upon Himself and paid for those sins with His own body. When He said on the cross, "It is finished," He was saying that the price had been paid.

The *only* way you can be righteous in God's eyes is by accepting and trusting in what Jesus did for you. His shed blood paid all your sin debt and opened the way for you to come to God. Jesus clothes you in His own righteousness; it's a gift.

You can put your trust in Jesus, my friend. He died so that you could live.

Pit Stop
POINT TO PONDER

Colossians 1:21-22 states that though you were one of the "enemies" of God, He reconciled you to Himself through Christ's death, and "as a result, he has brought you into his own presence, and you are holy and blameless as you stand before him without a single fault" (*NLT*). Trust His righteousness and shout "Hallelujah!"

June 30

Cast your cares on the LORD and he will sustain you.

PSALM 55:22

God gives you an open invitation, my friend, to give Him all your worries and concerns, because He can provide everything you need. No matter what your difficulty or what you're facing today, He says, "Cast your care on Me. I will sustain you."

There's nothing too difficult for Him, no problem He cannot solve. Turn to Him and trust Him.

> *Lord, You know my needs,*
> *and I pray, as I put my faith and trust in You*
> *that You will sustain me by the power of Your Spirit.*
> *I pray that You will equip me.*
> *I pray that You will strengthen me.*
> *I pray against fear. I pray against oppression.*
> *I pray that You will bring freedom and deliverance*
> *and victory and joy into my life.*
> *I pray that because of Your work in me, Lord,*
> *others will see the reality of Christ in and through me.*
> *I come against the enemy*
> *and ask that You would bind him*
> *and set me free in the power of Christ*
> *to serve You.*
> *In Jesus' powerful name I pray. Amen.*

Pit Stop
POINT TO PONDER

Oswald Chambers once said, "Faith never knows where it is being led, but it loves and knows the One who is leading." Do you have that sort of faith in God?

JULY

Telling Our Story

Whoever **hears** [Jesus'] word and **believes** . . .
has crossed over from death to life.

JOHN 5:24

July 1

The history of Christ's followers is the story of changed lives. The good news is that Jesus Christ came to this world to save sinners and transform their lives.

I can think back on my own life, recalling what I was before I came to know Christ. I'm so thankful that He totally, completely changed my life. The first verse I memorized after I became a follower of Christ was 2 Corinthians 5:17:

> Therefore, if anyone is in Christ, he is a new creation; the old has gone, the new has come!

What good news that is! The old is *gone;* He is making everything new. I'm still becoming new, still in the process. He is constantly shaping me into the person He wants me to be.

You, too, have a story to tell about how Christ has changed your life. The details may differ from mine, but it's essentially the same story: The old is gone; the new has come! Now Jesus Christ asks you to partner with Him, allowing Him to use you to proclaim His message of good news, the message that changes lives.

Pit Stop
PRAISE

Scripture says that just as Christ was raised from the dead, those who believe in Him are also raised to a new life, birthed into a life as a child of God. God is creating a new you. Thank Him for new life.

July 2

Jesus Christ came to this earth to reach sinful humanity. The song "Christ Receiveth Sinful Men," written by Erdmann Neumeister in the 1700s, urges us to sing that message over and over again, making it plain to all that Christ welcomes sinners!

> Sinners Jesus will receive;
> Sound this word of grace to all
> Who the heavenly pathway leave,
> All who linger, all who fall.
>
> Sing it o'er and over again;
> Christ receiveth sinful men;
> Make the message clear and plain:
> Christ receiveth sinful men.
>
> Come, and He will give you rest;
> Trust Him, for His Word is plain;
> He will take the sinfulest;
> Christ receiveth sinful men.

Yes, even me, even you, with all our sins! He cleanses us so that we can live in relationship with Him.

You may not be a singer, my friend, but doesn't your heart sing when you think about what God has done for you?

Pit Stop
PRAISE

"Even me with all my sin . . ." Praise Jesus for His mercy and grace!

July 3

> For it is by grace you have been saved, through faith—and this not from yourselves, it is the gift of God.
>
> EPHESIANS 2:8

I have a question for you today, and I want you to think hard about this one: What does the term "grace" mean to your life?

Imagine if we were sitting on a park bench and I had never heard a word about the Bible or the gospel. You tell me your story, that your life has been changed by the grace of God. But I have no idea what "grace" means. How would you explain it to me?

That's all for today. Just think about what God's grace has meant in your life. What would your life be like today if He had *not* shown you His grace?

Pit Stop — POINT TO PONDER

Without God's love, His goodness to you, His mercy and forgiveness, where would you be today? Who would you be? What would you be?

July 4

If being born into a good Christian family could get you into heaven, I would have had it made.

I was raised in a wonderful Christian home. My dad was a pastor, and by the time I was nine years old, my four older brothers were either in the ministry or away at school preparing for the ministry. I've been to church more than most people; when I was a kid, my dad was pastor of five churches at one time. He'd preach at three on Sunday morning or two in the morning, one in the afternoon, and two at night; and I was usually there. So I had plenty of church time.

Just as being born in a garage doesn't make you a car, so too being born in a Christian family doesn't make you a Christian. I certainly had more opportunities to hear the gospel than most people, but listening to it did not save me. Only grace could change my life. "He saved us, not because of the righteous things we had done, but because of his mercy" (Titus 3:5, *NLT*).

I believe in church, I love church, and I'm committed to helping my Savior build His Church. But it's only grace that gives me access to God. Only by His mercy is the old gone, the new come. That's grace—undeserved mercies and privileges.

If you answered my questions yesterday and thought about life *without* God's grace, thank Him today for His mercy. You have been saved, my friend, only because God had mercy on you. You did not deserve it, but He washed away your sins and gave you a new life.

Today, with a grateful heart, come to God in praise and worship.

Pit Stop
PRAYER

Father, I want to tell You how grateful I am that Your grace purged me from all of sin's stains and brought me into Your presence. You came to seek me and save me and to make me Your own—even though I didn't deserve it and I can never earn such favor. Thank You!

July 5

Have you ever been on death row? Yes, you have. I have, too.

Imagine that you are on death row in a prison in the United States. Your execution date is set, and you know you are going to die. But one day you hear the keys rattling, the door opens, and the guard tells you that you've received a pardon from the governor and you're free to go.

Would you not feel like shouting and rejoicing over the good news?

You *have* been on death row. But because you know Christ as your Savior, you have been pardoned, released and given freedom to live.

Jesus said, "I tell you the truth, whoever hears my word and believes him who sent me has eternal life and will not be condemned; he has crossed over from death to life" (John 5:24).

That's what Jesus did for every one of us on Calvary. Jesus stepped forward, opened the prison door and set us free. He said, "You are pardoned. Your sins are forgiven. You've been cleansed. You are set free."

That's grace. That's your story and mine, my friend. Now shout and rejoice over the good news!

Pit Stop
POINT TO PONDER

You have been set free by the grace of God and have crossed over from death to life. You've been given life! A few days ago, you thought about life without God's grace. Now, think about the new life you've been given, and ask God to open your eyes to all the wonderful blessings He has in store for you as His child.

July 6

Quick question: If you were asked to describe the character of God, what are the first words that come to mind? In the book of Psalms, David often talked about the attributes of God. For example, in Psalm 86:5, David wrote this about God: "You are forgiving and good, O Lord, abounding in love to all who call on You."

God is forgiving and kind. David also used the word "longsuffering" in this psalm to describe God (see *KJV*). God is not willing that any should perish and, with love, welcomes all who call on Him.

Occasionally I meet somebody who says, "Steve, I've done so many bad things. Could God forgive me?" Absolutely, my friend! Remember that He forgave the thief on the cross who was being executed for whatever he had done. Christ's cleansing work goes deeper than any stain.

If you know somebody who is in the depth of sin, God wants to forgive that person! That's His abundant love. He is kind and forgiving, abounding in love. His love is an everlasting love. God doesn't love the sin, but He loves the person. That's His mercy. His mercy is undeserved—not one of us deserves it. But He loves us that much.

That's the message you have to share with those who don't know Christ. That's who He is and what He wants to do.

Pray that God will give you the opportunity to share that message with someone today.

Pit Stop
POINT TO PONDER

When Jesus left this earth, He said that His followers would be His representatives to a world still in darkness. The message of God's forgiveness and mercy is in your hands. What will you do with that message?

July 7

In Romans 10:13, Paul wrote, "Everyone who calls on the name of the Lord will be saved." Saved from a life of sin, of pain, of sorrow. Saved from eternal punishment. Saved and given new life in Jesus Christ. Saved! In his hymn "Saved, Saved," Jack P. Scholfield describes this well:

> I've found a Friend, who is all to me, His love is ever true;
> I love to tell how He lifted me
> And what His grace can do for you.
>
> Saved by His power divine, saved to new life sublime!
> Life now is sweet and my joy is complete,
> For I'm saved, saved, saved!
>
> He saves me from every sin and harm,
> Secures my soul each day;
> I'm leaning strong on His mighty arm;
> I know He'll guide me all the way.
> When poor and needy and all alone,
> In love He said to me, "Come unto Me and
> I'll lead you home, to live with Me eternally."

You have been saved and are a child of the King. Perfect? No way! But Jesus is changing you, and you have been freed from death and brought to life. What a story you have to tell!

Pit Stop
POINT TO PONDER

Jesus came to set prisoners free. He died to free you from condemnation for your sins, and He can break all the prison bars that hold you. Christ saves you from a life chained to your old ways and old nature! That's the good news you have to tell.

July 8

> The first thing Andrew did was to find his brother Simon
> and tell him, "We have found the Messiah" (that is, the Christ).
> And he brought him to Jesus.
>
> JOHN 1:41-42

Many baby boys have been named Andrew because of this text in John 1:41-42. Andrew set an example for all of us, an example we should be living out as a way of life.

The first thing Andrew did after he found the Messiah, after he came to know Jesus, was to go and find his brother and bring him also to Jesus. Bring them to Jesus, my friend; that's what you are to do. There's nowhere else to bring them. Yes, you can bring them to church; that's a wonderful place. I believe in the church. But a person could join every church in the community and still not know Christ. A person could even be baptized, but that is not what will save.

Bring people to Jesus. Confront people with the cross of Christ. Confront them with the fact that the God of all creation died for them in order that they might be forgiven and cleansed and set free to live in a relationship with Christ.

As a follower of Christ, you are one of God's ambassadors. As His representative, you are to bring people to Jesus. You have found the Messiah. Now bring your brother and sister to meet Him.

Pit Stop PRAYER

Say this prayer, filling in the blank with the name of a person you can bring to Jesus: "Lord Jesus, I want to bring _____ to meet You. Give me opportunities, give me courage, give me wisdom, and give me the right words to say."

STEVE WINGFIELD

July 9

Does your life tell the story of transformation? Are you living out the message that Jesus saves us from sin and gives us new lives? Billy Graham once wrote:

> We are the Bibles the world is reading;
> We are the creeds the world is needing;
> We are the sermons the world is heeding.

We need to own the fact that we are the Bibles the world around us is reading. Many times today the world looks at the Body of Christ in North America and they don't like what they see. Too often the world sees us as angry, judgmental, hypocritical and boring. I hope we are not like that. I want to be real; I want to enjoy life to the full; I want to press hard and follow God in every way that I can. I want to exhibit the fruit of the Spirit, not the traits of the old-nature Steve.

You can be the light that Jesus described in Matthew 5:16—a light to "shine out for all to see, so that everyone will praise your heavenly Father" (*NLT*). Jesus said that you are a light for the world. Your transformed life should bring praise and glory to the One who saved you.

Let your light shine today. That's what Jesus called you to be and to do.

Pit Stop
POINT TO PONDER

"You are a chosen people, a royal priesthood, a holy nation, a people belonging to God, that you may declare the praises of Him who called you out of darkness into his wonderful light" (1 Peter 2:9). You belong to God. May your life declare His praises.

July 10

In Virginia where I live, every season seems to require preparatory work. In the spring, we take patio and porch furniture out of storage, tune up the lawn mower, and start planning our garden. Approaching summer means camping equipment is inventoried and tested. The fall requires calling the chimney sweep and giving the furnace a service checkup. By winter we've brought the patio furniture back into the basement and readied snow shovels and bags of salt. Because we want to be prepared as each new season approaches, we even change the clothes in our closets.

Disciples of Christ are to be prepared in all seasons. "Preach the Word; be prepared in season and out of season" (2 Timothy 4:2). That verse says to me that we're to prepare to share the good news of Jesus Christ at any time. Perhaps you sometimes use the excuse that "the time just isn't right." Now, that might be true; you need to be wise about what to say and when to say it. But too often, this is only an excuse. If you have an opportunity to preach the Word, you cannot wait until what you think might be a more favorable time to do so.

God is the One who grows the seeds, and He's promised to grow much fruit. Our job is to prepare ourselves to tell others how important it is to know Jesus Christ. God opens doors for us to tell our stories, and He says, "I will equip you; I will strengthen you. You will receive *power!*" How can we be timid with such a promise?

My friend, ask for His strength and power today and prepare to tell your story whenever God opens a door.

Pit Stop
POINT TO PONDER

When Jesus sent His 12 disciples into the countryside to do some of His work, He knew they would run into opposition, but He promised them, "God will give you the right words at the right time. For it is not you who will be speaking—it will be the Spirit of your Father speaking through you" (Matthew 10:19-20, *NLT*). Child of God, let Him speak through you!

July 11

You've probably heard or participated in debates about whether the heathen who have never heard the gospel will be saved. In answer to that, the British preacher Charles Spurgeon wrote, "It is more a question with me whether we who have the Gospel and fail to give it to those who have not, can be saved."

Pause and contemplate that statement. The more important question is whether those who have heard and received the truth *but not shared it* can be saved.

Now, we're saved by grace, through faith alone. Nothing we *do*—no works—could ever save us. Faith alone saves us—faith in what Christ has done for us. But because of the wonderful things Christ has done for us, we should be motivated to tell others the greatest story that's ever been breathed.

The story of salvation is the story for the brokenhearted, the prisoners and the captives. There are people in your life who desperately need to hear this story of hope. You know the story; the story of good news is your story! Tell it!

Pit Stop
POINT TO PONDER

Christ rescued you from darkness and death and gave you a new life as a child of God. Think about the people in your life who also need to find new lives. God put those relationships in your life so that you can partner with Christ in calling them back to God.

July 12

People will argue about almost anything, but there's one thing you can't argue with me about: my story. It's *my* story; it happened to *me*. This one thing I know: Jesus changed my life.

You have your story, too, about the difference Christ has made in your life. As you think about how to tell your story, use this simple outline as a guide:

1. Life before you came to know Christ
2. How you came to know Christ
3. Life since you've come to know Christ

I think the most powerful stories have a very limited *before*. Sometimes people spend too much time talking about life before they knew Christ, and it seems as though they glamorize sin. Instead, we should magnify what Christ has done in our lives. We should talk most about how God can not only save us but also keep us.

Work on your story. Write it out so that you can get comfortable with it and share it in about three minutes. If you're not comfortable with telling it, you won't be able to talk to others about it. You have a great story to tell; you've crossed over from death to life!

Pit Stop
PRACTICE

One of the most powerful methods of communication is storytelling, especially stories of your own experiences. Be Christ's witness by simply talking about your own new life. It may be something as simple as saying, "You know, God changed my attitude about . . ." or "God has been so good to me." Remember, you are sharing good news!

July 13

Several years ago, I had the privilege of praying with a young man in Hawaii. This man had just accepted the Lord, and I asked him if he had a Bible. He did not, so I took him to a Christian bookstore and I bought him one.

Right there in the bookstore, I started marking verses for him to read; and one of the verses I marked that day was Revelation 12:11: "And they overcame him [the devil] by the blood of the Lamb and by the word of their testimony."

I had never marked that verse for anyone before, and I haven't done it since; but that day, for that young man, I did.

"My friend," I said, "you just accepted the Lord. Why don't you tell everybody in this store what just happened?" He agreed, and I called for everyone's attention. "My friend wants to tell you what just happened to him." And right then and there, he shared his testimony to all the people in that store.

If you know Christ, you have a story to tell. God wants you to tell it and wants you to tell it well. When you do that, you have the power to overcome the enemy of your soul.

When you asked Christ into your life, He took up residence in you, and He gives you strength and power to overcome. But He also says that the word of your testimony helps you to overcome; in other words, telling your story helps *you* as well. If you're feeling discouraged or a little down in the dumps, share your testimony. And the enemy of your soul has to run away; he can't stand the story of God's mercy and forgiveness. Tell your story.

Pit Stop
POINT TO PONDER

God says that just as rain is sent to water the earth, He sends out His word of truth with a purpose and a plan. You are part of that plan! He has entrusted you to send out His message of mercy and love.

July 14

Listen to these words that Michael Green, senior research fellow at Wycliffe Hall, Oxford University, wrote in his book *Evangelism in the Early Church*:

> The enthusiasm to evangelize which marked the early Christian is one of the most remarkable things in the history of religions. Here were men and women of every rank and every station of life, of every country in the known world, so convinced that they had discovered the riddle of the universe, so sure of the one true God whom they had come to know, that nothing must stand in the way of their passing on this good news to others.[1]

Nothing must stand in the way of us passing on the good news to others! The early Christians lived that out, and God used them to exponentially expand His kingdom throughout the known world.

I spent time with a brother from Ethiopia, who told me the exciting news that the evangelical church in Ethiopia has grown to over six million people. God has been moving in power there. Then our brother prayed for the church in the United States, that we might recapture the zeal and the love of Jesus that compels us to go and tell others.

That's what happened in the New Testament, and the Church grew and spread across countries. God wants to do that again, my friend, and He wants to use you. Will you let Him use you?

Pit Stop
POINT TO PONDER

The early Christians took every opportunity to proclaim the news about Christ. In their homes, when they traveled, even when they were on trial or fleeing persecution, they proclaimed the message wherever they went. They had heard good news and couldn't keep quiet! Where will you be today? Ask the Spirit for opportunities and the words to proclaim the same good news.

July 15

You've probably heard the little statement, "What you are speaks so loudly I cannot hear what you say." I like to turn that around a bit and say, "What you are speaks so loudly, I cannot help but hear what you say." I hope that describes you.

God has called us to construct bridges of love to a lost and dying world. Once that bridge is constructed and once we have earned the right to be heard, then we can invite people across the bridge in the name of Jesus. If we build such a bridge, I believe we will have the privilege of seeing people respond to the invitation.

> [New life] is a gift from God, who brought us back to himself through Christ. And God has given us this task of reconciling people to him. For God was in Christ, reconciling the world to himself, no longer counting people's sins against them. And he gave us this wonderful message of reconciliation. So we are Christ's ambassadors; God is making his appeal through us. We speak for Christ when we plead, "Come back to God!" (2 Corinthians 5:18-20, *NLT*).

God gave us this wonderful message of reconciliation! You carry God's appeal to the lost. My friend, how can you not share such an amazing story?

Pit Stop
POINT TO PONDER

"Lead a life worthy of your calling, for you have been called by God" (Ephesians 4:1, *NLT*). You've been given a new relationship with God, brought out of darkness into His light and named His child. Does your life speak loudly of that new relationship?

July 16

Where is your mission field? You might say that you're not a missionary; you support missionaries, but you've never been called to the mission field. Oh, but you have! Listen to Jesus' command to all who belong to Him:

> Therefore go and make disciples of all nations, baptizing them in the name of the Father and of the Son and of the Holy Spirit, and teaching them to obey everything I have commanded you. And surely I am with you always, to the very end of the age (Matthew 28:19-20).

Go. That's the word. You are to be a go-agent. But where are you to go? You may not go to a foreign mission field, but God has strategically located you in the midst of people who need to know Him. Your mission field is made up of those people around you, those people you are in a relationship with. Maybe you are to go to your neighbor, maybe to your son, maybe to someone you work with.

And one day—and I say this lovingly, but I say it urgently—one day you will stand before the living God and give an account of what you have done to reach the mission field God gave you.

Make a list of people you know who do not know Christ. Begin to pray for them on a daily basis, and then pray that God will give you an opportunity to share your story with them.

Pit Stop PRAYER

Father, remind me every day that Your purpose for my life is that I point people to you. By the power of Your Spirit, bring Your love and compassion and mercy to all my conversations, my actions and my thoughts as I, Your child, represent You.

July 17

Gypsy Smith, an Irish evangelist, said that there are five Gospels and that the only one that some people will ever read is the fifth—the Christian. People are watching how you live your life, even those people who seem to slam the door to the gospel. Your life tells the story of how Jesus can save and forgive and change people.

"The preaching that this world needs most is the sermons in shoes that are walking with Jesus Christ." That reminder about the witness of our daily lives is from D. L. Moody.

Amen! The preaching most needed in our world today is the preaching that walks around every day in the shoes of Jesus' representatives on this earth. At our jobs, in our homes, in our churches—wherever we go, we need to let people know that Jesus is alive in us.

Not that we are perfect. We're not. We're not going to be perfect on this side of heaven. But may our heart's desire be to follow hard after the Lord, to love Him with all our hearts, and to serve Him with everything in us.

If that is the desire of your heart, then those who hear the sermon walking in your shoes will see Christ living in your life, and your story will tell the good news.

Pit Stop
POINT TO PONDER

Are you a sermon in shoes that walk with Jesus Christ?

July 18

You were buried with Christ when you were baptized. And with him you were raised to new life because you trusted the mighty power of God, who raised Christ from the dead.

COLOSSIANS 2:12, *NLT*

What a story you have to tell! You were dead and buried, and now you have a new life!

I attended a baptismal service at a river, and it was such a precious time. Three people had just given their lives to Christ and wanted to be immersed. They went down in that water, were "buried" and then raised up out of the water to their new lives. Without having a debate about the "right" way to baptize, I just want to say how powerfully the symbolism of that baptism spoke to me. We were dead because of our sins. But just as Christ was raised from the dead, so too we are raised to new life—a life bestowed by God in Christ.

You were dead, and Christ has made you alive! You were raised to new life by trusting the mighty power of God—the same power that raised Christ from the dead. That power now works in you.

So ask yourself these questions: You trusted God's power to save you, but do you trust it to work in your life now? Are you expecting God's powerful works as you walk with Him? God has a power that can create universes and raise people from the dead!

Thank God today for your new life. Watch for His mighty power at work in you, and give Him the glory as you tell the story of your new life.

Pit Stop: POINT TO PONDER

Here's another powerful image: "Those who belong to Christ Jesus have nailed the passions and desires of their sinful nature to his cross and crucified them there" (Galatians 5:24, *NLT*). The old has been nailed to the cross. Dead. And now you live a new life by His Spirit!

July 19

> You were dead because of your sins and because your sinful nature was not yet cut away. Then God made you alive with Christ, for he forgave all our sins. He canceled the record of the charges against us and took it away by nailing it to the cross.
>
> COLOSSIANS 2:13-14

In this new life you've been given, you don't have to carry around the burden of your sins. I know that's something many people struggle with. They come to Christ, they confess their sins, and they ask for God's forgiveness, but they cannot forgive themselves for things they've done. They live under a dark cloud of guilt and remorse.

My friend, that is not God's plan for your new life in Christ. He says that the old things are gone; all things are new. *All* things. He says that He has removed your sins as far as the east is from the west, *and remembers them no more*. He says that if you confess your sins, He will cleanse you from all the stains. He has canceled all the charges!

If you are living under a cloud of guilt today, ask Jesus to remove it. Ask Him to cleanse the stains in your life and to give you the joy of a new and abundant life walking with Him.

Christ has canceled the charges against you. That's what He's done for you. That's what He will do for anyone who calls on Him. Has God placed people in your life who desperately need to know that the record of their debts can be totally canceled? Will you tell them the good news?

Pit Stop
POINT TO PONDER

"God, with undeserved kindness, declares that we are righteous" (Romans 3:24, *NLT*). That's the richness of God's grace, my friend! That's the message you can share.

July 20

Have you ever stopped to imagine where you might be now or who you might be if you had never invited Christ into your life? What would life be like without Him? Or maybe you remember, all too well, what life was like before you knew Him.

> Because of our faith, Christ has brought us into this place of undeserved privilege where we now stand (Romans 5:2, *NLT*).

We have been made right with God through our faith in Him. There's nothing else we could do to make ourselves right with God. Because of our sinful nature, we could never work hard enough or be good enough to be right with Him.

But if we put our faith in Him, if we believe in Him, then He counts us as righteous (see Romans 4:24; 5:1). And that's all because of what Christ Jesus did for us; He paid the price we should have paid for our sins.

We now stand in a place of undeserved privilege. How exciting! In Romans 5, Paul goes on to talk about some of those great privileges we now have because of our faith. We'll discuss some of those privileges during the next few days. Make no mistake; we don't deserve any of them.

Thank God for His free gifts to you.

Pit Stop
PRAISE

In Psalm 103:1-5, David wrote, "Let all that I am praise the LORD . . . may I never forget the good things he does for me. He forgives all my sins and heals all my diseases. He redeems me from death and crowns me with love and tender mercies. He fills my life with good things" (*NLT*).

July 21

> Since we have been made right in God's sight by faith, we have peace with God because of what Jesus Christ our Lord has done for us.
>
> ROMANS 5:1, *NLT*

You have peace with God. No more insecurity, no more guilt, no more condemnation. You are at peace with the God of all creation.

Before you gave your life to Christ, your soul was in turmoil. Maybe you were afraid of God and you never felt at peace. But Christ has made this peace for you. You can lay your head on your pillow at night, knowing that your sins are forgiven. The charges against you have all been canceled. That's what Jesus did for you.

Put your faith in Christ alone. He brings peace with God. That's not something you can work up yourself. You can't buy it. You can't earn it. Nothing in this world can give you this peace. It's a gift from God, an undeserved privilege. What a difference that makes in your life, my friend!

Do you know someone who has no peace with God, who needs to know the story of what Jesus has done for them? Begin to pray for that person, and when God gives you an opportunity, tell the story of Jesus bringing peace to your life.

Pit Stop
POINT TO PONDER

Your God is the God of peace—peace for all of life. The psalmist wrote, "I listen carefully to what God the LORD is saying, for he speaks peace to his faithful people" (Psalm 85:8, *NLT*). Listen carefully to Him. He'll bless your life with peace.

July 22

> We also rejoice in our sufferings, because we know that suffering produces perseverance; perseverance, character; and character, hope. And hope does not disappoint us.
>
> ROMANS 5:3-5

No matter what happens in our lives, we have hope. So often, I wonder how people handle suffering and crises without faith. What if you have no faith in the Almighty? Do you go into shutdown mode, lock out the pain and hope that it will go away?

We are going to suffer. We have brothers and sisters all around the world who are suffering right now, even giving their lives for Christ. We may not be suffering that kind of persecution, but we will meet other kinds of suffering along our way. Sometimes it's physical suffering. Sometimes we suffer emotional pain. We might have trials on the job and in our homes. We are hurt, sometimes by others, sometimes by our own choices, and sometimes by things that seem to "just happen" in life.

But in all our suffering, we have hope! God pours His love over us. He's given us the Holy Spirit to strengthen and equip us. He has promised to walk with us through fire and flood, all the time working for our good in *everything*. He will never leave us, never abandon us.

How can anyone live without this hope? I don't know. But many, many people try. No one has ever told them about the hope we have been given by the God of all hope. If you're willing to tell your story, God can use you to bring His hope into someone's life.

Pit Stop PRACTICE

God is the God of hope. He keeps His promises—you can depend on that. Look for all His promises as you read the Scriptures, and take hope and encouragement from them.

July 23

> The sin of this one man, Adam, caused death to rule over many. But even greater is God's wonderful grace and his gift of righteousness, for all who receive it *will live in triumph over sin and death* through this one man, Jesus Christ. Yes, Adam's one sin brings condemnation for everyone, but Christ's one act of righteousness brings a right relationship with God *and new life* for everyone.
>
> ROMANS 5:17-18, *NLT*, EMPHASIS ADDED

Sin came into this world because of Adam's one act of disobedience. Do you see how one act by one person contaminated all of humanity? We have all sinned. But through one act by another man, Jesus Christ, righteousness now reigns in the lives of those who trust in Him.

Jesus Christ defeated sin! When He died, He broke the power of sin. Righteousness now reigns in the lives of those who believe in Him. All who receive God's wonderful grace and gift of righteousness will live new lives—lives lived in triumph. That says victory to me!

God wants you to live victoriously, my friend. Put your faith and trust in Jesus alone. Put the past behind you. Yes, sin is a reality in this world and in your life; but the victory Jesus Christ brings is also a reality, and He has said that He is stronger than the god of this world.

When you accepted His free gift of salvation, He put you in a place of undeserved privilege, the privilege of living a new life and living in victory over sin and death. Only those who believe and trust in Him have that privilege. What a story you have to tell!

Pit Stop
PRAYER

Lord Jesus, Your power breaks sin's hold on me. You have promised that Your power is part of my inheritance as Your child. I know that Your power is so much more than I can even imagine, but help me begin to see and understand the victory available to me in this new life.

July 24

In Romans 5 Paul gives us a great passage that tells our story so well. All of humanity is contaminated by sin, but "when we were utterly helpless, Christ came at just the right time and died for us sinners" (verse 6). We didn't even know Him, much less love Him, and yet He died for us. He offers us a free gift, and if we believe in Him, all the charges against us are canceled. God then sees us through Christ's righteousness, and we're given undeserved privileges.

There's one more thing mentioned in Romans 5 that is so good that we have to spend a few minutes meditating on it: "We can rejoice in our wonderful new relationship with God because our Lord Jesus Christ has made us friends of God" (Romans 5:11, *NLT*).

God has given us all these benefits and privileges as His sons and daughters, but perhaps the greatest benefit—the one that should cause our hearts the most joy—is that we now have a wonderful new relationship with God. We were once at war with Him; now we are His beloved children. God made us to live in relationship with Him, but that relationship was broken by sin. Jesus gave us a wonderful new relationship with our Creator.

Today, as you think about this Scripture, rejoice in your new relationship with your Creator, your Savior, your God. You don't deserve anything from Him, but when you were utterly helpless, He gave you His great, free gift of salvation. What a story!

Pit Stop
PRAISE

"Once you were not a people, but now you are the people of God; once you had not received mercy, but now you have received mercy" (1 Peter 2:10). You have a new life, a new identity, a new relationship with God. Praise Him!

July 25

Whoever claims to live in him must walk as Jesus did.

1 JOHN 2:6

First John 2:6 is a short verse, but with so much to think about.

You know, I fall so far short of walking as Jesus did. But my heart's desire—my prayer for every believer—is to walk in the way that He walked. As you think about Jesus' life here on earth and who He is today, you can't miss His compassion for people. He wept over Jerusalem, mourning that He wanted to bring them to Himself, but they would not come. He healed the sick and fed the hungry and forgave sin-sick souls. But His primary concern was always a person's eternal destiny.

This is one of the ways you can walk as Jesus walked: having compassion and concern for those who do not know Him. Scripture says that it's not His will that any should perish but that all should come to repentance. If you're going to walk the way He walked, you need to be concerned about the things He was concerned about, and He was most concerned about where a person would spend eternity.

Does that compassion of Jesus live in and move your heart, too? Are you concerned about the eternal destiny of your friends, family, neighbors and co-workers? That was the reason Jesus left heaven's glory to come to earth: He came to die for people who did not even know Him because He had compassion on all the sheep who had gone astray.

Today, ask the Spirit to give you Jesus' compassion for those who are still in darkness.

Pit Stop PRAYER

Lord Jesus, Your compassion extends even to those who stubbornly reject and oppose You. You wept over the city that refused to recognize You, the city where You would die. You wept at their stubbornness. Grow Your compassion and mercy in me!

July 26

The Lord says, "I have loved you with an everlasting love; I have drawn you with loving-kindness."

JEREMIAH 31:3

People often talk about finding the Lord. But the fact of the matter is He finds us. He found you; He sought you out. He drew you to Himself.

Yes, each of us must make the decision to say, "I surrender. I give my life to You, Lord. I want You to be Lord of my life." But make no mistake about it: He loves everybody on the face of the earth. He loves everybody who has ever lived. He created you because He loved you, and He longs for each of us to live in intimate relationship with Him.

Occasionally, people ask me if God will still love them if they do something He does not approve of. My friend, He doesn't love people based on what they do or don't do. He *is* love. Now, God might not like what we do; but He loves us, and there's nothing we can do that will cause God to stop loving us.

My question to you today is simply this: Are you in that relationship with God? If not, cry out to Him. He says, "Behold, I stand at the door and knock. If anyone hears my voice and opens the door, I will come in" (Revelation 3:20, *ESV*). All you have to do is ask. I don't care how you've messed up or what you've done. Just talk to Him and say, "Lord, forgive me. I want to live in a relationship with You. I want You to live in my life."

I promise you that He will come into your life with forgiveness, cleansing, healing, power and a new life.

Pit Stop
POINT TO PONDER

Ephesians 1:5 says that it pleases God to adopt us and bring us into His family. How very much He loves us!

July 27

As I read the New Testament, especially the book of Acts, I'm reminded again and again of how God used hospitality to advance His kingdom. The early Christians welcomed people into their homes, sharing meals and offering travelers a place to stay. In one of his letters, the apostle Paul specifically mentioned "Gaius, whose hospitality I and the whole church here enjoy" (Romans 16:23). When the Black Plague hit Europe and, at the height of it ten thousand were dying each day in Rome alone, Christians were the ones who went and ministered to the sick.

I believe God also wants to use this gift of hospitality today as a method to spread the gospel of Jesus Christ. Your hospitality invites people into your world, helps those in need and extends kindness to guests, even strangers. Hospitality not only creates opportunities to show Jesus Christ to those who do not know Him, but it also encourages your brothers and sisters.

"Practice hospitality," Paul wrote to the Romans (12:13). How can you do that? Maybe you'll take somebody to lunch today or invite someone into your home this week. You don't have to have a perfect home. The most wonderful meal I've ever had was in a four-room, fourth-floor flat in Romania, in the cold of winter when heat was limited. But we had a wonderful, wonderful meal. My hosts shared what they had, and they gave sacrificially so that we could enjoy a good meal together.

Start practicing hospitality, and watch how God uses that investment you make for the growth of His kingdom.

Pit Stop
POINT TO PONDER

"We live in a desert with many lonely travelers who are looking for a moment of peace, for a fresh drink and for a sign of encouragement. . . . Hospitality makes anxious disciples into powerful witnesses."
—Henri J. M. Nouwen (*The Wounded Healer*)

July 28

> Offer hospitality to one another without grumbling. Each one should use whatever gift he has received to serve others, faithfully administering God's grace in its various forms.
>
> 1 PETER 4:9-10

Offer hospitality . . . without grumbling. Be about the work God has given you without grumbling! Or, to put it in a positive way, find joy in serving Jesus. According to Paul's words in 2 Corinthians 9:7, God loves a cheerful giver. I don't think that verse is talking about only financial resources.

Each one should use whatever gift he has received. God has gifted us in all kinds of ways. The way in which you show hospitality or offer other service might be different from the way I would. But we are to use the gifts we've received. We'll be asked to give an account someday of how we've used whatever God has gifted to us.

To serve others. We are to serve others. Jesus said that He came not to be served but to serve. Now we represent Him to the world. We're not to be selfish. We're not to hoard and keep the gifts God has given us. If you have received the gift of God's grace, don't keep it to yourself. Share it with others!

Faithfully administering God's grace in its various forms. There's no limit to God's grace, and He exhibits it in many different ways. Even giving a cup of cold water in His name is serving Him.

God wants you to be a willing vessel, a person who will say, "Lord, I am here. Use me." Is that you?

Pit Stop
POINT TO PONDER

God has given you gifts to be used in Christ's work here on earth. "Do it with all the strength and energy that God supplies. Then everything you do will bring glory to God through Jesus Christ" (1 Peter 4:11, *NLT*).

July 29

Paul had been called by Jesus Christ to preach His message, and he did so, faithfully devoting all his life to that call. But his preaching landed him in lots of trouble. He was under house arrest in Rome and uncertain if he would be executed or set free. At the same time, there was also some trouble in the new church in Philippi. Paul heard that others were preaching, but they were doing it out of jealously and rivalry. So he wrote to the believers in Philippi.

Sometimes it's easy to have a pity party for yourself because of what's going on in your life, especially when you think you're doing what God has asked you to do. But Paul, chained to the guards and uncertain about his future, rejoiced that the gospel was being advanced! The gospel spread throughout the whole palace guard, an elite regiment of the Roman army, and even the brothers in the faith were being encouraged by the exciting things happening as people came to know Christ.

Paul was in jail and didn't know whether he would die. Yet he was encouraged and excited about what God was doing in his life and through his life. He said, "I trust that my life will bring honor to Christ, whether I live or die" (Philippians 1:20, *NLT*). The lesson is to be faithful, wherever you are. God is working in everything.

God wants to use you, my friend. Allow Him to do so. Living a life that will bring honor to Christ *no matter what happens* doesn't leave much room for pity parties.

Pit Stop
PRAYER

Lord, I want to live a life that brings honor to You, no matter what happens. May all I say, all I do, in every circumstance, be a sweet Christlike aroma rising up to You.

July 30

In John 6:40, Jesus gives us a glimpse into the Father's heart: "For my Father's will is that everyone who looks to the Son and believes in him shall have eternal life, and I will raise him up at the last day.}

What a great promise! I'm so energized when I look out at a group of people and proclaim Christ, and then a large number of that group make the most important decision in their lives and say yes to Him. I know for a certainty that they have been given new life and that at the last day they will be raised up to live eternally.

If you've met Christ, my friend, that is your hope, that is your destination, that is the drive that keeps you alive.

Be God's representative, proclaiming His plan of forgiveness and mercy, showing His wondrous work in your life, and telling of the hope He's given you so that you will have a host of people who will one day be in heaven because of you.

Our culture is moving further and further away from the cross. More and more people know less and less about the gospel message. More and more encounters with Christians are necessary, it seems, for individuals to get to the place of commitment.

You can be one of the links in that chain—that bridge between today's world and eternal God. Don't take that opportunity lightly. You may water, you may cultivate, you may give a word of encouragement. Whatever it is, God wants to use you to represent Him to a whole new generation so that this new generation will embrace the claims of Christ and come to know Him as Savior and Lord.

Pit Stop
POINT TO PONDER

God sent Jesus to the world on a mission of reconciliation. He found you in darkness and paid the ransom to bring you into His kingdom of light. You have a story to tell. Now Christ sends you into the world to carry on His mission. He's entrusted the story to you.

July 31

> Work at telling others the Good News, and fully carry out the ministry God has given you.
>
> 2 TIMOTHY 4:5, *NLT*

I don't believe God's plan includes our ever coming to rest at a place where we say, "I've done my part. I've finished what God asked me to do."

My challenge to you today is to keep your eyes on Christ, keep following after Him. Regardless of your age, there is still something God wants you to do. Stay engaged in your walk of faith and in the proclamation of the gospel as long as there's breath in your lungs.

God is able to keep you and strengthen you and equip you for the task. Christ's power works in you to declare His glory to all those around you:

> Now all glory to God, who is able, through his mighty power at work within us, to accomplish infinitely more than we might ask or think (Ephesians 3:20, *NLT*).

Wherever you are, don't let up, don't give up. Keep loving Jesus. Keep telling the story, whatever you do. And His power in you will accomplish more than you ever thought possible.

Pit Stop

The new life you have with Christ living through you never grows old or fades away. In fact, His light burns brighter and brighter as He makes you more and more like Himself. That light is meant to draw others to God. This is the mission God has asked you to join.

AUGUST

Investing Treasures

Store up for yourselves **treasures** in heaven.

MATTHEW 6:20

August 1

Godliness with contentment is great gain, for we brought nothing into the world, and we cannot take anything out of the world.

1 TIMOTHY 6:6-7, *ESV*

Have you seen the picture of a hearse pulling a U-Haul rental truck? That picture was probably just intended to get a laugh, but it is also a reminder of the irrevocable fact that we came to this world with nothing, and we leave with nothing. At least, that's how the world sees it.

But as followers of Jesus Christ, we still possess something even when our bodies lie in a hearse. We have the treasures we have invested and built up in heaven.

In 1 Timothy 6:6, Paul says that there's great gain in godliness with contentment: "True godliness with contentment is itself great wealth" (*NLT*). So, we ought to be investing in godliness; in other words, we want to be more and more like our Master. As we become more and more like Him, we find contentment in Him.

If I told you today about a stock that's guaranteed to grow exponentially over the next few months, you'd probably invest in it immediately. There's nothing wrong with that. But I'm telling you today that in godliness and contentment there is the greatest gain; and if you invest in godliness, your wealth will be eternal. Invest in godliness, my friend, and you'll get fantastic returns.

This world is not your home; you're just passing through. If you invest in godliness, your treasures will be waiting for you in eternity.

Pit Stop
POINT TO PONDER

Godliness is not just an attitude or character trait; it means devoting yourself to living God's truths. How do you train for godliness? Reading these devotionals is part of your training. Spending quiet time with God, prayer and reading His Word are other ways to train. And *practicing* the ways God has asked you to live is essential to your training.

August 2

Ever hear people say, "What's the bottom line?"

Well, let me give you the bottom line from Proverbs 22:4: "Humility and the fear of the LORD bring wealth and honor and life." That's the bottom line. You want riches and honor and life? Walk humbly with the Lord.

Walking humbly with God is something that every believer should seek to do. I want the reward. I want to hear God say one day, "Well done, my good and faithful servant." If I want to get that reward, then I need to walk humbly before Him now.

You can have your reward now or later. I choose to have mine later. I know that many people have invested a great deal of time and energy working for rewards and honors in this life. There's nothing wrong with earthly awards and honors. But the ultimate honors and rewards are those given in eternity. Fifty billion years from now, I'm going to be living on with God, and I want to enjoy my rewards there.

Those rewards come from walking humbly with the Lord now.

Make sure you're investing in the right place, my friend. God will honor that and will bless and reward you for it.

Pit Stop
POINT TO PONDER

Scripture has many references to rewards for pursuing godliness; some rewards come here in this life, while some wait in heaven. But you are shortsighted if you focus only on the rewards here and now. Heavenly rewards will last forever.

August 3

Some people might look at being born in the United States as a curse. I don't. I see it as a great blessing and a great opportunity.

Jesus said, "Everyone to whom much was given, of him much will be required" (Luke 12:48, *ESV*). We should thank God every day for the opportunity to do His work with our riches.

In Matthew 6:19-21, Jesus tells us:

> Do not store up for yourselves treasures on earth, where moth and rust destroy, and where thieves break in and steal. But store up for yourselves treasures in heaven, where moth and rust do not destroy, and where thieves do not break in and steal. For where your treasure is, there your heart will be also.

Where's your heart today? Be really honest with yourself, because your heart will be with your treasure. Where's that treasure?

Barb and I were on vacation with our family, and I looked at our four grandchildren and knew they had my heart. They are my treasure. My children also are my treasure. They too have my heart. I pray that this world also has my heart, because the Lord longs for this world to know Him, and I want to invest in the cause of His kingdom.

Where's your treasure? Where are you investing your life and heart?

Pit Stop
POINT TO PONDER

Your heart and devotion are tied irrevocably to your treasure. Your treasure determines your direction and decisions in life. Where are you storing your treasure?

August 4

> I am living for the moment when my Savior's face I see;
> Oh, the thrill of that first meeting, when His glory shines on me!
>
> AVIS B. CHRISTIANSEN

When I came across Avis Christiansen's verse, I wondered what it would be like to have been born blind and, when your sight was restored, to have the first face you see be that of your Savior.

In a sense, we are all blind. We have never seen the face of the One who saved us, the One to whom we've given our trust and our lives. As Peter said, "You love Him even though you have never seen him. Though you do not see him now, you trust him; and you rejoice with a glorious, inexpressible joy" (1 Peter 1:8, *NLT*). We've trusted our lives to someone we've never seen. We've built our hopes on Him and His promises.

Can you imagine what joy you will feel when you see His face? I'm living for that moment when His glory shines on me and I have the privilege of seeing His face. It's going to be overwhelming. As Avis Christiansen writes: "

> When His voice like sweetest music falls upon my waiting ear,
> and my name, amid the millions, from His precious lips I hear.

God knows your name! And one day, you'll hear Him call your name and you'll see His face.

Take some time today to be quiet before the Lord and think about that moment when He says your name to welcome you home.

Pit Stop
PROMISE

Take this promise from Jesus, the One you trust, to heart: "I will come back and get you, so you will always be with Me" (see John 14:3).

August 5

Although Fanny Crosby was blind for most of her life, she wrote more than 8,000 hymns. She's been quoted as saying that if she had a choice, she would have chosen to remain blind for her life on this earth so that the first face she ever saw would be that of her Savior. One of her hymns, "Saved by Grace," describes this moment of meeting Jesus face to face:

> Some day the silver cord will break,
> And I no more as now shall sing;
> But, oh, the joy when I shall wake
> Within the palace of the King!
>
> And I shall see Him face to face,
> And tell the story—Saved by grace.
> And I shall see Him face to face,
> And tell the story—Saved by grace.
>
> Some day: till then I'll watch and wait,
> My lamp all trimmed and burning bright,
> That when my Savior opens the gate,
> My soul to Him may take its flight.

Meeting Jesus is going to be a great experience! Take time today to think about that time when you will see everything more clearly.

Pit Stop
POINT TO PONDER

The night before Jesus' death, He prayed in Gethsemane. His prayer is a key to His heart: "Father, I want these whom you have given me to be with me where I am. Then they can see all the glory you gave me" (John 17:24, *NLT*). Does that thrill your heart? He wants you with Him!

August 6

What is heaven going to be like? Do you ever think about that? Whatever you imagine, it will be a thousand times better!

Scripture says that "no eye has seen, no ear has heard, no mind has conceived what God has prepared for those who love him" (1 Corinthians 2:9).

Jesus said that He was going back to heaven to prepare a place for those who know Him. He told us to build up our treasure there, where nothing can destroy it or steal it away; and He wants us to set our hearts on things above, not on this earth. He promised that He'd come back to take us to be with Him there in heaven.

And that's not all! We will be changed, too. Note these words from 1 John 3:2 (*NLT*):

> Dear friends, we are already God's children, but he has not yet shown us what we will be like when Christ appears. But we do know that we will be like him, for we will see him as he really is.

Are you planning to be there on that day? You'll see Jesus face to face, and Scripture says that you will be like Him. Oh, boy! How exciting that will be!

Today, think about this: Someday, you will be changed to be like your Savior. You'll be free of all that your human heritage has burdened you with, and you'll be all God created you to be! You can hardly begin to imagine—but try.

Pit Stop
PRAYER

Father, I can't begin to imagine the wonder of the day I come into Your presence forever—to see You face to face; to be surrounded with Your glory; to be changed from what I am now to what You created me to be; and to live in Your light! Keep my eyes on the hope of that great day.

August 7

I hope your giving is always done with great joy. To give is to invest in God's work; and if you have the privilege, the great honor, to be used by God in your giving, then that should make you hilariously happy.

God loves a cheerful giver—one that gives voluntarily and without reluctance (see 2 Corinthians 9:7). Here's Jesus' counsel about how to best use your wealth: "

> I tell you, use worldly wealth to gain friends for yourselves, so that when it is gone, you will be welcomed into eternal dwellings (Luke 16:9).

You know that you can't take anything with you when you die; you're going to leave behind everything you have. The only thing you can take to heaven is someone else. So use what you have been given in life to help someone else come to faith in Christ. You might never meet that person again until you get to heaven, but I believe that when you die, that person will be one of the friends who will welcome you home.

People talk about "building a life" here on this earth. But when you give in this way, you can know that you are not only investing in God's work but are also building a life in heaven.

Pit Stop
POINT TO PONDER

How do you store up treasures in heaven? First Timothy 6:18 gives one way: use your abundance here on earth to be generous and to do good things for others. (Abundance can be many things besides money.) In this way, you'll be storing treasures in heaven and building a good foundation for your future life in eternity. Why invest for a life just a few years down the road here on this earth? Invest for eternal returns!

August 8

For 40 days after Jesus' crucifixion, He appeared to the disciples, proving that He was alive and talking to them about the kingdom of heaven. His last words to them came one day out on the Mount of Olives.

The Bible says that Jesus was taken up at that time, into a cloud that took Him out of the sight of the disciples. The disciples stood there, looking up into heaven, until two men in white clothing suddenly stood with them and asked, "Men of Galilee, . . . why do you stand here looking into the sky? This same Jesus, who has been taken from you into heaven, will come back in the same way you have seen him go into heaven" (Acts 1:11). That promise has been the heartbeat and the hope of the Church for more than 2,000 years.

And what did Jesus say to His disciples? What are we supposed to do? Sit around and wait for His return? No, He says in the parable of the 10 servants that we are to "occupy till I come" (Luke 19:13, *KJV*). In other words, Jesus said, "Invest this; put to work what you have been given; do My business with what I have given you." He wants us to continue His work. He wants us to use every available means to reach every available person. We are to declare His glory to the people in our spheres of influence.

You need to proclaim the good news of Jesus by telling your story whenever you have an opportunity. Today, look for an opportunity to tell the story and invest your time and energy in the kingdom of Christ.

Pit Stop
POINT TO PONDER

In the parable of the 10 servants, the master called his servants together and "entrusted his money to them while he was gone" (Matthew 25:14, *NLT*). Jesus entrusted you with the message of the gospel. What are you doing with that message?

August 9

> Compassion costs. It is easy enough to argue, criticize and condemn, but redemption is costly, and comfort draws from the deep. Brains can argue, but it takes heart to comfort.
>
> SAMUEL CHADWICK

Getting involved in the lives of people who have need is costly. It will cost you time; it will cost you energy; it might cost you some of your financial resources. But this world is not your home; you're just passing through. And your treasures, thank God, "are laid up somewhere beyond the blue," as the old country song says.

Where have you invested? How's your portfolio doing? I'm not talking about what's going on down at the bank; I'm talking about the books in heaven.

Proverbs 19:17 says, "If you help the poor, you are lending to the LORD—and he will repay you!" (*NLT*). We cannot take any of our worldly resources with us when we die, but we can send wealth on ahead by investing in others, by spending resources to help others and by bringing others to Christ.

That's what God has called us to do. That's where investments gain wealth that never dwindles away, is stolen or loses its value.

Take some time today to check on the health of your heavenly investments.

Pit Stop
PRAYER

Lord Jesus, I get so caught up in my day-to-day schedule that it's easy to forget You've given me the responsibility of investing myself and my resources in Your work. Forgive me for dropping the ball. Today help me make wise choices in the use of my time, my energy and the abundance You've given me.

August 10

> If you read history you will find that the Christians who did most for the present world were just those who thought most of the next. . . . It is since Christians have largely ceased to think of the other world that they have become so ineffective in this.
>
> C. S. LEWIS, *MERE CHRISTIANITY*

Paul says in Colossians 3:2 that because we have a new life with Christ, we now should set our sights on the realities of heaven: "Set your minds on things above, not on earthly things." Think about the things of heaven rather than the things of this world. Earthly things can so easily distract us, but the next world is our eternal destiny. That's where we're going to spend eternity.

If you are focused on heaven and heaven's values, my friend, then you will be building those bridges that bring other people into the kingdom of heaven. You are a citizen of heaven, and as a citizen of that world living here in this world, you're a representative of your King, and your mission is to bring others to His kingdom.

This life is a breath, a vapor on a cold morning. Focus your thoughts on the next world and prepare for the next world. If you do that, you will be involved in this world as you represent Him.

As you go through your day today, ask yourself if your energies and thoughts and actions carry eternal value. Did you order your day according to heaven's values? Are you going to be about your Master's business today?

Pit Stop
POINT TO PONDER

"We are citizens of heaven, where the Lord Jesus Christ lives. And we are eagerly waiting for him to return as our Savior" (Philippians 3:20, *NLT*).

August 11

We are living in a desperate hour in a dangerous world. God has allowed you and me to live in this day to represent Him to the world around us—to a culture that is growing more and more distant from the cross of Christ.

People *are* looking at how you live your life. God's Word says that we are to guard our thoughts, because what goes into our minds comes back in ways that those around us can see. Staying in His Word will help to guard our thoughts and our actions.

As people look at your life, do they see the love of Christ radiating from you? Yes, hospitality will sometimes require you to step outside your comfort zone. Sometimes it will cost you financially. It will always cost you time and energy. But this is an important part of your work for the Kingdom. Your hospitality can be an encouragement to others in the Body of Christ, and it can also reach those who do not know Christ. God will use your investment of time and energy and comfort to exponentially expand His kingdom.

Today, pray that God will show you someone you can invest in—someone in your community, someone you work with, someone you go to school with, someone you have met who is not a follower of Christ. God has placed you in relationship with that person, and He may want to use you to represent Jesus by extending the gift of love and the gift of hospitality. That high calling is why you exist and why you have been brought into the family of God.

Pit Stop
POINT TO PONDER

Today, model the apostle Paul's dedication to spreading the gospel of Christ: "But my life is worth nothing to me unless I use it for finishing the work assigned me by the Lord Jesus—the work of telling others the Good News about the wonderful grace of God" (Acts 20:24, *NLT*). Jesus gave all believers the same assignment—to carry the story of new life to everyone in the world.

August 12

Scripture tells us that everybody has been given a spiritual gift. Some people have a multiplicity of spiritual gifts; but every person has at least one. And you are responsible for whatever gift God has given you.

Do you know the story Jesus told about the talents in Matthew 25:14-30? (A "talent" was a measure of money at the time of Christ.) One man received 10 talents, one was given five, and the last man was given only one. The first two got to work, invested the money, and doubled what they had been given. But the man with only one talent took it and buried it. The gifts that God has given you might be money, time, the ability to teach, a talent to make music, and a host of other blessings.

When the men who were given the talents came again before their master to report what they'd done, the master said, "To those who use well what they are given, even more will be given, and they will have an abundance. But from those who do nothing, even what little they have will be taken away" (Matthew 25:29, *NLT*).

The first thing you need to do is give your life to Jesus. Once you have done that, you become the dwelling place of God, and you are then His instrument in this world. You must own that, my friend. The world desperately needs people to point them to Jesus.

Yes, we're all cracked pots, and none of us is perfect. But I'm a cracked pot who has been redeemed through the blood of Christ. And He will use me and you, as weak and flawed as we might be, to serve one another and reach those who have not yet come to Him.

God has given you gifts to be used in His work. Just make yourself available, and He'll use you.

Pit Stop
PRAYER

Lord Jesus, it is my desire to be godly and to be devoted to living out the truth of your message. Take my life and the gifts You've given me; I bring them to You as a sacrifice of praise and thanks for what You've done for me. Use them for Your glory.

August 13

> When you give a banquet, invite the poor, the crippled, the lame, the blind, and you will be blessed. Although they cannot repay you, you will be repaid at the resurrection of the righteous.
>
> LUKE 14:13-14

In these verses, Jesus said that if you do something for the least of these, you've done it for Him. Payday is coming one day!

Most of us don't always live according to these instructions. When you have a banquet or a party, do you invite all the poor, the lame, and the blind to come? I don't either, but I hope I'm doing better at including those people I might have ignored before.

Whatever the setting, I think the principle Jesus is giving is that you are to be kind to people. Look for ways to be kind. Don't turn your eyes the other way when you see someone whose situation makes you uncomfortable. You might rationalize your looking away. You might think that perhaps a person with a help sign is mentally ill, a drug addict, an alcoholic or someone just trying to rip off people. No rationalizations! God has called you to be a blessing, and your responsibility is to do good. If someone abuses your kindness, that's between that person and the Lord.

I will tell you that when I help, I don't just hand out money. I'll sometimes buy someone a meal or do something else that helps fulfill a need. I think that's what Jesus is asking each of us to do.

This week, be sensitive to the needs of people around you and be intentional about looking for ways that you can be the love of Christ with skin on.

Pit Stop
POINT TO PONDER

Christ came to give light to the world, light that would bring life. That light is now in You. Does it shine from your life into the lives of those people you meet every day?

August 14

> He who despises his neighbor sins, but blessed is he who is kind to the needy.
>
> PROVERBS 14:21

He who despises his neighbor sins. Well, that should be obvious to anybody who is a follower of Jesus Christ. God doesn't want you to despise anybody; but if you despise your neighbor, you're living in sin; and I hope you'll confess it, get over it and ask the Lord to forgive you.

But the writer of Proverbs goes on to say something you might not have thought so obvious: "But blessed is he who is kind to the needy."

I know that there are needs all around, and you can't do something for every need you see. But you can do *something*. Find somebody who is needy and intentionally try to help. Just think of how much better this world would be if we all lived that way.

You might be tempted to think the government will just take care of the poor and needy, but I don't think that's something the government should be doing. The church of Jesus Christ should have been living this out all along. I do believe that. God has called the Church to be kind to the poor. Just read Scriptures. It's pretty obvious to me.

So look for some needy people and do something! Just do something—big or small—and God will honor it.

Pit Stop
POINT TO PONDER

Many people are financially needy, but many are needy in other ways. The lonely need someone to listen or an invitation to socialize; the new neighbors need an introduction to the neighborhood; the elderly man needs a ride to the grocery store; the single mother needs a babysitter or help with home repairs; visitors need a friendly welcome to church. Look for those needs, too, and you'll be blessed for your kindness.

August 15

> Cast your bread upon the waters, for after many days you will find it again.
>
> ECCLESIASTES 11:1

This wonderful promise from Ecclesiastes 11:1 became a reality to me the other day. A number of years ago, I had the privilege of praying with a person who made a commitment to Christ, and I then bought him a Bible. He lives a long way from me, and over time I lost contact with him and had not heard from him in almost four years.

For whatever reason, the Lord just stuck him in my heart and mind, and frequently I would pray for my friend. And then one day he called. It was like a family reunion, and the blessing that returned to me on that one phone call was inexpressible.

That's when I was reminded of the verse about casting your bread on the waters. Ecclesiastes 11:1 in the *New Living Translation* reads, "Give generously, for your gifts will return to you later." Paul wrote in his letter to the Corinthians, "Remember this: Whoever sows sparingly will also reap sparingly, and whoever sows generously will also reap generously" (2 Corinthians 9:6). Four years later, I was tremendously blessed.

Keep casting your bread. Keep sowing generously. Don't give up, and God will honor your gift, whether it's time or money or prayers or material gifts. And after many days, those seeds you sow will produce a crop that God will bring to harvest.

Pit Stop
PRAYER

Father, keep my eyes on the eternal. Help me trust in Your purposes, Your timing and Your harvest so that I will sow generously and freely and leave the results in Your hands.

August 16

> Give, and it will be given to you. A good measure, pressed down,
> shaken together and running over, will be poured into your lap.
> For with the measure you use, it will be measured to you.
>
> LUKE 6:38

Everything in God's creation gives. Did you ever stop to think about that? The sun gives light by day, and the moon and the stars give light by night. The heavens send rain and snow to water the earth; trees and plants grow and die and decay and give back to the earth. It seems to be natural that everything in all creation gives—except sinful humanity.

Sinful humanity urges you to get all you can, can all you get, sit on the lid and spoil the rest—and forget the rest of the world.

But we are to be good stewards of what God has entrusted to us. What you give will return to you, not just now but in the future as well. Let this principle of giving guide your life. One of the things God has given you is a new heart; and now you can learn to give as God intended all His creation to give.

Martin Luther said, "I have tried to keep things in my hands and lost them all, but what I have given into God's hands I still possess."

Today, decide to be a student of giving as a way of life.

Pit Stop
POINT TO PONDER

"We are not cisterns made for hoarding, we are channels made for sharing." —Billy Graham

August 17

You've probably heard a lot about the work ethic that made America great, but you also may have heard many people talking about the lack of work ethic currently. As a Christian, how do you go about your work?

I believe that in biblical terms, productive lives are not about worldly success as much as they are about service. God wants us to have servant hearts. We do what we do because we want to serve Him. We serve others because, ultimately, that is serving our Lord.

Jesus tells us in Matthew 25:40 that whatever we do for "the least of these brothers of mine" we do for Him (Matthew 25:40). That's a huge statement. Whatever I do, wherever I'm going and whatever I'm investing in, I'm doing it not only for a person but also for Christ.

Now, we're saved by grace through faith only; it's a gift and not a result of our works. But because we belong to Christ, we should be people who are known for devotion and faithfulness in what we do. We ought to do what we do with a degree of excellence. We ought to always give it our best shot.

That's one of the ways you reflect the fact that you have been bought with a price. You are no longer your own. Paul encourages industriousness, devotion to job, and productivity because a Christian is not working for a paycheck but for Jesus.

Ultimately, whatever you do, you do for Him. Today, give Him more than your second best.

Pit Stop
POINT TO PONDER

Devotion to doing good in the Lord's name springs out of a relationship with the Master. The doing good does not come first; the relationship comes first. Your relationship with God is your first priority. Serving others in His name then comes as an overflow of joy and generosity from the fullness of your relationship with Him.

August 18

> In the time we have it is surely our duty to do all the good we can to all the people we can in all the ways we can.
>
> WILLIAM BARCLAY

Our time is not our own. Our time is really in the Lord's hands. We are not guaranteed one more day or even one more breath. So in the time that we have, let us live carefully. As Paul writes in Ephesians 5:15-17:

> "Be careful how you live. Don't live like fools, but like those who are wise. Make the most of every opportunity in these evil days. Don't act thoughtlessly, but understand what the Lord wants you to do" (*NLT*).

I don't want to just waste time; I want to be used of God. I'm not saying you should never have any vacation or any time to relax. You do need to enjoy that part of life, too. But even during those "down" times, I think it is important to use your time wisely to allow the Lord to regenerate you so that you can be of greater service when the opportunity comes.

Do all the good you can to all the people you can in all the ways you can. You know, there's a lot of room there to be very creative. Of course, you can't do good for everybody; that's impossible. But you can be a blessing to as many people as you can. You can take advantage of every opportunity to serve others.

In serving others, you serve the Lord. Today, look for ways to serve others.

Pit Stop PRAYER

Holy Spirit, call my attention to opportunities I have today to serve others. Show me what I can do to bring light into the lives of those I meet throughout my day.

August 19

One of the psalms that I memorized as a young person and that has stuck with me all these years is Psalm 23. Verse 6 says, "Surely goodness and mercy shall follow me all the days of my life: and I will dwell in the house of the LORD forever" (*KJV*).

We have that blessed hope in Christ. I know that I am going to dwell in the house of the Lord forever. Two thousand years ago, Jesus said that He was going to prepare a place for us and that He would come again to take us with Him to that home. Oh, my! What a great, great promise.

How long is forever? It's forever, my friend. There will be no ending. God created you for eternity. You have a beginning but no end. You will either live on in eternity with God or you'll live on in eternity away from Him in a place the Bible calls hell. I want to live with Him forever, and I want you to live with Him forever as well.

Our hope always looks beyond today, to the time we will go home forever. In the meantime, we can claim the promises of Psalm 23. With wonderful promises for both today and eternity, it's a peaceful psalm and a wonderful way to rest in Him. If you haven't read it in a while, take some time to get alone with God and read Psalm 23.

Pit Stop
PROMISE

The Lord's goodness and mercy will bless all your days and bring you home to live with Him forever!

August 20

David Brainerd was an American missionary to Native Americans in the early 1700s and a man who lived his life while keeping his sights on the next. "I love to live on the brink of eternity," he wrote.[11] Brainerd knew that this world was not his home. He also wrote of his great desire to feel "more of a pilgrim and stranger here below; that nothing may divert me from pressing through the lonely desert, till I arrive at my Father's house."[12]

Your Father's house is your destination, too. Are you on your way?

Just before He left to go back to heaven, Jesus said, "I go to prepare a place for you. And if I go and prepare a place for you, I will come again, and receive you unto myself; that where I am, there ye may be also" (John 14:2-3, *KJV*).

There's a place for you in your Father's house, and if you've opened your heart's door to Jesus, you will spend eternity with Him. He promised that, and He cannot lie. You can stand on His promise.

You may often feel like a pilgrim and a stranger here; that is as it should be. You no longer belong to this world. The road might be through lonely desert, but your Father's house is your destination. As Billy Graham said, "Sometimes we get tired of the burdens of life, but we know that Jesus Christ will meet us at the end of life's journey—and that makes all the difference."[13]

You have a home that's being prepared for you in heaven: "No eye has seen, no ear has heard, no mind has conceived what God has prepared for those who love Him" (1 Corinthians 2:9).

Pit Stop
PROMISE

"For we know that when this earthly tent we live in is taken down (that is, when we die and leave this earthly body), we will have a house in heaven, an eternal body made for us by God himself and not by human hands" (2 Corinthians 5:1, *NLT*).

August 21

Most mothers whom I know live their lives for their children. At least through certain phases of children's development, mothers give up their own lives and devote all their energy and time to their children. It's a sacrificial life.

Mother Teresa, probably one of the greatest examples of a sacrificial life, is quoted as saying, "Unless a life is lived for others, it is not worthwhile." That's a pretty significant statement, one that should cause you to stop and reflect. I'm sure that you want your life to be worthwhile.

I was in Romania speaking at a pastors' conference with about 600 pastors in attendance. Someone asked the audience how many of them had come to faith at one of our meetings over the past 20 years in that country. Humbled, I sat there and wept as probably a fourth of the audience responded. Pastors and youth pastors now, they had first come to Christ at one of our crusades.

That spoke encouragement into my life. I want my life to be worthwhile. I want to invest in others. Returns on that kind of investment far out-value any investment I may have in the bank. To play a significant role in someone's life far outweighs anything else we might gain in this world.

That's why Jesus invested in you and me—so that we could give our faith to others.

Pit Stop
PRAYER

Father, keep my eyes on the unseen, the eternal. Focusing on You and Your promises and plans changes the way I look at my relationships here on earth. I want to become more a servant, less self-serving; more a witness to Your life and light, less weary and complaining a traveler; more You, less me!

August 22

Reflect on these words of Joseph H. Gilmore's famous hymn "He Leadeth Me":

> He leadeth me, O blessèd thought!
> O words with heav'nly comfort fraught!
> Whate'er I do, where'er I be
> Still 'tis God's hand that leadeth me.
>
> He leadeth me, He leadeth me,
> By His own hand He leadeth me;
> His faithful foll'wer I would be,
> For by His hand He leadeth me.
>
> Sometimes 'mid scenes of deepest gloom,
> Sometimes where Eden's bowers bloom,
> By waters still, o'er troubled sea,
> Still 'tis His hand that leadeth me.
>
> Lord, I would place my hand in Thine,
> Nor ever murmur nor repine;
> Content, whatever lot I see,
> Since 'tis my God that leadeth me.

Just think about this one thing today: Wherever you are, whatever you do, it's still God's hand that leads you, through this world and toward your eternal home.

Pit Stop PRAYER

May I be content and at peace, Lord, in knowing that it is Your hand that leads me and holds me secure.

August 23

Do you ever get tired? Of course, you do. We all do. I've had some long days of traveling, and I sometimes just get *really* tired—plain old weary. But in Galatians 6:9, Paul says, "Let us not become weary in doing good, for at the proper time we will reap a harvest if we do not give up."

Doing good can make you weary. You do get tired doing good. Any time you give of yourself, energy goes out. It's not easy.

There are times when you may think, *Oh, what's the use? I might as well give up.* Well, my friend, I want to give you this encouragement today: When the desire to give up comes, just rebuke it!

Yes, you will get tired physically, and it's okay to take a rest. But don't become weary in doing good. This world is looking for people who will do good and do good tirelessly. God asks us not to curse the darkness but to be men and women who light candles of joy and love and peace and hope. It's amazing what a little cup of cold water will do. And Jesus is the One who said that if we do it in His name, it's like doing it for Him.

Look around you for opportunities to do good. And don't give up. You will be the one who is blessed, along with blessing someone else.

Pit Stop PRAYER

Lord, lead my heart into understanding and expressing Your love. Grow Your patient endurance in me. Strengthen me, and protect me from discouragement, that I may be an effective part of spreading Your message to the world around me (see 2 Thessalonians 2:16-17; 3:5).

August 24

Look again at Galatians 6:9:

> Let us not become weary in doing good, for at the proper time we will reap a harvest if we do not give up.

Did you notice that Paul says "a harvest" will come "at the proper time"? We may often be impatient and want fast results. Especially when our energy and endurance begin to wane—when we become tired and weary—we may be tempted to give up. We cannot see the situation from God's perspective, but when the time is right, there will be a harvest.

There will be a harvest, *if you faint not.* I think it's possible to sow and sow and cultivate and water and work at a relationship but then give up and not reap a harvest. There's work involved. One person might plant, one might water, one might cultivate, and one might pull out a few weeds. We're all working together to represent Christ. But I believe it is possible to do all this and then give up before the harvest.

So how do you continue? You cling to God's promises. He promises to strengthen you. He promises to uphold you. He says that you will renew your strength; you'll soar like an eagle; you'll run without growing weary. Hold on to His promises and don't give up.

Don't give up on speaking into others' lives. God will use you to love them to Jesus.

Pit Stop PROMISE

The Scriptures were written to encourage and strengthen us, to revive our hope and faith in the Lord's promises. Soak yourself in His Word. It will revive, refresh, renew.

August 25

> What is more, I consider everything a loss compared to the surpassing greatness of knowing Christ Jesus my Lord, for whose sake I have lost all things. I consider them rubbish, that I may gain Christ and be found in him.
>
> PHILIPPIANS 3:8-9

There's a lot packed into Paul's words in Philippians 3:8-9. He says that he considered everything a loss compared to the privilege of knowing Christ. That's a phenomenal statement. Everything, a loss!

I don't care how wealthy you are, how poor you are, what you have or what you don't have—nothing can compare to the surpassing greatness of knowing Christ. The gift of life in Him is a treasure above all else.

Paul says that he considers everything else rubbish. He gives up everything to gain Christ and be found in Him.

Is there anything you're holding tightly that keeps you from getting to know Christ more fully? Is there anything you cannot give up to serve Him? Do you love Him above all else, above anything in this world?

This world is truly not your home. Your treasures are laid up for you somewhere else, and you will be there to enjoy your treasures in heaven forever and ever and ever.

Know Christ, serve Him, love Him. Walk in obedience to His will and plan and purpose for your life because to be with Him is worth giving up all else.

Pit Stop — POINT TO PONDER

Hear Jesus' question: "Of what use is it if you gain everything you want in this world but your soul is lost for eternity?" (see Matthew 16:26).

August 26

You've probably heard Sir Winston Churchill's oft quoted statement: "We make a living by what we get, but we make a life by what we give."

When you die, what will people remember about your life? How will your life be described? Will your life be noted for how much you *got* throughout your life? Or will you be noted for how much you *gave*?

A great epitaph for anyone who has been used by God would be, "He gave of himself" or "She gave of herself." That's all that needs to be said. Won't it be great if, when folks remember your life, they say, "He gave of himself and what he had to meet the needs of others" or "She allowed God to use her to advance His kingdom."

> If any of you wants to be my follower, you must turn from your selfish ways, take up your cross, and follow me. If you try to hang on to your life, you will lose it. But if you give up your life for my sake and for the sake of the Good News, you will save it (Mark 8:34-35, *NLT*).

What have you given up for the sake of Jesus and His kingdom? You give because God calls you to give, not because you hope to get something in return, but because you want to become the hands and feet of God. You allow God to use whatever you have to meet a need.

Give something away today, and ask God to keep teaching you how to give.

Pit Stop PRAYER

As your prayer today, use the beginning of Frances Havergal's hymn of consecration "Take My Life and Let It Be": "Take my life, and let it be consecrated, Lord, to Thee."

August 27

> Since, then, you have been raised with Christ, set your hearts on things above, where Christ is seated at the right hand of God. Set your minds on things above, not on earthly things. For you died, and your life is now hidden with Christ in God. When Christ, who is your life, appears, then you also will appear with him in glory.
>
> COLOSSIANS 3:1-4

Set your mind on things above, my friend. One of the most effective strategies the enemy of our souls uses against us is getting our minds off Christ and filling our thoughts and hearts with earthly things. Have you heard the phrase "That person is so heavenly minded, he's no earthly good"? I like to turn that around and say, "If we're so earthly minded, we're no heavenly good."

Keep your mind focused on Christ and His plans and purpose for you. Remember that the goal, the prize, is being with Him in glory. You are not living for the rewards and treasures of this world. You see far beyond, to the day you'll enjoy the place He's preparing for you.

Think on these things so that you can be who God wants you to be. God wants that mind of yours to be bathed by the love of Christ, to be bathed by the Word of God. Hear it, read it, study it, memorize it.

Today, think about what you think about. Make the choice to fill your mind with the things of heaven.

Pit Stop PRAYER

Father, may Your Spirit within me keep my heart and mind focused on the home You are preparing for me. I want to live as only a pilgrim and stranger here, looking forward to Your eternal kingdom.

August 28

> Those who live according to the sinful nature have their minds set on what that nature desires; but those who live in accordance with the Spirit have their minds set on what the Spirit desires. The mind of sinful man is death, but the mind controlled by the Spirit is life and peace.
>
> ROMANS 8:5-6

Where will you set your mind today? I hope you'll set your mind on the things that are above, on the things of the Spirit and on Christ, because that will enable you to continue to grow in your walk with Him.

It's a choice. You'll have to make the choice to spend time with Him. You'll have to choose what you will think about. You'll have to choose how you want to think about things that happen to you today. You are constantly tempted to focus on things society wants you to think about and to think according to philosophies of this world. Instead, choose to set your mind on what the Spirit desires.

Keep your eyes and your mind and your heart focused on Christ. Think about things of the Spirit and Christ's kingdom. Keep growing and keep maturing. Keep striving for that mark, for the prize of the high calling in Christ Jesus.

Let your mind be controlled by the Spirit, and He'll bring you life and peace.

Pit Stop
POINT TO PONDER

"Follow Me," Jesus said to the disciples He called. He calls the same way today; you must choose whether to follow or to hang back. You must choose whether His Spirit will lead you or whether you'll follow your sinful nature. The promise is this: The Spirit leads the way to life and peace.

August 29

> For you have been born again, but not to a life that will quickly end. Your new life will last forever because it comes from the eternal, living word of God. . . . So get rid of all evil behavior. Be done with all deceit, hypocrisy, jealousy, and all unkind speech. Like newborn babies, you must crave pure spiritual milk so that you will grow into a full experience of salvation. Cry out for this nourishment, now that you have had a taste of the Lord's kindness.
>
> 1 PETER 1:23; 2:1-3, *NLT*

Peter reminds us that we have been born again—born into the family of God. Your new life will not end; it will last forever! So get rid of evil behavior. Let God mold you into the image of Christ—to train for godliness, in other words—because this new life you're living will go on forever.

Peter mentions "pure spiritual milk." That's what you need in order to grow and mature. He says, "Cry out for this nourishment, now that you had a taste of the Lord's kindness." No matter where we are in our journey of maturing in Christ, we should cry out for nourishment in our faith. Study God's Word. Spend time with Him. Commune with Him in prayer. We are growing into a life that will last forever.

I'm convinced that the enemy of our souls will try to keep us so busy that we fail to spend time with the Master. We have choices to make. Every day, we make choices about where we want to go and who we want to be with. Now that you've tasted and know how good the Lord is, choose to spend more time with Him. Then your faith will grow and mature.

Cry out to Him for nourishment. Don't let anything come between you and time spent with the Master.

Pit Stop PRAYER

O Lord, Your mercy and love surround me all the days of my life. My heart is set on pilgrimage, so guide me in Your truth and teach me, until I come home to You forever.

August 30

We can learn much from King David about investing our treasure. David dreamed of building a temple for the Lord, a permanent place where the Ark of the Covenant would rest. But God told him he would not be the one to accomplish this; instead, his son Solomon would be the king who would see the dream come to fruition. David did not argue with God, yet he poured all his energy and wealth into preparing the way for Solomon to build the Temple (see 1 Chronicles 28–29).

Using every resource at his command, David gathered the gold, silver, bronze, iron, wood and precious stones necessary for the Temple. Then he said, "Because of my devotion to the Temple of God, I am giving all of my own private treasures of gold and silver to help in the construction" (1 Chronicles 29:3, *NLT*). And he also went to the people and asked them to bring all the offerings they could. The people gave freely and joyfully. In a prayer of praise, David shows a heart and mind set on heavenly things:

> O our God, we thank you and praise your glorious name! But who am I, and who are my people, that we could give anything to you? Everything we have has come from you, and we give you only what you first gave us! We are here for only a moment, visitors and strangers in the land as our ancestors were before us. Our days on earth are like a passing shadow, gone so soon without a trace (1 Chronicles 29:13-15, *NLT*).

Oh, Father! We are only here for a moment. Give us an eternal perspective like David's!

Pit Stop
POINT TO PONDER

The Lord says that someday the skies will disappear like smoke, the stars will dissolve, and the earth as we know it will be gone. "But my salvation lasts forever. My righteous rule will never end!" (Isaiah 51:6, *NLT*).

August 31

Are you living in anticipation of our Lord's return? Are you thinking about that? As I understand Bible prophecy, there is nothing left to be fulfilled other than His return. He could return at any moment.

We need to be ready. We need to have oil in our lamps and be prepared for Christ's return. Live with expectancy!

> For you died, and your life is now hidden with Christ in God. When Christ, who is your life, appears, then you also will appear with Him in glory (Colossians 3:3-4).

When you gave your life to Jesus, your old life died. Now the life you live is His; He *is* your life. His life is reflected through yours. And when He appears, you will appear with Him in glory.

That is the hope of the Church. All members of the Church live in expectancy of Christ's return, knowing that when He does appear, we'll be with Him in glory forever.

Let your light shine; His light is shining through you. Tell the story. Declare His glory. And look forward to your home in your Father's house forever.

Pit Stop PRAYER

Almighty God, You will rule forever! My life here is but a shadow, and I look forward to coming home to be with You. I give myself to the power of Your Spirit, that You will give me strength and wisdom to live a holy and godly life during my time on this earth. Amen.

SEPTEMBER

Running with Endurance

Run in such a way as to get the prize.

1 CORINTHIANS 9:24

September 1

> I have fought the good fight, I have finished the race,
> I have kept the faith.
>
> 2 TIMOTHY 4:7

In his book *The Beautiful Fight,* Gary Thomas gives a different perspective on 2 Timothy 4:7: "Most of us have heard the modern translation of 2 Timothy 4:7 that says, 'I have fought the good fight, I have finished the race. I have kept the faith.' An orthodox monk has pointed out that this is a 'strikingly Greek' expression that may be better understood as 'I have fought the Beautiful Fight.'"[14]

You know, I like that. We *are* in a beautiful fight, and we are going to win! I've read the last chapter. I know that Christ who is in us is greater than he who is in the world.

In the Christian's story of transformation and sacrificial service, there's drama, there's passion, there's struggle, there's vision—everything your soul needs to feel alive is found in Christ. Celebrate the life you have been given, the beautiful fight you are fighting!

"Each one of you will put to flight a thousand of the enemy, for the Lord your God fights for you, just as he has promised. So be very careful to love the Lord your God" (Joshua 23:10-11, *NLT*). Oh, my friend, stay in love with God. Know that He is empowering you; He is equipping you; He is strengthening you. Keep your eyes on Him and enjoy this beautiful fight that you're in. Stand firm. The Lord fights for you. You are going to win.

Pit Stop — POINT TO PONDER

As you fight the beautiful fight and run the race, the most important thing is your relationship with Christ. Keep close to Him, look to Him for strength and guidance, and heed His Spirit within you.

September 2

Even in the winter, I see people out running. I have a friend who's a marathon runner, and every now and then I think about training for a marathon; but then I lie down and the thought goes away.

I just don't like to run. I enjoy walking; when I walk, I can think and pray. But if I try to run, all I can think about is breathing and trying to stay alive.

But one thing I've never seen is a marathon runner with weights tied around his or her ankles. Scripture says that we are running a race, and we should "strip off every weight that slows us down, especially the sin that so easily trips us up. And let us run with endurance the race God has set before us" (Hebrews 12:1, *NLT*).

It's a good thing to occasionally look at what's going on in your life and be honest with yourself. Look in the mirror and ask yourself, *Is there anything hindering my walk with the Lord? Am I involved in anything that's keeping me from being all that God wants me to be?*

That's really what Hebrews 12:1 is talking about. Lay aside every weight and run with endurance. You don't want anything holding you back or slowing you down.

Is something holding you back from being what God wants you to be? Is something preventing your pursuit of all of God's purposes? Look in the mirror, and answer these questions honestly.

Pit Stop
PRAYER

Lord Jesus, as I think daily this month about fighting the beautiful fight or running the race, show me what weights I'm carrying that I need to throw off.

September 3

The Bible says that one of these days all of us are going to stand before the living God. Every knee shall bow and every tongue will confess that Jesus Christ is Lord. Run with endurance, as you run the race that takes us toward that day. As Paul writes:

> Do you not know that in a race all the runners run, but only one gets the prize? Run in such a way as to get the prize (1 Corinthians 9:24).

Are you running to get the prize? Just as athletes train their bodies, disciplining themselves so that they can win, so we must also train, discipline ourselves and "run with purpose in every step" (1 Corinthians 9:26, *NLT*). We're looking toward an eternal prize.

It's easy, in the busyness of our earthly days, to lose sight of our eternal goal. We deal daily with so many demands and distractions, and we are lured by pleasures and momentary satisfactions. Before we know it, our eyes are drawn away from the eternal prize.

I long to hear, "Well done, thou good and faithful servant." I want to represent Christ well in what I do. I want to be faithful to Him. In everything I say and in everything I do, I always want to proclaim the fact that Jesus is Lord of my life.

Today, let your life show that Jesus has changed you and you are a new creation in Him.

Run to get the prize.

Pit Stop
PRAYER

Father, You know that it's sometimes hard for me to see beyond today. Cares and concerns of daily life press in and eclipse my view of the eternal prize. I want to see things in light of Your everlasting reign, Lord. Keep my vision clear and my eyes focused on the eternal.

September 4

> Not that I have already obtained all this, or have already been made perfect, but I press on to take hold of that for which Christ Jesus took hold of me. Brothers, I do not consider myself yet to have taken hold of it. But one thing I do: Forgetting what is behind and straining toward what is ahead, I press on toward the goal to win the prize for which God has called me heavenward in Christ Jesus.
>
> PHILIPPIANS 3:12-14

Are you pressing on? When you read those words "I press on," what mental image do you see? I see an athlete who makes the body submissive so that it is well trained and equipped to do its best in a particular event. Why? To win the medal, crown or prize.

Earthly rewards soon fade, though. Paul says, in effect, "How much more should we strive for something that is imperishable?"

Take your relationship with Jesus Christ very seriously. Don't take it for granted. Choose to press on to be all that God called you to be. What is that for you? I don't know; I can't answer that. But He's promised to direct your steps and show you the best way to go. His plans for you are far beyond anything you can imagine, my friend. He wants nothing but the best for you.

Deepen your relationship with the Father and press on. Strive to win the prize. It's an eternal prize, one far greater than anything you can win or earn here below.

Don't ever give up. Don't ever quit. Press on!

Pit Stop PRAYER

Lord Jesus, I confess that one weight I carry is *yesterday.* I remember my failures, my sins, the times I've failed. But You have promised that You have washed my yesterdays clean and You, Lord, have forgotten them! Work in my heart and head, and help me to let go of those memories and feelings and look forward to what lies ahead with You.

September 5

*I hope you will be a missionary wherever your lot is cast. . . .
It makes but little difference after all where we spend these few
fleeting years, if they are only spent for the glory of God.
Be assured there is nothing else worth living for.*

ELIZABETH FREEMAN

What are you living for?

There's nothing wrong with working hard to get a paycheck and provide for yourself and your family. I know that these are tough times. You may have lost your job or are in some other financial difficulty and are concerned about providing for your family. But the greatest thing you can provide for your family is a living, intimate relationship with Jesus Christ. After all is said and done, that's what's going to count.

Are you representing Jesus Christ well wherever you go? When people see the way you interact with others and the way you communicate, are they drawn to the Savior? That is what being a missionary is all about. You are His representative. You are His ambassador. You have been called to be an ambassador of the living God.

God calls people to the pastorate. God calls people as medical missionaries. God sometimes calls people to make some form of ministry their life work. But most are called to be faithful servants while working in other capacities. No matter how we earn a living, *all* of us are in ministry because we represent Him. That's really what matters.

When you die, what will be most important is what you have done to represent Him in the way you've lived. That's your call in life. Take it seriously. And wherever you go today, remember why you're there.

Pit Stop
PRAYER

Almighty God, You are my Lord! Wherever I go today, remind me that I represent You, that You have placed me there for a purpose, and that Your love and mercy reach out to everyone I meet. Let me be a channel of that love and mercy.

September 6

These are difficult times for many people. Maybe you find yourself in a situation where funds are low. You have to buy food and make the house payment and pay the electric bill, and you can't see how even those basics will be covered. Maybe you have a seriously ill spouse and need to make decisions about medical treatments. Or perhaps an adult child has cut off contact with you and has given you no opportunity to rebuild the relationship.

You need encouragement and hope. Jesus says, "I want to be that hope. I want to be that encouragement for you." Jesus says to cast all your anxiety on Him, because He cares for you. That's a great invitation. As Paul wrote: "May our Lord Jesus Christ himself and God our Father, who loved us and by his grace gave us eternal encouragement and good hope, encourage your hearts and strengthen you in every good deed and word" (2 Thessalonians 2:16-17).

No matter what reason you need hope for today, ask Jesus to encourage you in your inner being. If you need a miracle, pray that God will give you a miracle, just to let you know that He's there. He's in the miracle business. God is your encouragement. He loves you and by His grace has given you eternal encouragement. Eternal! Not fleeting encouragement, but everlasting encouragement and good hope. The devil and all of his demons can't take that away from you, my friend.

God's Word is full of His promises to you. So claim His promises today; ask Him to give you eternal encouragement and good hope. Ask Him to surround you, equip you and be everything you need for this day.

Pit Stop PRAYER

Father, I need encouragement today. I'm carrying a heavy load and walking a dark path; all sorts of briars and rocks are making the going difficult and painful. Shine Your light on my path today. Give me a word of encouragement and hope and a sense of Your presence right here with me, giving me strength.

September 7

All of us walk through times of discouragement. Maybe you're even crying right now as you read these words. Grandparents may be crying over a grandson or granddaughter; maybe a mom or dad sheds tears over a son or daughter who is wandering away; maybe a wife weeps for a husband who is not walking with the Lord.

I want to encourage you right now not to grow weary in well doing, because in due season you will reap a harvest if you do not give up (see Galatians 6:9). Hold on, don't give up, keep praying, keep believing, and I believe God will reward you with answered prayer. As the psalmist wrote:

> Those who sow in tears will reap with songs of joy. He who goes out weeping, carrying seed to sow, will return with songs of joy, carrying sheaves with him (Psalm 126:5-6).

It may be your own trials and tribulations that are discouraging you. Yes, there are heartaches and pain in life on this earth. But in the midst of heartache and pain, if we put our faith and our trust in Jesus alone, He will give us songs of joy. It will happen. He has promised to give us that joy.

Jesus can give you joy overflowing, unspeakable and full of glory. That joy will enable you to sing the doxology in the dungeon and sleep well in the lion's den. He can give you joy in all circumstances, if you put your trust in Him.

Pit Stop
PRAYER

Lord Jesus, discouragement is almost crushing me. My own strength is gone and tears seem to have washed away all joy. I know my life is in Your hands and my only hope for strength and joy is in You, so I'm just going to cling to You and trust You.

September 8

> If Jesus Christ be God and died for me, then no sacrifice
> can be too great for me to make for Him.
>
> C. T. STUDD

Sometimes, you probably feel like having a little pity party for yourself. You may feel as if nobody's listening, nobody's paying attention to what you're doing, no one is supporting and encouraging you.

Years ago, I met a couple living in the Amazon jungle. They had been there for 25 years, faithfully translating the Scriptures for the purpose of planting a church and reaching people for Jesus. The question in my mind was, *What did it cost them to do this for all these years?*

Is God asking you to do something that you don't want to do? Maybe you are resisting because obeying will require sacrifices on your part. You may have to give up things you hold dear; you may have to give up your own plans for this day or for the future.

Even though I don't know the details of what God is asking of you and what sacrifices you might have to make, I can say this with certainty: No matter what He asks of you, there is no sacrifice too great for you to make for Him. Remember that He died for you!

So I challenge you to be faithful to Him, whatever He calls you to do. He will reward you with the joy of obedience.

Pit Stop
PRAYER

Say this prayer, filling in the blank with what you feel that God has called you to do: "Lord, I have heard You very clearly asking me to _____, but You know I'm still holding back. You know the reasons I'm dragging my feet. I know that my reluctance to obey is sin and is interfering with my relationship with You, lessening my joy and weakening my walk. I also know that faith means I must step out and act. Lord Jesus, increase my trust!"

September 9

> It is for freedom that Christ has set us free. Stand firm, then, and do not let yourselves be burdened again by a yoke of slavery. You were running a good race. Who cut in on you and kept you from obeying the truth?
>
> GALATIANS 5:1,7

It's important for each of us to examine where we stand, and for us to do this on a frequent basis. I try to do that on a daily basis as a part of my quiet time.

It is important to stay in tune with God's will, God's plan, and God's purpose for your life. Can you remember back to the time you committed yourself to the Lord? Maybe today you're not where you know you need to be. What happened to your race? Who or what cut in on you and caused you to either falter or stumble or maybe even run in the wrong direction?

Jesus Christ came into your life to set you free, and He doesn't want you to be encumbered by a yoke of bondage. If there's something weighing you down and holding you back from running in His freedom and truth, acknowledge it, ask Him to forgive you and walk away from it so that the power of His Spirit can be released in you and flow through you for the advancement of His kingdom.

If you will confess your sins, He will forgive and cleanse you (see 1 John 1:9). Then you can run freely.

Take time today to look at how your race is going. Talk with God about it, and let Him work in you.

Pit Stop
PRAYER

Father, I want to be able to say, "I run in the path of your commands, for you have set my heart free" (Psalm 119:32). What a beautiful picture! This is how I want to run the race. So continue to work in me, Lord, that I might run in the path of Your commands with a free heart.

September 10

What's on your mind today? What's uppermost in your thoughts? Is there something that is drawing your thoughts constantly? What's commanding the attention of your heart and mind right now? In Colossians 3:1-2, Paul tells us what should be on our minds:

> Since, then, you have been raised with Christ, set your hearts on things above, where Christ is, seated at the right hand of God. Set your minds on things above, not on earthly things.

Your old self is dead, and you have been raised to a new life with Christ. So your thinking and your heart's desires have changed as well.

We're to set our hearts on things above. What's your heart set on? Is it something in this world? Or is it something in the heavenly kingdom?

This world tries to get us to think about all this earthly *stuff*. But God says we need to be thinking about His ways, His plans and His purpose for our lives. We need to set our minds on things above, not on earthly things. According to Romans 12:2, we should not conform to this world but be transformed. How are we transformed? By the renewing of our minds. Our minds need to be focused on things above.

What are you thinking about? If you are going to represent Him well, you need a transformed mind and a heart set on His kingdom.

Spend some time today shutting out everything else and focusing on Him.

Pit Stop PRAYER

Lord, tune my head and my heart into Yours. I don't want to think like a citizen of this world but like Your child and a citizen of Your kingdom. Give me a heavenly perspective, an eternal view of even the small details of my life here on earth, because I know that even now, I am living an eternal life, one that will not end.

September 11

When Paul wrote to the church at Ephesus, he asked them to "pray in the Spirit on all occasions with all kinds of prayers and requests. With this in mind, be alert and always keep on praying for all the saints" (Ephesians 6:18). Then Paul said, "Pray for me, too" (verse 19).

If Paul were in this world today and were writing to us, what would he ask us to pray for? How do we pray for the Lord's people, "all the saints"? I think he would say, "Pray for boldness." He asked the church to pray he would be given the right words and would have boldness to speak the word of God with courage, conviction and passion (see verse 19). That's a prayer we can pray for all of Christ's disciples today, too.

But if he were alive today, I think Paul would have two more prayer requests. The first would be, "Pray that you not be overcome by the intoxication of success." You know, it's so easy to get caught up in all that's going on in our lives and think, *I can do this on my own.* Most of us do not have to pray about where we're going to get something to eat or where we're going to sleep tonight, but we must realize that without Him supplying our needs, we would be in desperate straits.

Paul's second prayer request would be, "Pray against the enemy, who wants to beat you up with the devastation of insignificance." In today's world, it's easy to think, *What can I do about such great need? Who am I to fight this battle? I know so little. How could the Lord use me?* The Lord made and chose every one of His children, and He wants to use each one in a significant way to advance His kingdom.

Pray these things today, for yourself and for me and for all the people of the Lord.

Pit Stop
PRAYER

Heavenly Father, You know that I battle two extremes. I'm so easily deceived by the lie of self-sufficiency and forget that my strength and power and victory come from You alone. Or I believe the lie that I can do nothing because I'm too insignificant. Forgive me, Father, and teach me how to live Your truth.

September 12

Acknowledge the Lord in the morning, and ask for His direction throughout your day.

I know, a lot of people are not at their best in the morning. They aren't morning people, and trying to have time with the Lord in the early morning isn't even a wise plan for them. Not matter when you have your extended time with Him, I believe it's so important to bring Him into your day at the beginning.

Start the day by directing your first thoughts in a prayer to the One who has given you life for that day:

> I cry to you for help, O LORD; in the morning my prayer comes before you (Psalm 88:13).

> I rise before dawn and cry for help; I have put my hope in your word (Psalm 119:147).

Maybe you do this even before you get out of bed! Acknowledge the Lord and His lordship over your life as soon as you wake up. Thank Him for the day and ask Him to direct your steps. It may only be a sentence or two: *Lord, I give myself and my day to You. Please guide me in the right steps today.*

God is your only strength, your help, your hope. He is the One who guides your feet and sustains you. Send your prayer up to Him in the morning, and it will change your day for the better.

Pit Stop
PRAYER

Lord, I give myself and my day to You. Would You guide me in the right steps today?

STEVE WINGFIELD

September 13

What are you looking at? What captures your attention? Day in and day out, we are probably tempted to look at all kinds of stuff. That's what the advertising industry is all about—trying to get us to look and desire and then buy. So much in the world around us clamors for our attention.

Yet even though we are living in this world, we belong to another kingdom, and we're commanded to fix our eyes on Jesus:

> Let us fix our eyes on Jesus, the author and perfecter of our faith, who for the joy set before him endured the cross, scorning its shame, and sat down at the right hand of the throne of God (Hebrews 12:2).

Jesus is the author and perfecter of your faith. His Spirit gave birth to your faith, and He will make it grow and mature. Don't lose sight of the One who has given you this faith.

And don't lose sight of what Jesus did for you. He willingly, joyfully, went to the cross. From my perspective, there can't be much joy in dying on a cross. But because He knew He was paying the price for your sins, He endured that.

Rejoice in what He has done for you, and don't take your eyes off Him. Then you will run with endurance.

Pit Stop PRAYER

Lord Jesus, You are the life-giving vine and I am a branch (see John 15:5). I want to be so closely connected to You that Your life flows through me and makes me strong and fruitful. Perfect my faith, Lord.

September 14

One man who certainly knew what it was like to run long, difficult races was Peter. We're sometimes pretty hard on Peter, but I can relate to him. Out of his passionate love for Jesus, he declared, "I'll never deny You. I would die for You!" (see Matthew 26:35).

Several years ago when I was in Israel, I was up early one day, having my devotions down by the Sea of Galilee. I sang the words from an old song: "What a day that will be when my Jesus I shall see. When I look upon His face . . ." The question came to me, *Will I be able to look at Jesus?*

Do you remember the rest of the story about Peter? Less than 24 hours after saying he would never deny Jesus, he was cursing and refusing to acknowledge that he even knew Christ. The cock crowed, and Jesus turned and looked at Peter.

I've asked myself many times how I would have felt if I'd been in Peter's shoes that morning. Yet there have been times when, in all honesty, I *have* denied Jesus, times when I didn't stand for Him as strongly as I should have.

The Bible says that Peter went out and wept bitterly; I would have, too. But Jesus still loved him. He didn't give up on Peter, and He hasn't given up on me or you. If you have denied Him, tell Him you're sorry. If you have not stood firm for Him or if you've been stumbling along in your race, ask Him to forgive you.

Jesus still loves you. He will forgive and keep on working in you. And "may he produce in you [and me], through the power of Jesus Christ, every good thing that is pleasing to him" (Hebrews 13:21, *NLT*).

Pit Stop PRAYER

Lord, Peter's story brought tears to my eyes because I too have denied You. You know I love You, but I was a coward. Forgive me. As I come to You now, I want to come to You with joy and a free conscience. Wash away the stains and make me stronger by Your Spirit.

September 15

> My dear children, I am writing this to you so that you will not sin. But if anyone does sin, we have an advocate who pleads our case before the Father. He is Jesus Christ, the one who is truly righteous. He himself is the sacrifice that atones for our sins—and not only our sins but the sins of all the world. And we can be sure that we know him if we obey his commandments.
>
> 1 JOHN 2:1-3, *NLT*

Are you walking in the light? Jesus wants you to walk without sin and to obey all His commandments, but we all stumble along the way. In such times Jesus is our advocate; He has already paid the price for our sins.

Keep going to God, saying, "Lord, I didn't mean to do that. I'm sorry. Will You forgive me?" He will forgive you. I love the image we're given throughout Scripture: He removes our sins, and He *forgets* them!

You know, I can remember all too well the times I've messed up, but God says that He will not only forgive but also forget. That may be hard for you to comprehend, but trust it, my friend. He loves you that much. All the charges against you are canceled when you go to Him, ask forgiveness and trust Him.

Whoever asks for God's forgiveness may come to receive it. If you do sin, you have an advocate. So come to Jesus, ask forgiveness and experience His cleansing.

Pit Stop PRAYER

Father, thank You for Your mercy and forgiveness. I can't comprehend how You can forget my sins, but I am going to trust Your promise and live out my new life walking with You in the light.

September 16

The words of the hymn "Turn Your Eyes upon Jesus," by Helen H. Lemmel, hold encouragement for all of us. The words are especially encouraging for those of us who are looking for light in the darkness—for a Savior and new life—for those of us who are struggling with temptation, and for those of us who are feeling tired in this race we're running.

> O soul, are you weary and troubled?
> No light in the darkness you see?
> There's a light for a look at the Savior,
> And life more abundant and free!
>
> Turn your eyes upon Jesus,
> Look full in His wonderful face,
> And the things of earth will grow strangely dim,
> In the light of His glory and grace.
>
> Through death into life everlasting
> He passed, and we follow Him there;
> Over us sin no more hath dominion—
> For more than conquerors we are!
>
> His Word shall not fail you—He promised;
> Believe Him, and all will be well:
> Then go to a world that is dying,
> His perfect salvation to tell!

Keep your eyes on Jesus, my friend.

Pit Stop PRAYER

Lord Jesus, I am constantly learning how You can change my life with Your presence, Your power, and Your Spirit. Keep me close, Lord, and call me back when I start wandering away.

September 17

You know, we read a lot about Jesus' disciple Peter, and the Peter we see in Acts seems like a completely different person than the Peter we see in the Gospels. Peter, the disciple, in spite of all his good intentions, failed to come through for Jesus during Jesus' arrest and trial. Peter had said he would die for Jesus, but at a crucial moment, he denied that he even knew the One he had called Master!

Yet Peter was one of the apostles who stood up to religious officials and said, "We're going to obey God, rather than men" (see Acts 5:29). He preached under threat of imprisonment and followed a vision that broke with tradition when he took the gospel to people who were not Jews.

The apostle Peter had received the power Jesus promised, the power of the Holy Spirit. Living under that power, Peter preached passionately and followed his Master fearlessly.

So when Peter writes a letter to God's chosen people, to all those who share his faith, he has encouraging words:

> By his divine power, God has given us everything we need for living a godly life (2 Peter 1:3).

Think about that verse today. Then take some time to be with Jesus, reading His promises to you and asking Him for everything you need to live the life He wants you to live.

Pit Stop PRAYER

Father, thank You for supplying what I need to live the way You want me to live. This is a huge promise, and I know I've barely begun to understand it. But I want to know, Lord. I want to grasp the greatness of this promise. Teach me.

September 18

In Deuteronomy 20:1-4, Moses gave the Israelites instructions on preparing for battle. They're good instructions for us as well:

> When you go to war against your enemies and see horses and chariots and an army greater than yours, do not be afraid of them, because the LORD your God, who brought you up out of Egypt, will be with you. When you are about to go into battle, the priest shall come forward and address the army. He shall say: "Hear, O Israel, today you are going into battle against your enemies. Do not be fainthearted or afraid; do not be terrified or give way to panic before them. For the LORD your God is the one who goes with you to fight for you against your enemies to give you victory."

I hear all kinds of gloom and doom these days, even in the Church. Yes, I know there are difficulties and there are battles on many fronts. But I want to tell you, my friend, to put your hope and your trust in the Lord and in Him alone. God told us not to live in fear. He promised to provide for our needs. He invites us to put our hope and our trust in Him. He is the One who brought us out of slavery and gave us new life. He conquered even death for us! He will be with us in the battle.

Don't fear the battle. Even when you face armies that are greater than yours, do not be afraid. In fact, God wants you to be on the front line as His representative.

Stand firm in the battle today! Do not be afraid; don't panic. God will be with you, fighting for you to give you victory.

Pit Stop
PRAYER

Lord, You have armed me with strength and trained me for battle. You've given me Your shield of victory and fought for me. Who is God except You, Lord? You are my rock, my fortress, my deliverer, my Savior. You are all to me (see Psalm 18).

September 19

Ron Luce is in teen ministry and speaks to young people all over the country. He says that we're in "a war for the heart and soul of a generation that we can win, if we all take action."

What are you doing to take action to win the hearts of a new generation? I really believe that God wants us to use every available means to reach every available person. And one of the challenges of today is connecting with the current generation of young people.

The real challenge is to live out what you profess. There's a sort of disconnect in America, and young people are quick to see it. There are too many believers whose mouths are saying one thing while their actions are saying something else. And not only young people, but people of all ages are watching those who bear the name of Christ.

How are you living? How are you representing Jesus Christ in all that you do? Ephesians 5 is filled with encouragement for us: "Live a life filled with love, following the example of Christ.... Live as people of the light! ... Carefully determine what pleases the Lord. Take no part in the worthless deeds of evil and darkness.... Be careful how you live. Don't live like fools, but like those who are wise. Make the most of every opportunity.... Don't act thoughtlessly, but understand what the Lord wants you to do" (verses 17).

How do you understand what the Lord wants you to do? Read the Word, my friend. Read it; study it; ask God to speak to you through it. You can help win the war, and you *must* help win the battle to reach a new generation for Christ. Your life must match what your mouth professes. It's going to take all believers representing Jesus Christ 24/7 as a way of life and allowing Him to live in us and through us as we declare His glory.

Pit Stop
PRAYER

"Oh, that my actions would consistently reflect your decrees! Then I will not be ashamed when I compare myself with your commands" (Psalm 119:5-6, *NLT*).

September 20

In Matthew 6, when Jesus gave His disciples a model prayer, one petition was this: "Lead us not into temptation, but deliver us from the evil one" (verse 13).

My friend Dr. Elmer Towns says that when he prays this prayer, he chuckles and thinks to himself how capable he is of finding temptation on his own; he doesn't need anyone to lead him to it!

"Lord, don't let me yield to temptation" is what this verse really means. You will be tempted, but God will *never* allow you to be tempted without also providing a means of escape from that temptation (see 1 Corinthians 10:13). Scripture is very clear on that.

So the question becomes whether you are making the *right* choice. There are times when you just need to lace up your tennis shoes and run. It's dangerous to see how close you can walk to a temptation without falling. Sometimes you just need to run away from it as fast as you can.

Lead us not into temptation, but deliver us from evil. You need to not only pray that but also practice it. You need to cooperate with what God wants to do in your life. If you think something you're watching on television is going to tempt you to do something you shouldn't do, turn off the TV. If you think a certain route home is going to lead past a temptation, take another route. Put some good common sense in that prayer, my friend.

Today, live out right choices. Flee from temptation. God wants you to live in victory.

Pit Stop PRAYER

Lord, You know I sometimes tiptoe too close to temptation. But I want to run this race without swerving toward distractions or outright sins that will hold me back. Give me an undivided heart that flees temptation.

September 21

Jesus told His disciples, "Ask and it will be given to you" (Luke 11:9). You know, I can ask for a lot of stuff. You probably can, too. But in order to see this promise in effect in our lives, we need to be in right communion with Him.

For about five years, I had been asking the Lord for an opportunity to take the gospel to Bristol Motor Speedway. When I first talked about it, many people said it would never work. NASCAR's too big, they said. It can't happen.

But I kept asking and knocking. *Lord, I believe this dream is from You. I believe this is an open door to take the gospel to the most popular sport in America right now. There are thousands of people gathered on race weekend, and they're camped there with nothing to do; and Lord, I want to take the gospel there!* And I kept knocking and kept asking.

Scripture says we should keep knocking and keep asking. Jesus once told a story about a man going to a friend's house at midnight to borrow bread. The friend was already in bed and didn't want to get up and open the door; but because the man kept on knocking, he finally got what he wanted (see Luke 11:5-8).

I kept on asking, and all of a sudden, at Bristol Motor Speedway, the door opened! That was the beginning of our Victory Weekends ministry. Sometimes, my friend, your timing may just not be synchronized with God's timing. If you're in communion with Him, you can ask and ask and ask. He does not grow tired of your asking.

Pit Stop
PRAYER

Say this prayer, filling in the blank with whatever you've been asking God for: "Heavenly Father, I have been asking for _____ for a long time. I know You hear my plea. I know You care about this burden on my heart. I am asking again today, Father. Hear my prayer."

September 22

> Just think how much more the blood of Christ will purify our consciences from sinful deeds so that we can worship the living God. For by the power of the eternal Spirit, Christ offered himself to God as a perfect sacrifice for our sins.
>
> HEBREWS 9:14, NLT

When we ask Christ to forgive us, He takes our sins and blots them out. He has the power to do that. He paid for those sins even though He was perfect Himself.

There are two sets of books in heaven (see Revelation 20:12-15). One is the Book of Life, and when you come to know Christ in a personal way, your name is recorded there. Then there are the books holding a record of all your deeds, your thoughts, your sins. Everything is written there, but when you come to Christ, He blots out the sins.

My finite mind has a hard time comprehending this principle. I can remember my black spots. I can remember where I have messed up. I can remember where I've sinned. Maybe you can remember such times too. But Jesus does not want us to live in bondage to past sins. He says He has removed all of that as far as the east is from the west and cleaned all the stains (see Psalm 103:12). We are forgiven. We are cleansed. We are set free.

So, you have to make a choice. Are you going to let those black spots define who you are? Or are you going to worship Him and allow His Spirit to work in you and equip you and strengthen you?

That's His plan, my friend. Will you accept it?

Pit Stop
PRAYER

O holy, almighty God, Your mercy and compassion provided a way for me to come to You free of guilt, spotless and without stain. Remind me daily that You came to set prisoners free and give new life. I thank and praise You!

September 23

> The LORD's unfailing love surrounds the man who trusts in him.
> PSALM 32:10

In Jeremiah 31:3, the prophet states that God loves us with an everlasting love. He doesn't love the stuff we do when we mess up, but He loves us. How great is His love for you! Higher, wider, deeper and longer than anything you'll ever know—there's nothing to compare to His love.

Take time today to reflect on the love of God. Think about the virtues of the love that Jesus Christ has for you.

The love that says, *I love you, period.*

The love that says, *I will never let you go.*

The love that says, *I will be with you to the end.*

The love that says, *I'm going to prepare a place for you, and I'll come back again.*

The love that says, *To be absent from the body is to be present with the Lord.*

Today, find a quiet place and let the deep, deep love of Jesus surround you. Let your roots go down deep into His love (see Ephesians 3:17). Embrace the hope you have in Christ. Thank Him for His love and grace and mercy.

Pit Stop PRAYER

As your prayer today, say these words from a hymn by George Matheson: "O Love that wilt not let me go, I rest my weary soul on Thee; I give Thee back the life I owe, that in Thine ocean depths its flow may richer, fuller be."

September 24

> I will give you a new heart, and I will put a new spirit in you. I will take out your stony, stubborn heart and give you a tender, responsive heart. And I will put my Spirit in you so that you will follow my decrees and be careful to obey my regulations.
>
> EZEKIEL 36:26-27, NLT

God promises to give you a new heart and a new spirit! What good news! Is that what you want? That's what the Spirit brings you, my friend. I believe the Holy Spirit is the least understood person of the Trinity. Yet Scripture says we are born again by the Spirit; it is the Spirit who lives in us and has given us a new heart and this new life in Christ.

If you want to get to know the Holy Spirit better, take some time reading about the Spirit's ministry within you. He's there to convict you of wrongdoing (see John 16:8-11). He teaches you truths about God and reveals Christ to you (see John 16:12-15). He indwells and guides your life (see Romans 8:14; 1 Corinthians 6:19-20). He gives assurance of your salvation (see Romans 8:16). He prays for you (see Romans 8:26). He distributes gifts to the Church members (see 1 Corinthians 12:1-11). He baptizes and places you into the Body of Christ (see 1 Corinthians 12:13). He seals and guarantees God's promise of eternity (see Ephesians 4:30). He fills your life with joy and power (see Ephesians 5:18-19). He regenerates and renews you (see Titus 3:5).

Those are some of the reasons why Christ has given you the One called Comforter and Counselor.

Today, rejoice in the Helper who lives in you.

Pit Stop
PRAYER

Comforter and Counselor, how can I live without Your life in me? Give me Your strength, guide me with Your wisdom, make my faith steadfast, and teach me how to live.

STEVE WINGFIELD

September 25

Do you ever feel as if you're doing battle with the enemy of your soul? Whether you feel like it or not, whether you think about it or not, there is a battle going on!

Keep in mind why Jesus came. He said He came that we might have life, and "have it more abundantly" (John 10:10, *NKJV*). He came to give us lives full of meaning, purpose and direction.

In the first part of that same verse, Jesus also said that the enemy comes "to steal and kill and destroy" (John 10:10). That's what the enemy is out to do: destroy us. But Jesus has promised us victory as we put our faith and our trust in Him.

Think about it: He has rescued us from death, giving us abundant life; His life and teachings model a way of life for us that will give victory in daily living; He gave us the Spirit, whose power is greater than that of the enemy; and His death was the greatest victory of all—because He died and then rose again, He defeated all Satan's powers.

He has made so many provisions for our victory!

You can learn from Jesus how to do battle with the enemy on a daily basis. Jesus spent 40 days in the wilderness, and Satan came there to tempt Him. Each time Satan presented a temptation, Jesus' response began with "It is written." He confronted and resisted the enemy with Scripture.

Choose a verse to think on each day so that you have some weapons to do battle with the enemy. Scripture is the sword of the Spirit, and He'll use it to give you victory.

Pit Stop PRAYER

Father, Your Word is more precious than riches. It keeps me on the right path, encourages me, reassures me of Your promises and Your unfailing love, comforts me in sadness, and gives me strength in times of trouble. Your Word is a shield against temptation and a comforting light in the darkness. By Your Word, my life is renewed and refreshed.

September 26

In Romans 12:2, Paul wrote that we should "not conform any longer to the pattern of this world, but be transformed by the renewing of our minds." In the last half of chapter 12, he provided a long list of ways we are to live out God's will: outdo each other in showing honor, extend hospitality to strangers, don't lag in zeal, be ardent in spirit, serve the Lord, rejoice in hope, be patient in suffering, persevere in prayer, contribute to the needs of the saints, live in harmony, rejoice with those who rejoice, don't be proud or conceited, don't take revenge, and live at peace with everyone.

But who among us can measure up to those ideals consistently? John Calvin was once asked how a person could possibly live this way. His response was that most of us move toward goodness at "a feeble rate."

As you read Romans 12 and think about your life, you might be tempted by discouragement, thinking you're not making the progress you should. But Calvin was optimistic. He wrote, "Let us not despair at the slightness of our success; for even though attainment may not correspond to desire, when today outstrips yesterday the effort is not lost."[15]

So tonight, as you put your head on your pillow, look back on your day. And even if you've made just a little progress, rejoice and be glad. Don't give up. Keep your eye on the mark, and God will continue the work He's begun in you *until it is complete on the day Christ returns!*

Pit Stop PRAYER

Father, I'm holding on to Your promise that You will complete the work You've begun in me.

September 27

We press on because Christ has made us His own. If you know Christ, my friend, remember that you have been bought with a price. You're no longer your own; you belong to Him. And He has plans for you! "I don't mean to say that I have already achieved these things or that I have already reached perfection. But I press on to possess that perfection for which Christ Jesus first possessed me" (Philippians 3:12, *NLT*).

So we press on. We're not perfect. Far from it. Christ was our perfect example, and God is shaping us into the image of Christ.

One year my daughter, Michelle, wrote a note in my birthday card, thanking me for setting a good example of always being positive and seeing the best in people, not the worst. Now, I think that's a discipline. I know you could look at my life at any time and find something to criticize, and I could probably look at your life and also find something to criticize. But how much better it is to look beyond what we might criticize and see God's love for that person.

When you look at others who belong to Christ, do you see them through God's eyes? Do you see that He's working His plan in their lives? Jesus looks at you in that way. Shouldn't you do the same for others who are following Him?

Today, if a critical thought about someone pops into your head, ask God to let you see that person with His vision, through His plans for them. It will change your thoughts and your feelings, too. And it will make you more like Jesus.

I'm not perfect. But I know who is, and I follow Him, pressing on toward His perfection.

Pit Stop PRAYER

Jesus, give me Your eyesight today. Let me see the people I meet as You see them, and extend to them Your grace, compassion and hope.

September 28

See to it that no one takes you captive through hollow and deceptive philosophy, which depends on human tradition and the basic principles of this world rather than on Christ. For in Christ all the fullness of the Deity lives in bodily form.

COLOSSIANS 2:8-9

Get to know Jesus. All the fullness of God lives in Jesus. All the treasures of wisdom and knowledge are hidden in Him (see Colossians 2:3). This is how we strengthen ourselves against the schemes of the devil, who wants to deceive and destroy us. We learn to know the One who is Truth.

In this world, we are constantly bombarded with human traditions, human thinking, and worldly principles. We are bombarded with thinking based on all that is hollow and deceptive, and if we're not careful, we can easily get sucked into the thinking of this world.

Know what the Word of God says. Study it. Hide the Word in your heart so that you will not sin against Him. Sharpen that sword of the Spirit so that you are armed for the battle, and no one can capture your mind through arguments and philosophies of this world.

Today, resolve to be a student of God's Word. Spend more time with the One who holds all wisdom and knowledge. Ask the Spirit to prepare you so that God can use you to the maximum for His honor and His glory and to the advancement of His kingdom.

Pit Stop PRAYER

Lord Jesus, You promised that Your Holy Spirit would lead me into all truth. I want to hold firmly to Your truth and not be swayed or deceived by this world's thinking. Even more dangerous is the enemy's ability to lull me into complacency so that I drop the sword of the Spirit without realizing the dangers. Keep me from the traps that are set for me. Keep me walking in the paths of Your truths.

STEVE WINGFIELD

September 29

When Paul wrote his first letter to the Corinthian church, he brought up some serious issues. One of those was a case of sexual immorality in the church: "Don't you know that a little yeast works through the whole batch of dough? Get rid of the old yeast that you may be a new batch without yeast—as you really are. For Christ, our Passover lamb, has been sacrificed. Therefore let us keep the Festival, not with the old yeast, the yeast of malice and wickedness, but with bread without yeast, the bread of sincerity and truth" (1 Corinthians 5:6-8).

Now, while Paul was talking about sin in the whole church, I want to talk to you about "a little" sin in your life.

Like yeast, "a little" sin works its way through all of your life. Get rid of it! Paul says to clear out the old and bring in the new. Make sure that all of the old is gone. "Therefore, if anyone is in Christ, he is a new creation; the old has gone, the new has come!" (2 Corinthians 5:17).

We cannot hold on to the old ways of thinking, the old habits, the old sins. Those ways bring death. Christ wants to give us new life, and He wants us to grow and mature in that new life controlled by His Spirit. He wants to completely transform our lives for His honor and His glory and to use us in the advancement of His kingdom.

You are God's workmanship! He has begun a work in you and He will complete it. Ask the Spirit to help you get rid of the old, and keep your eyes and heart focused on the Master.

Run to win the prize, my friend.

Pit Stop
PRAYER

Father, sometimes I feel pulled toward things of the old life or I find some of the old poisons brewing in corners of my heart and mind. But I do not want to live the old life—I want a new life with You! Clean out those old things and replace them with a desire to follow Your Spirit in everything I think and do.

September 30

We will feast at a great banquet someday. I'm going to be at the table, and I hope you're planning on being there, too. In the meantime, remember these words from the hymn "Surely Goodness and Mercy," by John W. Peterson and Alfred B. Smith:

> A pilgrim was I and a-wand'ring,
> In the cold night of sin I did roam.
> When Jesus, the kind Shepherd, found me,
> And now I am on my way home.
>
> Surely goodness and mercy shall follow me
> All the days, all the days of my life.
> Surely goodness and mercy shall follow me
> All the days, all the days of my life.
>
> And I shall dwell in the House of the Lord forever;
> And I'll feast at the table spread for me.
> Surely goodness and mercy shall follow me
> All the days, all the days of my life

Until we share that heavenly banquet, remember that as you walk through this world, God walks with you through everything. He has promised you so many things, if you will only trust Him.

Pit Stop PRAYER

Jesus, my Shepherd, lead me. Lead me beside still waters and to green pastures. Restore my soul. Lead me through the dark, lonesome valleys. When the way seems too long and too hard, remind me that You will give me whatever I need to take each step. Keep me strong and running this race with an undivided heart.

OCTOBER

Living in the Light

He has enabled you to share in the inheritance that belongs to his people, who *live in the light*.

COLOSSIANS 1:12, *NLT*

October 1

> For you were once darkness, but now you are light
> in the Lord. Live as children of light (for the fruit of the
> light consists in all goodness, righteousness and truth)
> and find out what pleases the Lord.
>
> EPHESIANS 5:8-10

There it is, my friend, in Ephesians 5:8-10—your story and mine and our mission here on earth, all wrapped up in three short verses. Once we were darkness; now we are light in the Lord. That's the life Jesus has given us!

Are you living as a child of light? The fruit of light in your life is goodness, righteousness and truth. As you go about your day today, think about goodness. As you face each situation—maybe a relationship in which there is discord, or perhaps a conflict that flares up, or just at times in the day when darkness seems to rule ask the Spirit to show you how to bring goodness into that situation. Ask Him to help you be a representative of righteousness and to speak the truth in love.

If you have accepted the free gift of Christ's righteousness, the Bible says that God directs your steps (see Psalm 37:23); so He has strategically placed you where you are to be His representative of goodness, righteousness and truth. Wherever you go today, think about that. What an awesome opportunity! What an awesome responsibility!

You never know what one word or one deed might do to bring goodness, righteousness and truth. Live as a child of the light.

Pit Stop
POINT TO PONDER

Goodness. Righteousness. Truth. Those three fruits come
not from your old self but from the light of Christ living in you.
Let that light shine into the lives of those around you.

October 2

> For the LORD God is our sun and our shield. He gives us grace and glory. The LORD will withhold no good thing from those who do what is right.
>
> PSALM 84:11, *NLT*

What a great promise this verse contains. What does your schedule look like this week? Are you wondering how you'll get everything done, how you'll juggle everything and manage to get through the week? Don't get caught up in the busyness of this life and miss the joy of a relationship with Jesus. Don't miss the peace that He can give you, a peace that saturates your life.

Living in this world, we have choices to make every day. We can get upset with the driver who cuts into traffic, or with the co-worker who is slacking off, or with the neighbor who often damages borrowed tools—or we can extend patience and forgiveness. We can take a shortcut at work, or we can spend extra time doing the job right. We can avoid the person we know needs help, or we can show kindness.

If you kept a list of every time you were faced with a choice of actions and reactions in just this one day, you'd be amazed at the length of that list—you make dozens of choices about how you will treat people. It's easy, though, to get so caught up by your own busy schedule or your own agenda that you don't stop to think about how Jesus would have you respond to others.

God wants you to be at peace with Him and at peace with others. Prepare each morning for the coming day; ask God to equip you for whatever you will face.

Pit Stop
POINT TO PONDER

All too often, we simply act and react out of habit, without even thinking about making a choice. Today, think about your choices in how you act and speak, and choose goodness, righteousness and truth.

October 3

In the devotional book *My Utmost for His Highest*, Oswald Chambers says of the Holy Spirit: "The Holy Spirit cannot be located as a Guest in a house. He invades everything. . . . He takes charge of everything; my part is to walk in the light and to obey all that He reveals."[16]

Think through that. You are the dwelling place of God. When you asked Christ into your life, He came, made His home with you and now lives in you by His Spirit. Oswald Chambers gives us a great image: The Spirit does not come as a guest but as an invader who occupies and controls all of your life.

The Holy Spirit cannot be relegated to one little isolated portion of our lives. We either move toward a more committed relationship to Christ, or we move away from Him.

You know, when I don't do what the Spirit says—when I resist the His guidance and teaching and convicting—things don't go well. If we could all just learn that one lesson. If only we could keep our end of that deal and always obey, always walk in all the ways He commands. We will fail, but His grace and mercy make Him a patient God—and we can also come to Him for forgiveness.

An old hymn sings a truth: "Trust and obey, for there's no other way to be happy in Jesus, but to trust and obey." You will fail at trying to fulfill that instruction in your own strength, but the Holy Spirit will help you to trust and obey.

Grow into a deep, intimate, vital relationship with Christ, my friend. Learn to hear His voice, to trust Him and to obey Him.

Pit Stop
POINT TO PONDER

Think again about the promise of what the Spirit will produce in your life: love, joy, peace, patience, kindness, goodness, faithfulness, gentleness and self-control. Oh, that He would invade every part of your being!

October 4

The apostle Paul gave us good advice in 1 Thessalonians 4:11: "Make it your ambition to lead a quiet life, to mind your own business."

Are you living a quiet life? Maybe you're thinking about your schedule for this week or maybe a storm of conflict has hit your place of work and you think, *A quiet life? That's impossible!*

I really do think we can have a peaceful state of mind in all of life's circumstances. It *is* possible, but it is *impossible* without Jesus. The power of His Spirit living in our hearts can bring peace in the midst of the busiest schedule or the most fearsome storm.

Some of the sweetest and most powerful memories I have are of people in the midst of one particular physical storm—each was facing death. I'll especially never forget one of those people, a successful businessman I met when I was going to college in Harrisonburg. I visited him in the hospital when he was not far from death, and when I asked him how he was, he replied, "I've never been sicker, but I'm at peace."

That kind of peace only comes from a relationship with Jesus. If you don't have it, I pray you will seek it.

Psalm 46:10 is the word for today: "Be still, and know that I am God."

Pit Stop
POINT TO PONDER

Quietude. Serenity. Peace. Those three things come to a life that rests in knowing who God is and whose you are.

October 5

When you commit your life to Christ, this verse becomes a reality:

> Therefore, if anyone is in Christ, he is a new creation; the old has gone, the new has come! (2 Corinthians 5:17).

Old things are gone; all things are new. *All* things. You are not the same person. Once you ask Jesus into your life, God puts the old you behind you. The pain, the failure, the sin of your past—they're all gone.

You know, we have the power to do something God says He can't do. Whoa. God can do anything, right? Yes, He can. But He has chosen to limit Himself.

According to Psalm 103:12, God will remove our sins as far as the east is from the west, and according to Isaiah 43:25 and Hebrews 8:12, God will never, ever remember them again. But *we* remember them. *We* remember past failures. *We* remember pains and sorrows that we caused other people by the wrongs we've committed. But Jesus has forgiven us, and He says, "I'll never remember it again."

My friend, if you know Christ, if you know the Son and He's taken up residence in your life, then He's given you new life. He's forgiven you. The old is gone and you are a new creation.

Grow in that new creation; and as you do, people will see that change in what you say and what you do. They will see Jesus in you.

Pit Stop
POINT TO PONDER

"For the darkness is disappearing, and the true light is already shining" (1 John 2:8). This describes what is happening in you as a child of God. You are a new creation, and the true light is shining in you, putting an end to the darkness.

October 6

Who or what is ruling your heart today? Somebody's in charge. Maybe it's that person who said something that ticked you off. Maybe it's your boss who is taking advantage of you. Maybe it's one of your children who knows how to push your buttons. If so, you have become that person's slave.

God wants to rule in your heart. He doesn't want you to be a slave to anyone but Jesus Christ. God made you to live in a relationship with Him, and He wants to sit on the throne of your life. It's His rightful place. Letting Christ rule your life is a choice you make daily. Yes, daily. Maybe you even must make the choice many times a day: Either you're going to be in charge, somebody else is going to be in charge, or Jesus is going to be in charge.

The enemy of your soul wants to take over the controls of your life. He wants to ruin you, but He will not have the power to do that if you put your faith in Jesus alone. "When he died, he died once to break the power of sin. . . . So you also should consider yourselves to be dead to the power of sin and alive to God through Christ Jesus" (Romans 6:10-11, *NLT*).

If God takes control, He wants His peace to be a way of life. That's what the Lord wants to do for you, but it's your choice. All you need to do is turn to Him and say, *Lord, I need You. I confess that I've blown it. I've sinned, and I invite You to take control of my life.*

I pray that today you will make the right choice and let Jesus have His rightful place on the throne of your life.

Pit Stop
PROMISE

Jesus said, "The thief's purpose is to steal and kill and destroy. My purpose is to give [you] a rich and satisfying life" (John 10:10, *NLT*). Make a choice whether to serve yourself, the thief or Christ the Shepherd.

October 7

God's Holy Spirit lives within you; and if you give Him control, you can have an abundant life, living out what God created you to be.

In Ephesians 5:18 we read, "Be not drunk with wine, . . . but be filled with the Spirit" (*KJV*). This may look like a strange combination of ideas to put together in one verse, but God gave us this comparison for a reason.

People who are drunk with alcohol fall under control of the alcohol. They're no longer in control of the way they think; they're no longer in control of the way they walk; they're no longer in control of the way they talk. The substance rules the person. Ephesians 5:18 tells us not to get drunk with wine or give it control of our lives.

Instead, we're to be filled and controlled by the Holy Spirit. When we come under His control, it affects the way we talk, it affects the way we think, and it affects the way we walk. That's why He wants to fill us with His Spirit and have the Spirit in control. He changes our way of life to be what He wants it to be.

Ask the Holy Spirit to fill you. Pray, *Lord, I want You to direct my steps and control me this and every day. I want You to control my tongue; I want You to control my thoughts; I want You to control what I do and where I go. I want You, not me, to be in control, Lord.*

Pit Stop
POINT TO PONDER

"If we want the Word of God to have authority in our life, there is only one way: obey it. If we want the Holy Spirit to have authority in our life, there is only one way: obey Him. If we always obey impulses of fear or doubt or resentment, what will have authority over our minds? Fear, doubt and resentment."

—Tom Marshall (*Living in the Freedom of the Spirit*)

October 8

Once when I was about four or five, my dad and I were walking down Main Street and a gentleman called out to my dad and asked for money to buy a cup of coffee.

We were in front of Texas Tavern, a hamburger joint, and my dad walked in the door to the counter. He had a little change purse, and I watched as he opened it and dumped out two dimes.

"Give my buddy a cup of coffee," he said. But I was thinking, *Man, he just gave all his money away.*

We went back outside and continued down the sidewalk. We had only gone about a block when my dad reached down and picked up a dollar bill that was lying on the street. He gave away twenty cents, and a dollar bill appeared on the street.

Dad said to me, "Son, remember this: You can never out-give God. He'll always supply your need if you give."

Jesus said the same thing. Listen to His words from Luke 6:38:

> Give, and it will be given to you. Good measure, pressed down, shaken together, running over, will be put into your lap. For with the measure you use it will be measured back to you (*ESV*).

That's a powerful promise. If you cheerfully give a good measure, God will always meet your needs. Be a cheerful and generous giver.

Pit Stop
PROMISE

Plant a few seeds, and you'll get a small crop. Plant generously, and you'll have a generous harvest. "God will generously supply all you need. Then you will always have everything you need and plenty left over to share with others" (2 Corinthians 9:8, *NLT*).

October 9

What role does the church play in God's will, plan and purpose for your life? No church is perfect; in fact, I tell people that if they find a perfect church, they should not join or they'll mess it up. Just as all of us aren't perfect, the church (made up of a lot of humans) is not perfect. Yet still, the church is important.

The writer of Hebrews encourages us not to give up meeting together with others who believe (see Hebrews 10:25). If you want God's guidance, then being a part of a church family is vital. I believe it is part of your discipleship.

If I have a big pile of wood and I set the pile of wood on fire, it will give off a whole lot of light and heat. But if I reach in and take out one of those logs and lay it to the side all by itself, its flames will soon die out. That's a great example of what the church is like. Together, we keep the fire burning. Alone, the flame dies.

Yes, the church is not perfect, but we need each other. The church is where we receive encouragement, where the flames of faith are fanned. We support each other and pray for each other. When Jesus spoke about a city on a hill that could not be hidden, could He have been talking about a whole group of lamps that, together, light up the entire countryside?

Be in communion with others who share your beliefs. They will help you in your walk with the Lord.

Pit Stop
POINT TO PONDER

God's Spirit gives each of us spiritual gifts. These gifts are not for our own benefit; they are given so that we can help each other. Jesus prayed for a spirit of unity among His followers, and as we depend on others' gifts to help us in our walk with Christ and the mission He's entrusted to us, the Spirit works to bind us together.

October 10

What's ruling in your life right now? Are you at peace?

In Colossians 3:15, Paul wrote, "Let the peace of Christ rule in your hearts, since as members of one body you were called to peace. And be thankful."

This is my prayer for you today:

Lord, I pray that Colossians 3:15 will become a reality in the lives and hearts of those who are reading this today. Whatever my friends are facing, I pray that they will sense Your presence and Your power in their lives. Let Your peace rule in each heart.

Protect them. Watch over them. Equip them. Strengthen them. Fill them with Your presence. Guard their hearts and their minds in Christ Jesus. Lord, I pray that You will give to them, at this very moment, the peace that passes all human comprehension.

And, Lord, as they go about their day, whether they face sickness or pain or struggles at home or at work or in economics, I pray for peace that cannot be explained away.

In Jesus' name, amen.

Pit Stop
POINT TO PONDER

Jesus is the Prince of Peace. He promises to give peace to those who believe in Him, and it's one of the fruits of His Spirit living within each child of God. Knowing His presence and power in your life is the only way to have peace in this life on earth.

October 11

God offers you forgiveness and loving acceptance. The God of all creation loves you and wants to live in relationship with you. He accepts you for who you are. He loves you, in spite of all those warts, all those mistakes, all those problems. Why would anybody turn down such love and acceptance?

In Joshua 1:9, we read these words:

> Have I [God] not commanded you? Be strong and courageous. Do not be terrified; do not be discouraged, for the LORD your God will be with you wherever you go.

The God of all creation now lives in your heart, and He says, "I will never leave you. I will never forsake you." My friend, if you've asked the Son of God to come into your life, then He resides in you now and He promises He will never leave you. He will be with you wherever you go, whatever you do, in every circumstance.

Maybe you're lonely, maybe you have been hurt, maybe you're sick, maybe you are worried about the future. Why don't you say to Him right now:

Lord, I need Your presence. I need Your power. I need to know that You are there. So, God, give me that comfort. In Jesus' name, amen.

Pit Stop PROMISE

"If I go up to heaven, you are there; if I go down to the grave, you are there. If I ride the wings of the morning, if I dwell by the farthest oceans, even there your hand will guide me, and your strength will support me" (Psalm 139:8-10, *NLT*).

October 12

Here's a great quote from Martin Luther:

> Either sin is with you, lying on your shoulders, or it is lying on Christ, the Lamb of God. Now if it is lying on your back, you are lost; but if it is resting on Christ, you are free, and you will be saved. Now choose what you want.

Where is your sin? Are you carrying it around on your back? Are you allowing the enemy to beat you up, constantly reminding you that you're not worthy? For once, the enemy speaks the truth. None of us is worthy.

But if you have given your life to Jesus Christ, then Jesus has taken your sins off your shoulders and taken them upon Himself. That's what the cross is all about, my friend. Jesus paid the price for your sins: "Christ's one act of righteousness brings a right relationship with God and new life for everyone" (Romans 5:18, *NLT*).

You must choose want you want. If you want Christ to set you free from the burden of your sins, then confess Him with your mouth and believe in your heart. Believe that He is the Son of God and that He died for you. And believe that there's an empty tomb and He's alive. Because He lives, you too can live.

Ask Jesus to come into your life to take up residence and take over the controls. He will take your sins and set you free.

Pit Stop
PRAISE

"He personally carried our sins in his body on the cross so that we can be dead to sin and live for what is right. By his wounds you are healed" (1 Peter 2:24, *NLT*). He carried your burden of sins so that you could be healed!

October 13

> We have peace with God through our Lord Jesus Christ.
> ROMANS 5:1

God's purpose is for you to receive eternal life and live in peace with Him. If this is His purpose, why are so many people not enjoying that peace?

In the book of Genesis we read the story of Adam and Eve. God created them to live in relationship with Him, but they chose to disobey. That choice led to separation from God. People today are still separated from God.

But, my friend, if we turn to Christ, He hears our prayer, and we can be restored to that relationship He intended us to enjoy. He designed us to live in relationship with Him.

You can do that by communing with Him in prayer and by reading His Word. He's given you His Word that you might grow and mature and be all that He created you to be. He wants to live in you; He wants you to have that communion with Him; He wants you to know His presence and peace as a way of life.

If you don't have peace today, you can make the choice to establish that relationship through Jesus Christ. You will have peace with God. That's God's promise to you.

Pit Stop
POINT TO PONDER

No thing and no person in this world can give the peace God gives to a heart that rests in relationship to Him.

October 14

Why are so many people unhappy? If everybody wants to be happy (and I think they do), then why are so many not happy?

The answer may seem complicated at first. There can be all kinds of reasons why people are not happy. Many people have looked for happiness in all the wrong places. They think wealth or power or popularity will make them happy, but when they get all those things, they realize they are still not happy. So what *does* make us happy?

> O, taste and see that the LORD is good! Blessed is the man who takes refuge in him (Psalm 34:8, *ESV*).

Where are you finding your refuge today? Happy is the person who takes refuge in the Lord. The Lord is good, my friend. Taste, and see how good He is!

When I'm with my friends in Africa and someone says, "God is good," others will add, "All the time!" And it's true. He is. Taste and see that God is good. You will find true, lasting happiness, happiness that nobody can take away from you. It's not a happiness that's going to vanish if the stock market crashes or you don't get the promotion.

Take refuge in Christ alone today and taste the goodness of God.

Pit Stop
POINT TO PONDER

We learn how good the Lord is only by learning to know the Lord.

October 15

> They devoted themselves to the apostles' teaching and to the fellowship, to the breaking of bread and to prayer.
>
> ACTS 2:42

If you're looking for ways to be an instrument of God's goodness, ways to speak into people's lives and be a blessing, pay attention to Acts 2:42. The early Christians devoted themselves, not only to teaching and prayer, but also to fellowship and the breaking of bread.

I love being out in God's creation, and I feel close to God in the mountains or at a lake. But there's something about fellowship with other Christians that strengthens my relationship with the Lord in a way that solitude does not.

Fellowship encourages us. Scripture says that we are to motivate one another toward good works and encourage each other in our walk with the Lord (see 1 Thessalonians 5:11; 1 Peter 2:12). That's the purpose of being a part of the Body of Christ. Just as "iron sharpens iron" (Proverbs 27:17), so too we are strengthened by being with other believers. Fellowship with someone else of like faith will bolster our own faith.

That's why the early Christians met regularly and broke bread together—so that they would spur each other as they walked in faith.

So be intentional about seeking out someone to spend time with who will help you in your walk with the Lord.

Pit Stop
POINT TO PONDER

Paul often addresses people as partners in the gospel (see Philippians 1:5). We are partners not just with each other but also with God as He uses us to further Christ's mission on this earth. We are all born of one Spirit, and the Spirit uses each of us to encourage, teach, build up, inspire, counsel, comfort and strengthen other partners in the gospel.

October 16

In John 14:27, Jesus encouraged His disciples with these words: "Peace I leave with you; my peace I give you. I do not give to you as the world gives. Do not let your hearts be troubled and do not be afraid."

Oh my, what beautiful, beautiful words. Maybe you're reading this today with an anxious, distressed or uneasy heart. Hear this from Jesus: Don't let your heart be troubled.

Christ came as the Prince of Peace. Whether we live or die, whether we are in the midst of tribulation or the midst of calm, God's Spirit can bring peace to our lives.

Jesus said He came to give us abundant life. He promised that that abundant life includes protection, refuge, comfort, hope, strength, joy and the ever-present love of the God of all creation.

Even if you face death, you have peace if Christ is your Savior. To be absent from this body is to be present with your Lord. You don't have to fear an earthly death; you'll be with Jesus for eternity. Death has lost its sting; the grave has no victory.

Whether you live or die, Jesus says, "Peace I leave with you."

The world cannot offer such peace. Nothing and no one can give you the peace that Jesus can give you. In effect, He says, "Don't stress out or be unsettled; don't let uncertainty rule your life. Put your hope and trust in Me."

Read John 14:27 again. Memorize it, if you haven't already. Listen to the voice of the One who loves you so much He died for you. Allow the power of God's Spirit to work in your life and give you peace.

Pit Stop
POINT TO PONDER

Oswald Chambers wrote that whenever we have unhindered contact with Jesus, His peace becomes real: "a peace which brings an unconstrained confidence and covers you completely, from the top of your head to the soles of your feet."[17] Let nothing come between you and Christ!

STEVE WINGFIELD

October 17

Christ alone can bring lasting peace—peace with God—peace among men and nations—and peace within our hearts.

BILLY GRAHAM

We are living in a world that is torn apart by war, by mistrust, and even by religion. In the name of religion, people spread hatred and division. Homes and families are threatened by conflict and discord, and the hearts of so many people hold only turmoil and unrest.

Peace? How can there be peace in this world?

Only in Christ can we find lasting peace. Only a relationship with Jesus Christ can bring peace to our lives. The peace offered by Jesus is a peace that passes all understanding; there's no way we can comprehend or explain it. To the world, it may seem illogical and impossible. But God, by the power of His Spirit, can give you peace.

We can be at peace with God, knowing that our sins are forgiven. Peace is one of the fruits of the Spirit, and we can be instruments of peace in our daily interactions with others.

I hate conflict; I just detest it. It bothers me to no end. Jesus says that He wants to bring peace—even peace among nations.

Peace only comes, my friend, from Jesus Christ. When He comes into your life, He will "guide [you] to the path of peace" (Luke 1:79, *NLT*). If you don't have peace, cry out to Him right now and simply ask, "Lord Jesus, would You give me Your peace?"

Pit Stop
POINT TO PONDER

In Luke 1:79, the father of John the Baptist prophesied that Jesus would "guide us to the path of peace." Jesus is called the Prince of Peace. Only in Him do we find peace with God, peace with others, and peace of mind and heart. He is the only One who can lead us along the path of peace.

October 18

> Who except God can give you peace? Has the world ever been able to satisfy the heart?
>
> GERARD MAJELLA

Who except God can give peace? What can satisfy the heart? You can't go into a drugstore and buy what the heart longs for. You can't work hard enough to achieve peace. You can't take enough vacations to finally gain peace.

Once when I was traveling and in an airport, I noticed a man dressed as though he were headed for a Caribbean vacation spot. He was talking on the phone, and he was in a rage. I don't know what the situation was, but I was reminded that even though he was probably headed for a beautiful Caribbean beach and wonderful food and all kinds of leisure activities, he was not going to have any peace unless he dealt with what was in his heart.

Maybe you have looked many places and tried many things in order to find peace. Nothing in the world can give you peace, my friend. Nothing and no one but Christ satisfies the heart. Jesus said to the lady who washed His feet with her perfume, "Your faith has saved you; go in peace" (Luke 7:50).

Jesus alone can grant peace. When we put our faith and trust in Him, He is able to give us His incomprehensible, deep, abiding, boundless peace.

Pit Stop
POINT TO PONDER

The tumult and confusion of life is anything but peaceful. Jesus knew that, but He promised a peace of mind and heart: "Let not your heart be troubled," He said. "You will have trouble in the world, but be of good cheer, because I have conquered the world" (see John 14:27; 16:33). Life might be tumultuous, but your heart and mind can rest in His peace.

October 19

> Now may the Lord of peace himself give you peace at all times and in every way. The Lord be with all of you.
>
> 2 THESSALONIANS 3:16

Our God, Jesus, is Lord of all. He is the Lord of peace. Do you need His peace today? I don't know what you're facing. It may be surgery. It may be sickness, financial loss or family problems. Maybe your life is just filled with stress and anxiety. You need a touch from the Lord of all creation, the Lord of peace.

Horatio Spafford's hymn "It Is Well with My Soul" talks about peace that comes like a river. Spafford wrote the lyrics shortly after several devastating losses in his life: his four-year-old son died, a fire in Chicago ruined him financially, and his four daughters drowned when the ship they were on sank. The song reminds us that even though sorrows roll over us "like sea billows," it is still well with our souls. Our sins are forgiven; God is with us and brings hope, comfort, strength, guidance and peace.

Julian of Norwich wrote, "Peace reigns where our Lord reigns." Prophecies said that the Messiah would be the Prince of Peace. Does He reign in your heart today? Has He brought His peace to your life? If not, invite Him into your life and give Him full control. If He is on the throne, He will reign with peace.

My prayer for you is the same as Paul's in 2 Thessalonians 3:16: "May the Lord of peace himself give you peace at all times and in every way. The Lord be with you."

Pit Stop PRACTICE

Review the plan for peace outlined on January 1: Pray. Tell God what you need. Thank Him for everything He has done for you. Then the peace of God will guard your heart and mind.

October 20

> Look at those who are honest and good, for a wonderful future awaits those who love peace.
>
> PSALM 37:37, NLT

Do you want a future? Well, of course you do. We all do. Psalm 37:37 reveals that a wonderful future awaits those who love peace. Jesus said, "Those who work for peace ... will be called the children of God" (Matthew 5:9).

Take some time today to do a personal inventory of your peacemaking:

- When you walk into a room, do you bring peace, or does your presence declare war?
- Do people ever seek you out because they feel a calmness and peace in your presence?
- When you enter a conflict, does peace enter, or does the conflict escalate?
- At your office, job or home, or even in your car, is there a sense of peace that surrounds you or a tight tension?

God has a future for those of us who are instruments of peace. He has plans to work in and through us. His purpose is to use us to advance His kingdom. What a privilege!

You can only be one of God's instruments of peace, though, if the Prince of Peace rules on the throne of your life. Have you given Him that place?

Pit Stop
POINT TO PONDER

Jesus had a very special word for those who work for peace: "They will be called children of God" (Matthew 5:9).

October 21

> Love must be sincere. Hate what is evil; cling to what
> is good. Be devoted to one another in brotherly love. Honor one
> another above yourselves.
>
> ROMANS 12:9-10

Love must be sincere. What does that mean to you? We have some guidelines here as we seek to sincerely love others.

Hate what is evil; cling to what is good. Here is the choice again, between darkness and light. We all know there are certain things we say or do that are only of darkness. Instead, choose to live as a child of light in how you treat others.

Be devoted to one another in brotherly love. Don't be selfish. Don't try to impress others. Be humble (see Philippians 2:3). Jesus commanded His followers to love each other just as He had loved them. Whew. Do you think you can love like Jesus does? Unconditionally, forgiving and forgetting, laying yourself down for someone else? We can only love like that through the power of His Spirit living in us!

Honor one another above yourselves. Here is where most of us get into trouble—myself included. I like me. The selfish part of me always wants to put me first, to look out for myself first, to think I'm better than others. But how much better things would go in my life if I could always live out this command to honor others above myself.

As a follower of Christ, you have been called by God to show the love of Christ to others. Paul said that he had to die daily so that the life of Christ could live in Him. That's what you need to do, too, to live out sincere love.

Pit Stop PRAYER

Lord Jesus, Your commandment was that we love each other as You love us. This is not something I can do on my own. I can only show Your love to others if You love through me. But I am willing, Lord, to be a channel for Your love to others. Teach me to love Your way.

October 22

Sometimes I get up at night or in the early morning before dawn and I don't turn on the light. I don't want to disturb Barb, so I stumble around in the darkness. Now, I'm pretty familiar with our house, so I can manage most times without a light; but one night the vacuum cleaner had been left out and it was sitting in the normal path I take. Well, you can imagine what happened. I was trying not to disturb Barb, but that time she and I were both quite disturbed!

Walking around in darkness is just inviting a big stumble, isn't it? Jesus says He provides light for us. He doesn't want us to walk in darkness; we've been rescued and brought into the light: "Whoever loves his brother lives in the light, and there is nothing in him to make him stumble" (1 John 2:10).

This verse tells me several things: Sincere love for others is a sign that we're living in the light. God loves us, and He's called us to live in love. One of the characteristics of the children of light, of those living in light, is that they show God's love to those around them.

This verse also says to me that the more we love as Christ asks us to, the brighter our light shines. He provides the light; and the more I'm in Him, the brighter His light shines in me. It is the Spirit of Christ working in us who produces that love, and as we give Him control of our lives, as He molds us into the image of Christ, we walk less and less in the darkness and more and more in the light.

Today, ask the Spirit to produce more and more of His fruit in your life.

Pit Stop
PRAYER

Lord, I stumble over *myself*. When I let my own selfishness dictate my actions, when I think I have certain rights or when I put my own concerns above others, then I am also walking in the darkness, and my love is stumbling over all those obstacles. Shine Your light and Your love into me, and help me clear the path so that I can be an open channel of Your love.

October 23

We've spent several days talking about love, so let me spend today concentrating on how important it is that we love one another:

> Dear friends, let us love one another, for love comes from God. Everyone who loves has been born of God and knows God. Whoever does not love does not know God, because God is love (1 John 4:7-8).

Oh, my! How well we love is a test of how well we know God!

As I try to dissect that verse and wrap my mind around it, I'm convinced that the apostle John (by the power of the Holy Spirit) is pointing out that it truly is impossible to experience love in its completeness unless we are living in relationship with Jesus Christ.

I'll say that again: Complete, divine love can only be experienced if we are living close to Jesus Christ.

There are different forms of love—parental love, love between friends, romantic love—but loving in the way Jesus said to love can only happen when the Spirit of God works in us.

So first of all, we need to get our relationship with Jesus right. Only then can we move on to be the husband, wife, friend, mom, daughter or whatever else God has called us to be. The vertical relationship has to be established first, and then that relationship can release love into the horizontal relationship.

Pit Stop
POINT TO PONDER

Love is a fruit of the Holy Spirit working in your life. Like the branch that can only bear fruit when it draws its life from the vine, you can only love if Christ's life flows through you.

October 24

Whoever does not love does not know God.
1 JOHN 4:8

Love is so important in our walk with God because we are to reflect His love to the world. If people look at your life, do they recognize that you know God?

Do another inventory of your life. This time, ask yourself how you are living out God's divine love. First Corinthians 13:4-7 (*NLT*) describes that love in action:

> Love is patient and kind. Love is not jealous or boastful or proud or rude. It does not demand its own way. It is not irritable, and it keeps no record of being wronged. It does not rejoice about injustice but rejoices whenever the truth wins out. Love never gives up, never loses faith, is always hopeful, and endures through every circumstance.

Those may be familiar words, but ask the Spirit to keep them fresh in your mind and remind you of them today, whenever you have the opportunity to show love.

Pit Stop
POINT TO PONDER

Read again the actions of love listed in 1 Corinthians 13:4-7. Which is the most difficult for you? Are you impatient? Do you hold grudges or demand your own way? Be honest in your answer, and then pray for the Spirit's help in overcoming that hindrance to showing Christ's love.

October 25

> Whoever lives by the truth comes into the light, so that it may be seen plainly that what he has done has been done through God.
>
> JOHN 3:21

Jesus spoke these words to explain to His disciples that God's light had come into the world, but people loved the darkness more than the light. They preferred their evil actions to what God wanted them to do. But those who live by the truth, Jesus said, come into the light; and it will be plain that God is working through and in them.

As we live in the light, our lives reflect the power and glory of God. He works in us, according to Philippians 2:13, to align our wills with His will and to give us power to act according to His commandments.

Have you been discouraged because of some temptations that keep tripping you up? Are you feeling weak? Do you feel as if you're just not strong enough, not "good" enough to be an effective witness for Christ? Hear this, my friend: God is working in you, and He has no intention of stopping that project until it is completed! He says that His power works in your weakness. He will give you strength. The changes He brings to your life *will* be a witness to everyone, showing that God's power has been at work in you.

Don't give up. Continue to live in the light. Continue to seek God's truth. Continue to study His Word and spend time with your Lord. Christ is living in you.

Pit Stop
POINT TO PONDER

God brings people into your life to help you in your walk. Be open to sharing with other believers your struggles, your temptations, your weakness—yes, even those times you fail your Lord. This mutual openness and encouragement is part of living in the light, and the Spirit will use it to strengthen you.

October 26

A simple question for you: Are you obeying Jesus' commands?

Jesus says that obedience is a reflection of love for Him, and lack of obedience shows a lack of love. Here are His words in John 15:9-11:

> As the Father has loved me, so have I loved you. Now remain in my love. If you keep my commands, you will remain in my love, just as I have kept my Father's commands and remain in his love. I have told you this so that my joy may be in you and that your joy may be complete.

Are you obeying what God asks you to do? Maybe that's not a simple question, after all. Maybe that's a complicated question, but it's an important question for you to ask yourself and to answer honestly.

Obedience really does say, *I love Jesus.* And He told us to obey Him. He obeyed the Father and set the example for us, so we should want to be obedient to whatever He has asked us to do.

Find some time today to get alone with the Lord and deal with this question about obedience. Ask Him, *Lord, am I obeying You in what You've asked me to do? Am I walking in obedience? I want my obedience to Your will and Your way and Your plan and purposes for my life to be a reflection of my love for You. Show me if there's any disobedience in me.*

Then walk in obedience and experience the joy of living out your love for Christ.

Pit Stop
POINT TO PONDER

"God's commands are designed to guide you to life's very best. You will not obey Him, however, if you do not believe Him and trust Him. You cannot believe Him if you do not love Him. You cannot love Him unless you know Him." —Henry Blackaby, Richard Blackaby and Claude King (*Experiencing God: Knowing and Doing the Will of God*)

October 27

In our own strength, we often falter in our obedience to Jesus' commands. We battle daily with the old self who chooses to walk in darkness. We need to cry out to God, as David did, and ask for His strength and guidance. "I am weak, but You're mighty, Lord. You are my rock and my fortress; for the sake of your name, lead and guide me" (see Psalm 31:3). As William Williams states in his hymn "Guide Me, O Thou Great Jehovah," God can help us obey His commands:

> Guide me, O Thou great Jehovah,
> Pilgrim through this barren land.
> I am weak, but Thou art mighty;
> Hold me with Thy powerful hand.
> Bread of Heaven, Bread of Heaven,
> Feed me till I want no more.
>
> Open now the crystal fountain,
> Whence the healing stream doth flow;
> Let the fire and cloudy pillar
> Lead me all my journey through.
> Strong Deliverer, strong Deliverer,
> Be Thou still my Strength and Shield.

Give the Lord songs of praises for what He's already done! And whatever you're facing, wherever you go, let your prayer be, *I am weak, but You are mighty. Guide me, O Thou great Jehovah*. He will be your guide and direct your steps. Allow Him to do so.

Pit Stop PRAYER

I am weak, but You are mighty. Guide me, O Thou great Jehovah.

October 28

As Jesus faced His death, the uppermost thing in His mind was the unity of those who followed Him. His prayer in Gethsemane contained this request: "May they be brought to complete unity to let the world know that you sent me and have loved them even as you have loved me" (John 17:23).

That prayer is still waiting to be fulfilled 2,000 years later. I thank God for diversity and distinctiveness; I thank God that we're not cookie-cutter Christians. But the bottom line is this: If you love Jesus, you're my brother or sister. We may have some theological differences here or there; but if you know Jesus, we are one family.

For too long believers have acted as if the church down the street or across town is the enemy. Your brothers and sisters in Christ are not the enemy. You may see things a little differently, but we are to be one in Christ, completely unified in Jesus. Why? So that the world may know.

My friend, keep the main thing the main thing. And the main thing is Jesus. The main thing is your relationship with Jesus. The main thing is bringing Jesus' message to this dark world.

Work at not arguing with another believer. It's okay to have differences of opinion. But remember that other Christians are your brothers and sisters in Christ and we all have one mission. It will be our unity, our oneness, our bond of love that, more than anything else, says to the world that Jesus is real.

So, starting today, love those brothers and sisters around you. Ask the Spirit to give you new eyes to see our bonds of unity in the kingdom of light, not the ripples of disagreement.

Pit Stop
POINT TO PONDER

Sometimes the human body actually attacks and fights itself. Those diseases are sometimes fatal. Christ intended the members of His Body to be one unified, effective *whole*. Struggles between the parts of His Body cripple both the Body and its witness.

October 29

> There is neither Jew nor Greek, slave nor free, male nor female, for you are all one in Christ Jesus.
>
> GALATIANS 3:28

When we come into a living, intimate relationship with Jesus Christ, a oneness takes place and makes us each a part of a huge family made up of every kindred, every tribe and every tongue. I am part of a global community where there is no Jew, there is no Greek, there is no slave or free, there is no male or female, for we all belong to Christ.

Knowing I am a part of a nation of people that surrounds this globe brings me great encouragement. I have dual citizenship. Yes, I will always be an American citizen. I'm thankful that I was born in this wonderful country and that God has brought blessings into my life; I have so much to thank God for. But I have dual citizenship because this world is not my home; I am just passing through, and I belong to God's kingdom of light.

Christ has brought all of us from darkness to light. We all have "put on Christ, like putting on new clothes" (Galatians 3: 27, *NLT*). We are all part of the same body, have life in the same Spirit, and look forward to the same hope, "confidently looking forward to a city with eternal foundations, a city designed and built by God" (Hebrews 11:10, *NLT*).

If you are part of that family, take time today to pray for your brothers and sisters around the world as all believers seek to put on the character of Christ and live as citizens of the kingdom of light.

Pit Stop
PRAYER

> Let the words from Henry van Dyke's hymn "Joyful, Joyful, We Adore Thee" be your prayer today: "Thou our Father, Christ our Brother, all who live in love are Thine; teach us how to love each other, lift us to the joy divine."

October 30

This is the message we have heard from him and declare to you: God is light; in him there is no darkness at all. If we claim to have fellowship with him yet walk in the darkness, we lie and do not live by the truth. But if we walk in the light, as he is in the light, we have fellowship with one another, and the blood of Jesus, his Son, purifies us from all sin.

1 JOHN 1:5-7

Are you walking in the light? We have a choice: to walk as children of the light or to walk in the darkness. If we walk in the darkness, we have no fellowship with God, no matter what we might say with our mouths.

Knowing His Word enables us to walk in the light; He gave us the Word so that we might hide it in our hearts and not sin against Him. We need to know the truth, study the truth and obey the truth. Then we will walk in the light as He is in the light. Then we will reflect His light to bring glory to our Father.

If you have asked Christ to forgive your sins and come into your life, you are a child of light, not darkness! He has rescued you from the dominion of darkness and brought you into His kingdom of light. You've been given a new life to walk in the light of Christ.

Today, spend time in the Word that is the light for your path. Then live conscious of your choices and choose to walk in the light.

Pit Stop PRAYER

Lord, I choose to be faithful to Your commands. Give me understanding and lead me along the paths of Your truths, for that is where my happiness is found (see Psalm 119:30-35).

October 31

God is an almighty God to be reverenced. He's a holy and just God. But He is also "a friend who sticks closer than a brother" (Proverbs 18:24), a friend who will never leave you or forsake you.

When you asked Christ to forgive your sins and come into your life, He took up residence in you. Now you are the dwelling place of God. He will never leave you. He will never disappoint you. What a friend! As Joseph M. Scriven wrote in the hymn "What a Friend We Have in Jesus":

> What a friend we have in Jesus, all our sins and griefs to bear!
> What a privilege to carry everything to God in prayer!
> O what peace we often forfeit, O what needless pain we bear,
> All because we do not carry everything to God in prayer.
>
> Are we weak and heavy laden, cumbered with a load of care?
> Precious Savior, still our refuge, take it to the Lord in prayer.
> Do your friends despise, forsake you?
> Take it to the Lord in prayer!
> In His arms He'll take and shield you; you will find a solace there.

What a promise, my friend. Christ will take you in His arms and shield you. That's a friend who sticks closer than a brother.

Pit Stop PRACTICE

Take everything to your friend Jesus. He'll never abandon you; He'll carry your burdens; He'll give you strength and solace and peace.

NOVEMBER

Rejoicing in God's Unfailing Love

Give **thanks** to the Lord, for he is good.

PSALM 107:1

November 1

November—the month of Thanksgiving.

What are your Thanksgiving traditions? Maybe a little turkey. Maybe a little football. But above all, I hope you'll establish the tradition of being thankful to almighty God, setting aside some time when you truly just thank Him for His blessing and provision: "Give thanks to the LORD, for he is good! His faithful love endures forever. Let them praise the LORD for his great love and for the wonderful things he has done for them" (Psalm 107:1,8, *NLT*).

This month, make a special effort to focus on your blessings rather than on your trials and hardships. Count your blessings. Maybe keep a written list of those blessings, and add more each day as you think of them. As the song "Count Your Blessings" says, "Name them one by one, and it will surprise you what the Lord hath done."

I hope this will truly be the month of thanksgiving. Feel free to use my prayer as your own every day this month:

Father, I thank You for my family, for my friends, and for good health. I thank You for my job, for the ability to earn what I need in life. I pray that You'll go with me today and open my eyes to a source of joy. Help me to be thankful. Lord, I humbly thank You for this nation and for the privilege of being a part of this country. Help me to use what You've placed in my hands for Your honor and Your glory and for the advancement of Your kingdom. In Jesus' name, with thanksgiving, amen.

Pit Stop
POINT TO PONDER

Again and again, the Israelites of the Old Testament were reminded that God had rescued them from slavery to be God's special people, His "treasured possession" (see Exodus 19:5). He rescued you, my friend, for the same reason and has named you His child. This month, focus on the wonderful things He has done for you, His treasure.

November 2

Celebration is an important discipline. I want to briefly remind you of six stories found in Luke 14–15.

In the three stories in Luke 14, the people didn't understand celebration. They just didn't get it. Jesus healed on the Sabbath and His critics got mad, not glad. A person who wanted a seat of honor at the banquet didn't understand the whole point of the banquet. And then there was the banquet that nobody wanted to come to; everyone had excuses!

In Luke 15 there are three different stories about people who did celebrate. The first is about a lost sheep. In this story a shepherd left his 99 sheep in the fold to look for one that was lost; and when he found it, he celebrated.

A second story is about a lady who lost a coin. It was most likely a precious coin she had received as an engagement gift, so she swept her house clean; and when she found the coin, she called her friends and said, "Come celebrate with me."

The third story is about a prodigal son. When he came home, his father saw him while he was still a great distance away and ran and embraced him and welcomed him home and planned a celebration party. All these stories include celebration when what was lost was found.

Are you living out celebration? You were lost, my friend. Now you are found! You were dead, but now you're alive! What a cause to celebrate every day!

Celebrate your life in Christ this month. Enjoy it, and be thankful today and every day.

Pit Stop
POINT TO PONDER

Most of us celebrate birthdays. If we celebrate the beginning of a life that will soon end, how much more we should celebrate the birth of a new life that will go on forever!

STEVE WINGFIELD

November 3

Are you planning any feasts this month? I hope you are. Feasts are "made for laughter" the Scriptures say (Ecclesiastes 10:19). Proverbs 17:22 also says that a merry heart is just as good as a dose of medicine. A good ol' belly laugh can do wonders.

I really believe that as followers of Jesus, you and I should be exhibiting joy as a way of life. Joy doesn't always express itself in laughter, though. In the midst of pain, there can still be joy. In the midst of sorrow and great loss, you *can* have joy. Does that sound like a disconnect? "Many are asking, 'Who can show us any good?' Let the light of your face shine upon us, O LORD. You have filled my heart with greater joy than when their grain and new wine abound" (Psalm 4:6-7).

When the world might think you have no reason for joy, you have a deep-seated joy, knowing that Jesus Christ is with you in everything—*everything*—you walk through in life. He's the author and finisher of your faith. He'll take care of you, even to the end, and the devil and all his demons cannot separate you from His care. I believe you can even laugh in the face of danger, at times.

You can have that kind of relationship with Jesus Christ—a relationship that will give you peace in the midst of storms and joy in the midst of sorrows. He is your comfort, your strength, your shield, your guide.

Whether in feast or famine, whether your heart is merry or sorrowful, the joy of the Lord will be your strength!

Pit Stop
PRAYER

O Lord, I rejoice because You have rescued me, and I will trust in Your unfailing love. I will sing my thanks to You because You have been good to me (see Psalm 13:5-6).

November 4

Surely one of the most inspiring hymns ever written is Haldor Lillenas's "Wonderful Grace of Jesus." Just singing this song makes me rejoice.

> Wonderful grace of Jesus,
> Greater than all my sin;
> How shall my tongue describe it,
> Where shall its praise begin?
> Taking away my burden,
> Setting my spirit free;
> For the wonderful grace of Jesus reaches me.
>
> Wonderful the matchless grace of Jesus,
> Deeper than the mighty rolling sea;
> Wonderful grace, all sufficient for me, for even me.
> Broader than the scope of my transgressions,
> Greater far than all my sin and shame,
> O magnify the precious Name of Jesus.
> Praise His Name!

Jesus' grace is greater than all your sins. He took away your burden and set your spirit free. Praise His name!

Pit Stop
POINT TO PONDER

From His grace, Jesus has given you the gift of peace and heaven. He has purchased a place for you as God's beloved child. Thank Him for His wonderful, matchless, deep, high, all-sufficient grace!

STEVE WINGFIELD

November 5

Rejoice in the Lord always. I will say it again: Rejoice!
PHILIPPIANS 4:4

Philippians 4:4 is an easy verse to quote, but sometimes it's pretty difficult to practice. Yet this attitude of joy is not an option in the Christian life; it's a command. We're commanded by God to be people who rejoice—who have the joy of the Lord as our strength.

Such joy comes as a result of an intimate relationship with our risen Savior, the Lord Jesus Christ. Be full of joy! I'll say it again: Rejoice!

Rejoicing may not come easy today. You may be in pain. You may have mental anguish. You may have sorrow beyond sorrow. You may have to rejoice in faith. If it's difficult to rejoice today, look up into the heavens and be honest. Don't lie. Say to your Father:

Lord, I don't feel like it, but by faith I want to rejoice in You. I want to rejoice in the fact that You've forgiven my sins. I want to rejoice that my name is written in Your Book of Life. I want to rejoice in the fact that I'm going to spend eternity with You. I want to rejoice in You, Lord. I choose to rejoice.

Pit Stop
POINT TO PONDER

"Let the godly rejoice. Let them be glad in God's presence. Let them be filled with joy" (Psalm 68:3, *NLT*). Your joy comes not from your circumstances but from knowing the presence of God in every circumstance.

November 6

Have you seen the glory of the Lord? How do you respond to His power and glory? "I have seen you in the sanctuary and beheld your power and your glory.... I will praise you as long as I live, and in your name I will lift up my hands" (Psalm 63:2-4).

In the book of Numbers, we read a story about a different reaction to God's glory. The Israelites were ready to cross the Jordan into the land God had promised them. But scouts had gone into the land and reported that there was trouble ahead; the land was inhabited by giants who would be impossible to conquer.

Only Caleb and Joshua tried to encourage the people. "The Lord is with us! Don't be afraid!" they said. But the people would not listen; they were angry and plotted to choose a new leader and go back to Egypt. They even planned to stone Joshua and Caleb.

Then "the glory of the LORD appeared in the tabernacle of meeting before all the children of Israel" (Numbers 14:10, *NKJV*). Everybody saw the glory. But how did they respond? God said that they held Him in contempt. They saw the glory of the Lord but chose not to walk with Him! In His anger, He vowed to destroy them with a plague.

God wants you to experience His glory, and He wants His glory to draw you closer to Him. He wants you to put your hope and your trust in Him and know that He is going to take care of you and that He's going to provide for you. Spend time today dwelling on the glory of your God. Allow Him to speak into your life. Don't run from Him. He is the author and finisher of your faith. He is where hope and joy can be found.

Pit Stop
PROMISE

"Even the wilderness and desert will be glad.... The wasteland will rejoice and blossom with spring crocuses. Yes, there will be an abundance of flowers and singing and joy!" (Isaiah 35:1-2, *NLT*). What a beautiful image of the transformation the glory of the Lord brings to your life, to your dark days, and to your soul! Seek His glory today.

November 7

Jonathan Edwards said this about the redeemed: "For as their Redeemer is mighty, and is so exalted above all evil, so shall they also be exalted in him."[18]

As I read those words and realize that we are exalted in God, I'm reminded of a verse from an old gospel song:

> Redeemed, how I love to proclaim it!
> Redeemed by the blood of the Lamb;
> Redeemed through His infinite mercy,
> His child and forever I am.

Redemption means you've been bought back. You were a child of this world; you were a child of sin. Jesus Christ stepped forward and with His own blood and His death on the cross of Calvary, He paid the price to buy you back from this world. You now are redeemed! You are His!

The devil is defeated, and you are redeemed through the blood of Jesus Christ. If you are redeemed, if you know Christ in a personal way, if you have the assurance that your sins have been forgiven, if you have put your faith and trust in Jesus alone for salvation, then I want to encourage you to just take a moment and thank Him for the gift of redemption. Just say, *Thank You, Lord, for paying the price to redeem me.*

Now have a great day and rejoice in your redemption.

Pit Stop
POINT TO PONDER

Can you think of a greater gift? Jesus rescued you from the kingdom of darkness, paying the ransom to buy you back. Then He named you His child and promised that you will someday share in His glory!

November 8

> Always be joyful. Never stop praying. Be thankful in all circumstances, for this is God's will for you who belong to Christ Jesus.
> 1 THESSALONIANS 5:16-18, *NLT*

Thank God for the privilege of living in a nation that sets aside a day to give thanks to almighty God for His goodness and mercy and grace. Don't let that day become just another national holiday. The intent of it—the origin of the day—was with a group of people who got together to give thanks to almighty God for His sustaining grace, mercy and provision for them during the year. That's our heritage. That's what Thanksgiving Day is all about.

My prayer is that during all of this month, we will grow thankfulness and gratitude in our heart. We set aside one day to focus on thanksgiving, but I hope we'll develop a joyful thankfulness that bursts out of us every day of the year.

I know you have difficulties in your life. Many things can take your eyes off of thankfulness, and the devil will whisper his lie that you just have too many troubles and hardships to be thankful. My friend, don't let the enemy squash praise and thanks for what God has given you and done for you.

You belong to Christ Jesus! Always be joyful!

Set aside some time every day this month to thank God for what He has done for you and in you.

Pit Stop
POINT TO PONDER

Romans 8:15 says that you are not a fearful slave of God; instead, He adopted you as His own child and gave you His own Spirit. Ask God to give you a greater sense of being His child and belonging to Him.

November 9

> The wages of sin is death, but the gift of God is eternal life in Christ Jesus our Lord.
>
> ROMANS 6:23

Thank God that Christ brought forgiveness! Thank God over and over again for His free gift of salvation. It's not His will that anyone should perish; He wants all to come to repentance. His free gift is extended to all who will believe.

Many people in today's world misunderstand God's gift of grace. They think that somehow they have to earn salvation or they can purchase it by doing good things. They can't get their hearts around the fact that grace is a gift from God.

None of us could ever become good enough to get to God. We can't better ourselves in order to be acceptable to God; we can't pull ourselves up by our own bootstraps. No, the gap that separated us from God was too immense.

I don't care how good you are, I don't care how righteous you think you are—the gap between you and a totally holy God cannot be bridged except by what Jesus Christ did for you. The cross bridged the gap, my friend. It brought you from death to life.

Rejoice in the great, free gift God has given you.

Pit Stop: PRAISE

"I am overwhelmed with joy in the LORD my God! For he has dressed me with the clothing of salvation and draped me in a robe of righteousness" (Isaiah 61:10, *NLT*). Only Christ can do this for you; there is no other way and no other person who can give this gift of eternal life.

November 10

> I pray that you, being rooted and established in love,
> may have power, together with all the saints, to grasp how wide
> and long and high and deep is the love of Christ, and to know
> this love that surpasses knowledge—that you may be filled to
> the measure of all the fullness of God.
>
> EPHESIANS 3:17-19

Ephesians 3:17-19 is one of my favorite portions of Scripture, and it's my prayer for you and for all who follow hard after the Lord.

I pray that you will be rooted and established—in other words, that you will know what you believe and why you believe it.

I pray that you'll have the power to glimpse the magnificence of the love of God. It's impossible to comprehend such love; it surpasses human knowledge. Yet my prayer is that you'll be able to grasp how high and deep and wide and long is that love that went to the cross for you.

The cross of Christ declares His love like nothing else. Imagine going to that cross. Above Christ's brow, which is bleeding from the crown of thorns, write, "The height of His love." Stoop down beneath Christ's feet, which walked those dusty roads, and write, "The depth of His love." Look at the outstretched hand on the left, pierced by a nail, declaring the breadth of God's love; and the right hand, proclaiming the length of His love. On the cross, God's heart beats and bleeds for you. He says, "I love you with an everlasting love."

That's the love of God, my friend. He wants you to understand how much He loves you. Today, think about the cross and the depth and height and length and width of God's love for you.

Pit Stop
PRAYER

Lord Jesus, I want my roots to grow deep into You, drawing my life and strength from Your love for me. You alone are my solid Rock, my salvation, my hope. I cannot comprehend Your great love for me, but I am so, so grateful for it.

November 11

> All the earth bows down to you; they sing praise to you, they sing praise to your name.
>
> PSALM 66:4

All the earth bows down to the Lord! All the earth sings His praises! Are you a part of that?

When Jesus entered Jerusalem, the people were so excited about seeing Him that they welcomed Him by singing praises to Him. But the Pharisees were upset about that and wanted Jesus to quiet down the people. Jesus told them, "If these people remain silent, the rocks will cry out" (see Luke 19:40).

Let us never be silent and allow that to happen on our watch. Don't let the rocks cry out and give Jesus praise because we have been too quiet. Psalm 19:1 states that "the heavens declare the glory of God." They do! The trees bow before Him and the rivers give Him praise. All the earth bows down, worshiping the Creator and Master. How much more should we be caught up in praise and adoration for what He has done for us?

Think about everything He's done for you. Your sins are forgiven; you've been cleansed; you've been set free. He's given you everything you need to live a godly life. Heaven is your home. When you're absent from this body, you'll be present with Him.

Worship Jesus, my friend, and rejoice in His presence, both now and forever.

Pit Stop
PRAISE

"Let all that I am praise the LORD; may I never forget the good things he does for me. For His unfailing love toward those who fear him is as great as the height of the heavens above the earth" (Psalm 103:2,11). Take the time to read all of Psalm 103. Read it aloud, and think about all God has done for you. It is your story, my friend.

November 12

You have an invitation today: Come. How I love the word "come." It's one of God's favorite words. "Come."

> Come, let us bow down in worship, let us kneel before the LORD our Maker; for he is our God and we are the people of his pasture, the flock under his care (Psalm 95:6-7).

What joy to know that He is caring for us! That He is our provider, He is our sustainer, He is a friend who sticks closer than a brother. And He invites us to come and bow down in worship.

Come and bow down and worship Him.

Lord, I thank You for this day. I do worship You. I worship You, my Savior, who gave Himself so that I might have abundant life. I kneel before You, my Maker. You are my God, and I am one of Your people. You are my Shepherd, and I am one of Your flock. I thank You for Your care. I worship You, I love You, I adore You. Father, thank You for this day that You have made. I will rejoice and be glad in it. Speak into my life and direct my steps. May the words of my mouth and the meditation of my heart be acceptable in Your sight, O Lord, my strength and my Redeemer. In Jesus' name, amen.

Pit Stop
POINT TO PONDER

"Happy are those who hear the joyful call to worship, for they will walk in the light of Your presence, LORD" (Psalm 89:15, *NLT*). There is no greater joy in this world than to walk in the light of God's presence. If joy is lacking in your life, hear His invitation: "Come." Spend time in His presence.

STEVE WINGFIELD

November 13

Do you live with any regrets? Are there times you think about your past and get discouraged? Do you wish you could live parts of your life over again? Let this Scripture speak encouragement to you: "The LORD says, 'I will give you back what you lost to the swarming locusts, the hopping locusts, the stripping locusts, and the cutting locusts. It was I who sent this great destroying army against you. Once again you will have all the food you want, and you will praise the LORD your God, who does these miracles for you. Never again will my people be disgraced'" (Joel 2:25-26, *NLT*).

Think about that promise: "I will give you back what you lost to the swarming locusts." The picture of locusts eating away all living vegetation is an illustration of what sins do to a life. "The fields are ruined, the land is stripped bare" (Joel 1:10, *NLT*). Sin devastates a life, exactly what the enemy purposes to do.

Maybe you came to Christ later in life, and now you reproach yourself: "I've wasted so much of my life!" You know, my friend, if you'll give your life totally to the Lord, if you'll follow hard after Him, He has promised to repay you for the years the locusts have eaten away. There's joy in serving Jesus; there's joy in living for Jesus; there's joy in walking with Him. Put your hope and your trust in Him and don't look at the past. Thank God that He delivered you and gave you new life.

Keep your eyes and your heart focused on Jesus. Walk with Him and let Him meet your every need. He does mighty things for those who love Him!

Pit Stop
PRAISE

Christ took the punishment you deserved. He took the wounds that ended His earthly life so that you could have a new life in the Spirit and be healed of the sin disease that doomed you. Trust Him, and don't look back, except to give Him thanks and praise and adoration for what He did.

November 14

I love the word "joy." Something about the word even sounds joyful, don't you think? My favorite Christmas carol (I know, it's not even December yet) is "Joy to the World." I just love joy. "

> I pray that God, the source of hope, will fill you completely with joy and peace because you trust in him (Romans 15:13, *NLT*).

Joy is one of the fruits produced by the Spirit; and you and I, as representatives of Christ, should be demonstrating to the world what true joy looks like. Is your heart filled with joy this morning?

Now, I know that life brings on all kinds of difficulties. Maybe you're sick, maybe you are in need of a job, maybe there's some painful conflict in your family. All kinds of issues could be going on today, things that are not joyful experiences. But those issues do not have to limit your joy.

Come to Jesus and get joy! Joy unspeakable and full of glory. Joy that money cannot buy. Joy that the world cannot take away or steal from you. That joy is yours; live in it!

Because joy is a fruit of the Spirit, we can really only obtain it through a living, vital, intimate relationship with the person of Jesus Christ. When we trust in Him, He fills us with a joy and peace that can be found nowhere else.

If you have not experienced the joy that only God can give to you, open your heart to His Spirit. You can trust Jesus with your whole life, my friend. He will bring you great peace and joy.

Pit Stop
POINT TO PONDER

Your joy and peace rest on the hope God has given you: hope for the past—sins forgiven; hope for the present—God's presence and care; and hope for the future—your Father's constant guidance and a final coming home to His presence.

STEVE WINGFIELD

November 15

> Be glad and rejoice with all your heart. . . . The LORD has taken away your punishment, he has turned back your enemy. The LORD, the King of Israel, is with you. . . . He is mighty to save. He will take great delight in you, he will quiet you with his love, he will rejoice over you with singing.
>
> ZEPHANIAH 3:14-17

Oh, my! Have you thought about God rejoicing over you?

God takes great delight in you and rejoices over you with singing! He's so happy when you know Him and when you're walking with Him. When I read this verse, I get a picture of God just breaking out in song over me. What encouragement!

And God can quiet your heart. This week may have brought uneasiness or turmoil or terror. Maybe you heard the "C" word this week; maybe you were the victim of a crime; maybe you think you've failed in a colossal way. Whatever you're going through, He can quiet your heart with His love.

Oh, my friend, I want you to go through today knowing that God delights in you. He is mighty to save. As He takes joy in you, He wants you to be overcome with the joy of knowing Him and living in relationship with Him. He loves you that much.

Take some time today to reflect on what He's done. Tell Him you need His joy to flow in you. Ask Him for an extra dose of joy today!

Pit Stop PRAYER

"Bring joy to your servant, for to you, O Lord, I lift up my soul" (Psalm 86:4). Father, quiet my heart. I feel so empty of joy right now, but You've promised that Your Spirit will bring joy. I give myself up to You, to be filled by You and Your peace and joy.

November 16

> Because of his great love for us, God, who is rich in mercy, made us alive with Christ even when we were dead in transgressions—it is by grace you have been saved. And God raised us up with Christ and seated us with him in the heavenly realms in Christ Jesus, in order that in the coming ages he might show the incomparable riches of his grace, expressed in his kindness to us in Christ Jesus.
>
> EPHESIANS 2:4-7

Ephesians 2:4-7 is a passage packed with encouragement and a great description of how God has related to the world.

No matter what your bank account looks like, whether you're rich or poor, to have received from God's rich mercy is absolutely awesome. Because of that richness in mercy and because of our faith and our trust in Jesus alone, He made us alive with Christ, even when we were dead in trespasses and sins. We were dead. And He made us alive!

We are saved only by God's grace. We can't earn it; we will never deserve it. God gave His grace to us freely. That incomparably rich grace was expressed in His kindness to us through Jesus Christ our Lord, who canceled all the charges against us.

That is what you have received, what you own, what you possess—because of who Christ is in you. Rejoice in it! Celebrate it! Let the world know that because of Jesus, you are who you are. Not all you want to be; not all you're going to be. But Christ living in you is your hope of glory. Experience the joy of God's grace today wherever you go.

Pit Stop
POINT TO PONDER

Think about these lyrics from a hymn by C. F. Butler: "Since Christ my soul from sin set free, this world has been a heav'n to me; and 'mid earth's sorrows and its woe, 'tis heav'n my Jesus here to know."

November 17

> Come, let us sing for joy to the LORD; let us shout aloud to the Rock of our salvation. Let us come before him with thanksgiving and extol him with music and song. For the LORD is the great God, the great King above all gods. Come, let us bow down in worship, let us kneel before the LORD our Maker; for he is our God and we are the people of his pasture, the flock under his care.
>
> PSALM 95:1-3,6-7

Do you hear the joy of obedience to our God, the Lord our Maker? Sing for joy to the Lord!

Do you sing? You might not think of yourself as a singer. The more I read Scripture, though, the more I really believe singing is an important part of our relationship with God.

You may not be able to carry a tune in a bucket. God's not concerned about that. He's concerned about the desire and the expression of your heart. You sometimes hear joy described as the heart singing. God wants your heart to sing.

Try singing. Even if you are self-conscious about it, get alone, choose a praise CD, and let your songs of praise go up to the Lord. Sing aloud to the Rock of your salvation.

Pit Stop
POINT TO PONDER

Scriptures say that the heavens above and the earth beneath, the mountains and rivers and trees of the forest—all of creation—sing for joy in the Lord. Join the chorus and rejoice in all that the almighty Father is and does.

November 18

Do you begin your day with thanksgiving? Besides shouting your joy to the Lord, come before Him every day with a thankful heart. Here's a little help to remember how to pray. Keep the acronym ACTS in mind. These letters represent four things to include in your prayers:

Adoration—Begin every one of your prayers with adoration of the Lord. Begin your day with adoration. Even before you get out of bed, fill your morning breaths and first thoughts with adoration of the Lord. Praise Him for His greatness. Tell Him you love Him.

Confession—If you know exactly what you need to confess and ask God to forgive, do it. If you need to ask Him to search your heart and see if there is anything He needs to purify and cleanse, do that as well.

Thanksgiving—Psalm 28:7 says that the Lord is your strength and shield; you trust Him with all your heart, and He helps you. No wonder your heart should be filled with joy, and bursting into a song of thanksgiving should come naturally.

Supplication—God wants you to bring your anxieties, your requests and your needs to Him. He's promised to hear your cries and help you.

Sometimes it is easy to forget about thanksgiving. Sometimes your troubles seem so dark that you have a hard time remembering to be thankful. Paul wrote in 1 Thessalonians 5:18 that we should be thankful in every circumstance. That might seem impossible, but Colossians 2:7 says that if your roots go deep into Christ and you build your life on Him, you will overflow with thankfulness!

Come before God with thanksgiving today.

Pit Stop PRACTICE

If you haven't started yet, grab a paper and pen right now and begin daily to write down one thing that you thank God for.

November 19

So many people misunderstand a relationship with Jesus Christ. They fear bondage. Restriction. Severity. Nothing could be further from the truth! "Thou wilt shew me the path of life; in thy presence is fullness of joy; at thy right hand there are pleasures for evermore" (Psalm 16:11, *KJV*).

Psalm 16:11 is a little verse that offers so much. Why would anyone turn down a relationship that brings all of this? Just look at some of the promises of what a relationship with Jesus brings.

Thou wilt shew me the path of life. That's a promise. Jesus will show you the way. Scripture promises that. You don't have to wonder; you don't have to hope you're on the right path; you don't have to ask, "Am I doing what God wants me to do?" You can know, my friend. He will show you.

In thy presence is fullness of joy. A little bit of joy? No! Fullness of joy. Overflowing joy. So much that you'll have to drink from your saucer because your cup will overflow with joy.

At thy right hand there are pleasures for evermore. All too often, people look for pleasure in the wrong places. Pleasures that will never fade are at Jesus' right hand.

Today, remember that you're living in God's presence. Experience joy and pleasure in your relationship with your Savior.

Pit Stop
PRACTICE

Taste and see how good the Lord is! The fullness of joy and pleasures of living in His presence must be *experienced*. You can't talk yourself into these things; they are not produced by willpower. Joy in His presence comes from talking to Him and listening to Him, putting Your hopes in Him, trusting Him with your future, and depending on Him for strength and wisdom. Live in His presence, and see how good He is.

November 20

The way to be happy in Jesus is to follow the Lord with all of your heart, seek to do His will, and trust and obey Him. Proverbs 8:32 tells us, "Happy are those who keep my ways."

This is where we'll find happiness, because we were made to live in intimate, living relationship with the Lord Jesus Christ. We have a God-shaped vacuum within us, and we can try to fill it with all kinds of stuff; but until Jesus is allowed His rightful place in our lives, we will always have this void, this vacancy, this emptiness that nothing else can fill. And until Jesus is given His rightful place, true happiness will never be found.

If you want true happiness, you'll keep the ways of the Lord. This is my prayer for us all today:

Lord God, thank You for all the rich blessings You bring to each of us. Every day, You have supplied our needs, and we thank You for that. Forgive us when we turn our backs on the bounty You provide and look for happiness in all the wrong places, in the ways of the world. Guide us in Your Word, and open our eyes to the words You have given us, for in them we know that we will find true happiness. In Jesus' name, amen.

Pit Stop
POINT TO PONDER

Jesus said that He is the true light that banishes darkness, the living water that quenches all thirst, and the living bread that satisfies and gives eternal life (see John 1:9; 4:10; 6:51). You've probably tried to satisfy your soul with other things; but until it is Christ who fills you, you will still be wandering in the darkness, thirsty and hungry.

November 21

You will go out in joy and be led forth in peace; the mountains and hills will burst into song before you, and all the trees of the field will clap their hands.

ISAIAH 55:12

Can you see in your mind the picture Isaiah paints with his words? When you leave the house today, will you go out in joy? Can you imagine all of nature exploding into song and the trees clapping along as you drive to work? What a way to start your day!

But maybe there were some cross words spoken and the enemy already has things tense this morning. Those things happen, I know that. That's the enemy's way of stealing your joy. God doesn't want you to live that way. He says that you'll go out in joy and be led forth in peace. Just take a moment to tell Him, *Lord, I want to restart my day. I didn't get things started off real good this morning, but I want to go out in joy. I want to be led forth in peace.*

Then I hope you will feel the mountains and the hills bursting into song and the trees clapping their hands. As you go out in joy, I hope you'll see some visible reminders of God's blessing on your choice to follow hard after Him.

Pit Stop
POINT TO PONDER

Satan would love to squelch your joy, and he uses all kinds of external circumstances to try to do it. But remember that joy comes from Christ's presence in you, and the Spirit works to produce goodness, righteousness and truth. If you need to ask forgiveness, do it. If you need to ask God to give you a new perspective, ask. Let the Spirit fill your life with His fruit.

November 22

At one point, the disciples asked Jesus to teach them how to pray, and He gave them that well-known prayer we still pray today. In Matthew 6:9, He begins, "This, then, is how you should pray: 'Our Father in heaven . . .'"

Although the model prayer He gave begins with "Our Father," this could also be translated "Abba," or "Daddy." Jesus was communing with His dad. I don't want to demean in any way the sacredness of the Lord's Prayer, but I want you to pick up on the intimacy of that phrase.

Some people might have a difficult time imagining God as their Father. In those good aspects of your dad here on this earth, you may get a little glimpse of God. But there's no dad that measures up to the qualities of our Father in heaven. He is our God; He loves us.

"When you pray, pray in this manner," Jesus told us (see Matthew 6:9; Luke 11:2). What He was doing was getting us in the right frame of mind to commune with the God of all creation. This is not something we should take lightly. But we are also coming to *our Father*.

We come into God's presence, knowing who we are to Him. He is the God of all creation, yes, but He has adopted us as His children; and we have a personal, intimate relationship with Him.

Today, when you pray, rejoice that the God of all creation is your Father and wants you to come to Him.

Pit Stop
POINT TO PONDER

Amazing grace! God's grace has brought you from being His enemy to being His beloved child.

November 23

> The LORD your God is a merciful God; He will not abandon or destroy you or forget the covenant with your forefathers, which he confirmed to them by oath.
>
> DEUTERONOMY 4:31

I know that the words recorded in Deuteronomy were originally spoken to the children of Israel, but just as God had a covenant with them, He also has a covenant with you and me. And there are some encouraging words for us in this verse.

The Lord is a merciful God. Thank God for His mercy! Where would we be if He had not extended His mercy to us? *Lord, we thank You that You are a merciful God!*

The Lord will not abandon us or forget the covenant He's made with us. God made a covenant with you when you asked Christ to come into your life, and He promises that He will not forget that covenant. He's not going to turn His back on you. Oh, what a way to live, with the confidence that God will remember you and never leave you!

Your covenant with God was also confirmed by oath, the oath of His own Son's blood. This covenant is written in the *blood of Jesus Christ*, and you can be assured that your Savior, your Redeemer, your Rock, your friend will never forget or abandon you.

Live in the joy of the certainty of God's covenant with you.

Pit Stop
POINT TO PONDER

Scriptures say that Jesus is the guarantee of God's new covenant with you, and the Holy Spirit dwelling within you is the guarantee of your position as His child. He will see you through to the end. God keeps His promises (see 1 Corinthians 1:9).

November 24

God loves you so much that when He sees you fall and knows your sins, He still loves you. As Charles Wesley states in his hymn "Depth of Mercy":

> Depth of mercy! can there be
> Mercy still reserved for me?
> Can my God His wrath forbear,
> Me, the chief of sinners, spare?
>
> I have long withstood His grace,
> Long provoked Him to His face,
> Would not hearken to His calls,
> Grieved Him by a thousand falls.
>
> There for me the Savior stands,
> Shows His wounds and spreads His hands.
> God is love! I know, I feel;
> Jesus weeps and loves me still.

The length and the height and the depth and the breadth of God's love, my friend, are never-ending.

Mercy, mercy. That's what God gave you. Receive it and thank God for it. Walk in forgiveness and rejoice in His mercy.

Pit Stop
PRAISE

First Peter 1:3 is a great verse that sums up God's mercy, our hope and our life: "Praise be to the God and Father of our Lord Jesus Christ! In his great mercy he has given us new birth into a living hope through the resurrection of Jesus Christ from the dead." Memorize it.

November 25

God wants us to have a positive attitude. I really believe that. You may think that it's just not part of your personality to be upbeat and optimistic, and I'm not saying that we have to shout hallelujahs once or twice every hour. But I really do believe God wants us to live in victory. We're His children, and He doesn't want us to live in discouragement and defeat:

> Finally, brothers, whatever is true, whatever is noble, whatever is right, whatever is pure, whatever is lovely, whatever is admirable—if anything is excellent or praiseworthy—think about such things (Philippians 4:8).

What are you thinking about? Do you dwell on things that will build you up in the faith? Thinking about true, noble, right, pure, lovely, admirable and praiseworthy things will help you mature in your walk with Christ. Anybody can look at the negatives in life, but when you look to Jesus and let Him work in your life, He shapes you.

Think about such things. What things? For starters: Think about the day that Christ saved you. Think about the home He's preparing for you in glory. Think about the fact that He has plans for you, plans to prosper you, plans to give you hope and a future (see Jeremiah 29:11). Think about His promises to strengthen you, to guide and protect you, to be with you to the end.

Look to Christ. Look to Christ and live abundantly and positively and victoriously. Life is found in Him only. Focus on Him, and think about such things.

Pit Stop
POINT TO PONDER

The world around you certainly does not think the way you do. The world dwells on the opposite of true, noble, right, pure and lovely. Will you follow worldly thinking or will you let the Spirit fill and change you as you practice thinking as Christ wants you to think?

November 26

In this month of Thanksgiving, when we've focused on joy in God's goodness to us, I hope you have taken time to thank Him for what He's provided. It's so easy to get caught up in the materialistic mentality all around us and to forget who has given us everything we have.

Moses warned the Israelites about forgetting the Lord God as they moved into the Promised Land: "You're being brought into a good land by your God, but don't forget to thank and praise Him for what He's giving you" (see Deuteronomy 8:7-11). Moses' words were for the children of Israel, but they are also for us today. Read the following and think about how closely it mirrors today's world:

> When you have eaten and are satisfied, praise the LORD your God for the good land he has given you. Be careful that you do not forget the LORD your God. . . . Otherwise, when you eat and are satisfied, when you build fine houses and settle down, and when your herds and flocks grow large and your silver and gold increase and all you have is multiplied, then your heart will become proud and you will forget the LORD your God (Deuteronomy 8:10-14).

Do you hear the attitudes of today in that passage? "I've done it." "My hard work and hustle have accomplished this." And in a land of plenty and abundance, sadly, people forget the God who has blessed them. The Lord has brought us into a good land, both literally, in our country, and spiritually, in our new lives in Christ. It's so important that we say, *Thank You, Lord, for everything You've done and all You've provided.* It's so important that we realize that all we have comes from Him.

Today, "praise the LORD your God for the good land he has given you."

Pit Stop
POINT TO PONDER

When you fail to praise God for His goodness in providing for you, you miss the joy of seeing His heart of love that cares for His children.

STEVE WINGFIELD

November 27

> Consider therefore the kindness and sternness of God: sternness to those who fell, but kindness to you, provided that you continue in his kindness. Otherwise, you also will be cut off.
>
> ROMANS 11:22

Boy, this verse in Romans has some pretty harsh words, but there is encouragement for us as well.

Consider the kindness that God has shown you. There is no way I could list all the good things that God has done for me. (By the way, have you been keeping that list of blessings this month?) He has been more than kind to me. He's been more than forgiving to me. He's been more than gracious to me. I am blessed because of my relationship to Jesus Christ.

But I look at those around me who have chosen not to receive what God has offered, and I see that they are already being punished by their own wrong decisions. You don't have to look very far to find people who are suffering the consequences of bad choices, reaping the harvest of what they sowed.

God's blessings of joy and contentment are there, my friend, if you choose them. Yes, He sends the rain on the just and the unjust, but there is great gain in following hard after the Lord. Choose life or death. Choose God's kindness or His sternness. Choose peace and joy, or choose to live without the peace and joy that only Jesus can give.

Pit Stop
POINT TO PONDER

Consider these words by Albert B. Simpson: "What will you do with Jesus? Neutral you cannot be; some day your heart will be asking, 'What will He do with me?'"

November 28

> LORD, You have assigned me my portion and my cup; you have made my lot secure. The boundary lines have fallen for me in pleasant places; surely I have a delightful inheritance. You have made known to me the path of life; you will fill me with joy in your presence, with eternal pleasures at your right hand.
>
> PSALM 16:5-6,11

We do have so much to thank God for. I hope that you can say the lines have fallen for you in pleasant places and that you praise God for every blessing. Yet I know many of us have struggled this year, in many different ways. So, as you pause on this day to give thanks, praise God for His constant presence in your life.

Even if you are in the midst of a difficulty today, I hope you can look at God's goodness and His provision and His blessing.

He is your inheritance.

He shows you the path of life.

In His presence is fullness of joy.

Find time to sit in His presence. Let Him, by the power of His Spirit, minister to your needs and bring you full and overflowing joy.

Pit Stop PRAYER

Use Psalm 16:5-6,11 as a prayer to your Father, and let the Spirit fill you with His joy and peace.

November 29

> Keep me as the apple of your eye; hide me in the shadow of your wings.
>
> PSALM 17:8

Our deep and abiding joy flows out of our relationship with our Savior. Several times He said, "I've told you these things so you will have joy." The more closely we walk with Him, the deeper our relationship grows, and the more abundant our joy. We love and trust Him, even though we have never seen Him. Still we know that we abide safely in Him, "in the shadow of [His] wings." As William O. Cushing wrote in his hymn "Under His Wings":

> Under His wings I am safely abiding;
> Tho' the night deepens and tempests are wild,
> Still I can trust Him; I know He will keep me;
> He has redeemed me, and I am His child.
>
> Under His wings, under His wings,
> Who from His love can sever?
> Under His wings my soul shall abide,
> Safely abide forever.

Safe, abiding in God, my friend. No one can separate you from His love. Sing for joy in the shadow of His wings.

Pit Stop
POINT TO PONDER

"In counting blessings I stumbled upon the way out of fear. Can God be counted on? Count blessings and find out how many of His bridges have already held."—Ann Voskamp (*One Thousand Gifts: A Dare to Live Fully Right Where You Are*)

November 30

In Psalm 34:1, David says, "I will extol the LORD at all times; his praise will always be on my lips." Did you note those two little phrases "at all times" and "always"?

Dr. S. M. Lockridge was an African-American pastor and a friend of mine who died several years ago. He used to say, "I'm just so happy, I can't help it. I gotta say something. It's just gotta come out."

He told a story about being at a White House service when Dr. Billy Graham was speaking on the 23rd Psalm:

> First time I'd ever been to the White House, and I thought I was supposed to be dignified. But the Lord kept stirring in my life and I was sitting there and Dr. Graham was talking about the Lord saying He was with me, even through the valley of the shadow of death and He'd never leave me; and finally, I just let it go and said "Amen!" You know, it caught on.

That will work anywhere, my friend. When we're just so caught up in God's love, we can't help but let people know that we love Jesus. That's what it's all about. Acclaiming Him. Being so overwhelmed with the love of God that we cannot help but let it out.

Did you keep a list of blessings this month? If you did, take out that list right now and read over it and thank God for His loving care.

And—I know this might sound impossible, but I want to encourage you—try to rejoice in God at all times and in every circumstance. Who knows, it could become a way of life!

Pit Stop PRACTICE

You may have found that writing down God's blessings every day makes you more aware of and thankful for His guiding and providing hand. Keep on thanking God daily and rejoicing in His love and care.

DECEMBER

Producing Lasting Fruit

I chose you and appointed you to go and
bear fruit—fruit that will last.

JOHN 15:16

December 1

What is your mission in life? Is that a tough question? As you think about your answer, consider what Jesus says in John 15:16: "You did not choose me, but I chose you and appointed you to go and bear fruit—fruit that will last. Then the Father will give you whatever you ask in my name."

That's another way of saying that Jesus has asked us to represent Him in this world by bearing the fruit He desires. The only way we can do that is by staying close to Him, spending time with Him and getting to know Him. Jesus also said that He is the vine, and we are branches; and branches will only produce fruit if they're connected to the vine (see John 15:1-17).

Jesus wants you to be a fruit-bearing Christian—not just a Christian who has pretty leaves, but a Christian who points people to Jesus. As one of His ambassadors to the world, you acknowledge His lordship in your life and tell others about Him.

You may carry out this mission in a way different from other Christians, but if you know Christ, you have been redeemed for the purpose of bearing fruit, fruit that will endure. How's your fruit-bearing? If your life was pictured as a grapevine right now, would the world see many clusters of grapes? Or would the world have to search to find even one or two clusters?

Keep in mind that in real vineyards, pruning is a necessity. Those parts that do not bear fruit must be trimmed. Apple trees and pear trees and even some flowers produce more abundantly when they're trimmed well. Is there anything in your life that needs to be trimmed? Jesus wants to prune you, to get you into shape to serve Him better.

Pit Stop
POINT TO PONDER

Pruning is not something the branch chooses to do on its own; it is the gardener who sees what is necessary for growth and productivity and then prunes and shapes the branch. Turn yourself over to the Master Gardener's skill and wisdom. He has plans for you!

December 2

As you prepare your heart to celebrate this joyous Christmas season, think about your expectations.

When we were kids, we made Christmas wish lists. We'd get a catalog in the mail and look through it and make our lists after looking at it. Then our wish lists were narrowed down to things our parents thought were reasonable; but we each had a hope list as well, and the hope lists went well beyond anything our parents recommended or thought possible.

How about having a wish list and a hope list for your faith? Those lists don't have to be limited; you can dream big! Remember, the Lord said that He can accomplish what you think impossible: "This is the word of the LORD to Zerubbabel: 'Not by might nor by power, but by my Spirit,' says the LORD Almighty" (Zechariah 4:6).

God is the *Almighty*. If you belong to Christ, you are living in a relationship with the King of kings and Lord of lords, and He wants to bless you and use you for His honor and His glory.

One of the ways God wants to use you is by making you sensitive to the needs of those around you. Yes, your hope list might include a big miracle for yourself, but here's a challenge for this Christmas season: Be part of a miracle. Let God's Spirit use you to be His love with skin on.

Think about it. What are your wishes and hopes for your faith? Does your list include being a part of the mighty works God does by His Spirit?

Pit Stop Prayer

Lord, use me during this season and give me the gift of being part of a Christmas miracle.

December 3

> I have been crucified with Christ and I no longer live, but Christ lives in me. The life I live in the body, I live by faith in the Son of God, who loved me and gave Himself for me.
>
> GALATIANS 2:20

Praise the Lord! Christ lives in you! He lives in me! What good news that we are free of our old selves, set free to live out the life of Christ within us. The evangelist Daniel W. Whittle captured this sentiment in his hymn "Christ Liveth in Me":

> Once far from God and dead in sin,
> No light my heart could see;
> But in God's Word the light I found,
> Now Christ liveth in me.
>
> Christ liveth in me,
> Christ liveth in me,
> Oh! what a salvation this,
> That Christ liveth in me.
>
> As rays of light from yonder sun,
> The flow'rs of earth set free,
> So life and light and love come forth
> From Christ living in me.

Rejoice in the truth of the words in this old hymn, my friend. And let your heart sing the words into your soul.

Pit Stop
POINT TO PONDER

Consider these words from Corrie ten Boom: "Trying to do the Lord's work in your own strength is the most confusing, exhausting, and tedious of all work. But when you are filled with the Holy Spirit, then the ministry of Jesus just flows out of you."

December 4

The Christmas season almost always includes special foods and festivities. We celebrate with family and good friends and neighbors. But Hebrews 13:2 says, "Do not forget to entertain strangers."

Jesus said that giving a hungry person something to eat, giving a thirsty person something to drink, or inviting a stranger into your home is the same as doing it for Him (see Matthew 25:35-40). Do you ever think about showing hospitality to people you don't know? Or to people you don't know well? Or to people you would never think of inviting, because they're just so, well, different than your usual crowd of friends?

Entertain strangers. Invite someone you had not planned to invite. I know, this might make you a little uncomfortable. But I don't want Jesus to say to you one day, "I was a stranger and you did not invite me in" (Matthew 25:43).

Bless someone with the gift of hospitality this month, and it may be the best gift you give this season. God will honor that invitation. His Spirit will be there, too.

Pit Stop
POINT TO PONDER

Hospitality can be shown in more ways than opening your home—it's opening a door into your time and space. Can you be patient when a stranger interrupts your schedule? On a flight or in a waiting room, what if the person next to you needs a listening ear? At church, are visitors greeted and "invited in" or are they left to be spectators? Might "hospitality" even mean a friendly wave to let someone into traffic ahead of you?

December 5

Let each one of you speak truth with his neighbor.
EPHESIANS 4:25, *NKJV*

Even in the Christian community, we often cover up our true feelings and fail to communicate honestly, but Scripture says that each one of us is to speak truth. Are you speaking truth as a way of life? The *New Living Translation* says to "stop telling lies." That's pretty clear.

One of the ways we might be dishonest is in what we say when we're angry, upset or disappointed. We're dishonest when we don't acknowledge our feelings. So, how do we handle that?

Remember to keep it honest. When you're angry, don't deny it. Say, "This really makes me mad. I'm upset about this." It's okay to be honest about how you feel. Scripture, in fact, says that we're to be angry but not let sin control us. It's okay to have those kinds of emotions. Learn how to express anger and deal with it, and don't let it control you.

Speak truth. One way we can speak truth is when somebody offends us and we do not cover it up, but honestly speak what we feel and think so that we live an honest life. We can speak kindly, we can speak with discretion, but we must speak truth.

Be honest in your communication with your spouse, with your children and with people you work with. Your day will be much better if you'll just be honest about whatever's going on and let God begin to heal any rift there might be.

Pit Stop PRAYER

Lord Jesus, give me wisdom in handling emotional situations.
Nudge me when I am lying, even to myself, about my feelings.
Teach me to speak the truth in kindness.

December 6

Do everything without complaining or arguing.
PHILIPPIANS 2:14

Oh, my. Philippians 2:14 contains a stinger, something that often challenges me.

Complaining is addictive. And once we start complaining, things can spiral downhill really, really quickly. Complaining robs God of blessing. Instead of committing ourselves afresh to the Lord, we doubt His wisdom and prevent Him from doing His work.

Somewhere I read this tip for dealing with a complaining spirit. Ask yourself this question: *If someone gave me a dollar every time I complained and collected a dollar every time I showed gratitude, would I be rich or poor?* That's a great question. Answer it honestly to yourself.

Complaining affects your health. Did you know that? Proverbs 14:30 says, "A peaceful heart leads to a healthy body; jealousy is like cancer in the bones" (*NLT*). A calm and undisturbed mind and heart are the life and health of the body.

Choose today not to complain, and instead offer words of gratitude and appreciation and praise. I promise you, at the end of the day, you'll be a lot better off than if you spend the day complaining.

Pit Stop PRAYER

Lord, I know that the words I speak come from the thoughts I think. Dig deep with Your Spirit and transform my thinking. Replace any complaining spirit You find in me with a spirit of gratitude and praise.

December 7

Has anyone snapped at you this week? Or taken advantage of you? Or lied about you? Or criticized you unfairly? How did you react? Jesus gives us instructions for handling situations like that: "I say, do not resist an evil person! If someone slaps you on the right cheek, offer the other cheek also. You have heard the law that says, 'Love your neighbor' and hate your enemy. But I say, love your enemies! Pray for those who persecute you! In that way, you will be acting as true children of your Father in heaven. For he gives his sunlight to both the evil and the good, and he sends rain on the just and the unjust alike (Matthew 5:39,43-45, *NLT*).

This one is impossible for me to accomplish in my own strength. I just don't have it in me to follow Jesus' guidelines. If somebody slaps me, I'm ready to slap back. That's my personality, a part of my sinful nature that the Lord still needs to conquer.

But it is possible to live Jesus' way through the power of the Holy Spirit. I have to rely on Christ to give me the strength; otherwise, I'll be fighting back. And in order for Him to shape me into the kind of person He wants me to be, I must spend time with Him, letting Him change my thinking and my heart.

So the question for you is this: Who are you going to rely on in this kind of situation? Yourself? Or Jesus? My experience is that I'm always much better off relying on Him. I can testify to that.

Rely on the living God today, and depend on His strength to bear the fruit He desires in your life.

Pit Stop PRAYER

Lord, You ask us to live above normal. I cannot do that on my own. I always fail, even though I want to follow Your commands, so I'm depending entirely on Your Spirit and Your power to help me live Your way. Thank You for Your promises that You will work in me!

December 8

If you could somehow paint every thought you have today, what sort of picture would be formed by your thoughts by the end of the day? What do you think about? Do you *choose* the paths for your thoughts?

Scripture tells us to focus on the good: "If anything is excellent or praiseworthy—think about such things" (Philippians 4:8). We are to be intentional about what we think about and focus on.

When we think too much about the negative things in life, it's easy to get dragged down. When somebody does something that offends us or takes advantage of us, dwelling on that will drag us down. But when we meditate on praiseworthy things, our attitude will be so much better.

Pick out something today that's praiseworthy. Maybe you want to choose a song and just let that melody ring in your heart throughout this day. This is not just positive thinking, but it's also focusing your attention on Jesus, the author and finisher of your faith.

Focus on Jesus. In Him you'll find joy, contentment and happiness.

Pit Stop
PRACTICE

"Since you have heard about Jesus and have learned the truth that comes from him, throw off your old sinful nature and your former way of life, which is corrupted by lust and deception. Instead, let the Spirit renew your thoughts and attitudes. Put on your new nature, created to be like God—truly righteous and holy" (Ephesians 4:21-24, *NLT*). Focus on putting on your new nature.

December 9

When we are filled with the Spirit, our lives will bear the fruits of the Spirit listed in Galatians 5: love, joy, peace, patience, kindness, goodness, faithfulness, gentleness and self-control. Are those on your faith hope list?

What kind of fruit are you producing? When people think of you, do they think of love? Are you a joyous person? When you enter a room, does peace also enter? Do people see patience and forgiveness, gentleness and kindness in your relationships with others? In your life, do you exhibit goodness, faithfulness and self-control?

All of those fruits, my friend, are exactly what Jesus Christ wants to produce in you and me. When we are filled with the Spirit and are living under His control, we can bear that fruit:

> Those who live according to the sinful nature have their minds set on what that nature desires; but those who live in accordance with the Spirit have their minds set on what the Spirit desires (Romans 8:5).

The Spirit desires to produce His fruit in your life, and His fruit is the opposite of what your sinful nature desires. Open your heart and mind to the Spirit; ask Him to produce His fruit abundantly. That's what this world desperately needs to see in those who profess the name of Christ.

Give the Spirit control, and He will produce His bountiful fruit in your life.

Pit Stop PRAYER

As a prayer, use a stanza from this hymn by George Croly: "Spirit of God, descend upon my heart; wean it from earth; through all its pulses move; stoop to my weakness, mighty as Thou art; and make me love Thee as I ought to love."

December 10

These days, the world insists on saying, "Happy holidays." I always reply, "Merry Christmas to you." There are some things we should just not give up. As you enter the Christmas season, I encourage you to keep Jesus as the reason for the season. Don't let this secular, humanistic, materialistic world drain the joy of Jesus from your celebration:

> The Lord will surely comfort Zion and will look with compassion on all her ruins; he will make her deserts like Eden, her wastelands like the garden of the Lord. Joy and gladness will be found in her, thanksgiving and the sound of singing (Isaiah 51:3).

He will make her deserts like Eden. Isn't that a beautiful picture?

Think of ways you can creatively spread God's joy wherever you go. Let a melody of thanksgiving sing in your life. Be careful of getting so caught up in gift-giving, entertaining, decorating and concerts that you miss Jesus in this season. Let your life represent the joy and gladness that the baby Jesus brought to the world.

This season, take the opportunity that God has given to you to be a missionary in a world that has rejected Jesus. Many people are looking for peace and hope, and they're asking questions. Jesus needs you to introduce them to Him.

Each day this month, take extra time alone with Jesus so that you can keep your eyes on Him, the reason for this season.

Pit Stop PRAYER

Lord Jesus, the news of good tidings and great joy is a message for all year, and my desire is to devote my life to being Your messenger wherever there are deserts and wastelands. Use me, Lord!

December 11

Do you ever get angry? Of course, you're human, right? You get angry. Maybe you're angry right now.

But if your anger controls the way you think and the way you act, your anger will hinder what God wants to do through you. Scripture says, "Be angry, and do not sin" (Ephesians 4:26). We have these additional instructions in Ephesians 4:26-27:

> Do not let the sun go down while you are still angry, and do not give the devil a foothold.

Jesus got angry. When He went into that temple and created havoc, overturning the moneychangers' tables and driving them out of the Temple, He was angry (see Matthew 21:12-13). But He did not sin.

We all get angry. But when we allow anger to control our day, our actions, our thoughts and our speech, then we have sinned. Instead, we must practice forgiveness as a way of life and settle those accounts before we go to bed.

You know, there is great freedom in forgiveness. So if anger has led you to say or do something that you shouldn't have said or done, why don't you go to that person today and say, "I was wrong. Will you forgive me?" The end of the year might also be a good time to ask the Lord to show you if you still need to extend forgiveness to someone who has wronged you.

Pit Stop
PRAYER

Spirit, I know my human anger does not achieve Your purposes. Show me if there is any anger or grudge that You want to deal with right now, and give me the grace to forgive or to ask for forgiveness.

December 12

Do you know anybody who could use a good ol' dose of humility? I think all of us do. But have you thought about yourself?

The ideal is that, regardless of how high your station in life might be, you must always, always treat others with dignity and respect.

The Lord taught His disciples how to do that. He's a perfect example of humility. He was the King of the universe, the author, the creator, the sustainer of everything that ever was and ever will be; yet He never raised Himself above others. He really did exemplify the qualities of modesty and respectfulness at all times.

Jesus' life should be an inspiration to all of us. When we believe that we have it all or that we know it all, we must remember Jesus and His walk on this earth. He had it all, He knows it all, and He willingly gave it all up to serve others. As David wrote in Psalm 25:8-9:

> Good and upright is the LORD. Therefore he instructs sinners in his ways. He guides the humble in what is right and teaches them his way.

Be willing to be taught and led by the Lord. Allow Him to be your all in all. Humble yourself before Him and seek His face so that He will teach you His way.

Pit Stop
PRAYER

Father, I want to be part of what You are doing on this earth, but my pride and self-centeredness get in the way. Prune me in whatever way is necessary, because I want to represent You well in everything I say and do.

December 13

Consider these declarations of blessings from Jesus:

> Blessed are the poor in spirit, for theirs is the kingdom of heaven. Blessed are those who mourn, for they will be comforted. Blessed are the meek, for they will inherit the earth. Blessed are those who hunger and thirst for righteousness, for they will be filled. Blessed are the merciful, for they will be shown mercy. Blessed are the pure in heart, for they will see God. Blessed are the peacemakers, for they will be called sons of God. Blessed are those who are persecuted because of righteousness, for theirs is the kingdom of heaven. Blessed are you when people insult you, persecute you and falsely say all kinds of evil against you because of me. Rejoice and be glad, because great is your reward in heaven, for in the same way they persecuted the prophets who were before you (Matthew 5:3-12).

Here is a simple prayer you can pray:

> *Lord God, help me to follow Your Word and obey Your will. Make me aware of the obstacles that stand in the way of my obedience, and help me find the best way around them. Please forgive me when I fail. And thank You, Lord, for the rewards, both material and spiritual, that come from obedience. Help me to obey You. In Jesus' name, amen.*

Pit Stop
POINT TO PONDER

Reflect on Jesus' words to His disciples in John 14:15: "If you love me, obey my commandments" (*NLT*).

December 14

In the night sky over Bethlehem, angels sang about peace on earth when Jesus was born. Yet the Christmas season is one of the most peace-less times of the year. There's more stress, more depression and more suicides during this time of year than at any other time.

> You will keep in perfect peace all who trust in you, all whose thoughts are fixed on you! (Isaiah 26:3, *NLT*).

I think this is one of the greatest promises in the Bible. This season celebrates the birth of Jesus, the Prince of Peace. The peace God brings into our lives surpasses all understanding; there's no way to explain it or comprehend it because it's of God. It's not something we can create by ourselves; it's not something we'll find in any other thing or person.

God will keep you in perfect peace. Can you imagine a perfect peace? It will not disappear when things get stressful; it won't be ruffled by circumstances. You need such a peace to guard your heart and mind this season—and all the rest of the year.

The secret is to focus your mind on the author and finisher of your faith. Keep your eyes and thoughts on Jesus. Don't let the enemy control your mind.

As you go through your day, if you're feeling stressed or tense, stop and take a deep breath and have a few minutes of quiet time with Him. Just do it. And ask Him to speak His peace into your life.

Pit Stop
POINT TO PONDER

The key to perfect peace is trusting in God. When you find the security of trusting Him, you can say with the psalmist, "[The Lord] is my refuge, my place of safety; he is my God, and I trust in him" (Psalm 91:2, *NLT*).

December 15

John 15 is one of my favorite chapters in all the Bible. (My wife, Barb, says they're *all* my favorite chapters, and maybe she's right.) John 15:16, the theme for this month, is a great word to all of Jesus' disciples. Jesus says that He chose us and appointed us to bear fruit that will last.

Not only did Jesus talk about bearing fruit, but He also spoke about a progression in our fruitfulness, from fruit to more fruit to much fruit. You know, you can count the seeds in an apple; you can cut the fruit open and count the exact number of seeds in the fruit. But have you ever thought about the fact that you cannot know how many apples are in a seed? You do not know how much fruit one seed you plant will bear in the future.

Jesus said that He chose us to represent Him, and "When you produce much fruit, you are my true disciples. This brings great glory to my Father" (John 15:8, *NLT*). The secret to bearing much fruit is to remain in Him. "I am the vine; you are the branches. If a man remains in me and I in him, he will bear much fruit; apart from me you can do nothing" (John 15:5).

Take time today to read all of John 15. There are some great promises in that chapter. Remain in Jesus today, tomorrow and all of your days so that you can bear much fruit and bring great glory to your Father.

Pit Stop
PRAYER

Lord Jesus! I am going to cling to Your promise that if I remain in You, You will remain in me. Grow my faith and give me Your life as I depend on You and desire to follow Your commands.

December 16

Saint Basil said, "He who sows courtesy reaps friendship, and he who plants kindness gathers love." So here's a simple little assignment for you today: Sow courtesy.

Open a door for someone. Let someone into line ahead of you. Offer someone a cup of cold water. Carry packages for someone. Let someone merge into traffic. Sow courtesy.

You know, this world would be so much more pleasant if everyone would just show more courtesy. The workplace, grocery store, highway, parking lot, even your home—every place is a fertile ground where you can sow the seeds of kindness. I know, you're sometimes on a tight schedule and you've learned to ignore the world around you as you hurry through the day; but today, look for situations when you can be more courteous.

You can do it—you can! Choose to show courtesy and choose to plant some seeds of kindness. "A man reaps what he sows" (Galatians 6:7). You want kindness? Sow kindness. You want friendship? Sow friendship. Sow the crop to reap a harvest.

God will give the increase. If you sow generously, you will reap generously (see 2 Corinthians 9:6). And often the harvest is bountiful—you are not the only one who reaps what you sow. One act of courtesy or kindness might lead to a whole chain of kind and courteous acts by many people throughout the day!

Sow courtesy—generously.

Pit Stop PRAYER

Father, by Your Spirit, remind me that I carry Your name and represent You to the world. Everything I do and say, whether large or small, scatters seeds in the fields that You want to harvest. I want to be part of Your work in those fields. Give me wisdom in all the little things today.

December 17

A really personal question today: Is your life full of peace, quietness and confidence?

> The fruit of righteousness will be peace; the effect of righteousness will be quietness and confidence forever (Isaiah 32:17).

If you've asked Christ to come into your life, He has made you righteous. That's what He did for you on the cross. You might be far from perfect, but because Christ was perfect and yet willing to pay the price for your sins, His righteousness is now given to you. None of us deserves it, but His sacrifice gives us right standing in God's eyes.

The righteousness that He gave you brings you peace. And the effect of righteousness will be quietness and confidence forever. God doesn't want you to be living in anxiety and fear. His righteousness in you should be producing quietness and confidence. You can experience that by letting Him have control of your life. You can trust Him; He has promised He'll always work for your good.

Allow Him to do His work in you, my friend, and you'll have quietness and confidence in Jesus.

Pit Stop
PROMISE

My friend, you can be confident of God's promises: "The LORD will fulfill his purpose for [you]" (Psalm 138:8). "He will keep you strong to the end and bring you blameless into His presence" (1 Corinthians 1:8). He who began a good work in you will carry it on to completion (Philippians 1:6). Sing hallelujah and rest in His promises.

December 18

> The fruit of the Spirit is love, joy, peace, patience, kindness, goodness, faithfulness, gentleness and self-control. Against such things there is no law.
>
> GALATIANS 5:22-23

If you live in the Spirit's power, He will produce fruit in your life.

Now, I will flat out admit that my life doesn't always bear the fruits mentioned in Galatians 5:22-23. I remember one day I was talking to a friend on the phone while I was driving. Going up a hill, I was following a truck. It was a 55 MPH zone, but we were only doing 15 MPH. And I couldn't pass.

In our conversation, my friend suddenly asked, "What's wrong?"

"Nothing's wrong," I said. But my friend had heard something in my voice. I was not living out the Spirit's fruit, because my great impatience was very evident.

If you could stand back and look at a picture of the fruit on your tree, what would you see? Be honest with yourself. Would there be love? Joy? Peace? Would there be patience? Kindness? Goodness? How about faithfulness, gentleness and self-control? Those are the things God wants to produce in your life.

Today, open yourself to the Spirit's teaching. He will show you what needs to be pruned in your life and where you still need to allow Him to work to bring forth His fruits.

Pit Stop PRAYER

Holy Spirit, I long for more of the life and the fruit You bring. Fill me, teach me, prune me, strengthen me.

December 19

There's something within each of us that wants to do our very best and achieve, even be first. But Jesus said that servanthood brings the greatest rewards. He told His disciples, "If anyone wants to be first, he must be the very last, and the servant of all" (Mark 9:35).

In regard to servanthood, the story of Dan Mazur really spoke into my life. Dan was leading a team of mountain climbers up Mount Everest. Climbers plan for this trip for years; and when Dan's team started their climb, conditions were ideal and they looked forward to reaching the peak, something relatively few people have accomplished.

Only two hours from the top, they came across a man by the name of Lincoln Hall, a climber who had collapsed the day before on his way down. His own team had thought he could not be saved and had even reported him dead. Alone and hallucinating, he had no equipment and was suffering from frostbite and dehydration.

Without hesitation, Mazur's team gave Hall some of their oxygen, food and water. By the time more help arrived, reaching the peak was out of the question for Mazur's team. They had sacrificed years of planning and preparation to save a life.

What would you give up to save a life? Dan Mazur and his team had wanted to climb that peak, but they made a choice to give up their goal for the good of another person. Every day, you're faced with such decisions. The decisions may not all be life-and-death matters, but they all matter in the life you live in Jesus' kingdom.

Will you live according to the world's standards or according to Christ's? Will you serve or demand to be served? Will you be first or last?

Pit Stop
POINT TO PONDER

Give yourself first of all to God, as His servant. Mother Teresa wrote, "Give yourself fully to God. He will use you to accomplish great things on the condition that you believe much more in His love than in your own weakness."

December 20

God created us to be successful. I'm not talking about the success that results in money and a mansion on the hill, although God does sometimes give that. I'm talking about success in bearing much fruit, in representing Jesus well, and in being effective and productive in advancing His kingdom. That's the success He wants to bring to your life.

In his letter to all who have faith in Christ, Peter outlined this formula for success in walking with our Lord:

> For this very reason, make every effort to add to your faith goodness; and to goodness, knowledge; and to knowledge, self-control; and to self-control, perseverance; and to perseverance, godliness; and to godliness, brotherly kindness; and to brotherly kindness, love (2 Peter 1:5-7).

The qualities Peter lists—goodness, knowledge, self-control, perseverance, godliness, kindness and love—are fruits that, like those mentioned in Galatians 5:22-23, are hard to produce on our own. We need the power of the Spirit to grow these things in our lives. Maybe we need to add these things to our faith wish lists.

Take some time to read through that list of fruit slowly and meditate on each one. Then read God's promise: "The more you grow like this, the more productive and useful you will be in your knowledge of our Lord Jesus Christ" (2 Peter 1:8, *NLT*).

Success promised!

Pit Stop PRAYER

Lord Jesus, only Your Spirit can grow these things in my life; this fruit does not come from human nature. I want to live by Your Spirit, not by my old nature. Give me the strength to say no to the old ways of living and the trust to rely on You to provide all the resources I need to live my new life.

STEVE WINGFIELD

December 21

One of the verses that I love to claim for people is Philippians 1:6, where Paul expresses the confidence we have that God will continue the good work He's begun in us, and that He will carry it on until it's finally finished on the day of Christ's return!

You're a recipient of the love of God. He abounds in love and compassion; He loved you even before you knew Him. Paul goes on to say that God gives love to you so that you might give it away:

> I pray that your love will overflow more and more, and that you will keep on growing in knowledge and understanding. For I want you to understand what really matters, so that you may live pure and blameless lives until the day of Christ's return. May you always be filled with the fruit of your salvation—the righteous character produced in your life by Jesus Christ—for this will bring much glory and praise to God (Philippians 1:9-11, *NLT*).

Once again, the Bible makes it clear that God's work in you is meant to produce fruit that will bring praise and glory to God. He's given you a great and boundless love, and He wants you to extend that love to others.

What you've received, choose to give away. Ask Jesus to give you understanding of what really matters and to continue His work in your life.

Pit Stop
PRAYER

Lord Jesus, here I am in the middle of a busy season of the year. Today and every day, turn my eyes away from worthless things and give me an understanding of what really matters.

December 22

> The image of the crucified Christ is found much rather in men who imitate Him in their daily walk than in the crucifix made of wood.
>
> RAYMOND LULL

Raymond Lull was a missionary in the late thirteenth century who made three trips to Africa. On the last trip, a furious mob stoned him to death. He lived and wrote those words long ago, but how true they still are today!

You may have a cross hanging around your neck or from your rearview mirror right now. There's nothing wrong with that; it's a great way to testify to the fact that you're a follower of Christ. But whether or not you are devoted to imitating Christ is shown more accurately by how you walk every day.

I want to be an imitator of Christ. I have a long way to go; I'm the first to confess that. But that's my mission and my heart's desire; I long to be more like Him.

The more time we spend with Christ, the more we will become like Him. Hebrews 11:6 says that God "rewards those who earnestly seek him."

Earnestly seek God. Tell Him that your heart's desire is to imitate Him in your walk today and every day.

Pit Stop PRAYER

Spirit of the living, almighty God, grow this life I take from the vine so that Your character shines in me and Your amazing love overflows and spills into the lives of those around me.

December 23

> Against the backdrop of people who avoid work, cut corners, and do half-hearted jobs, a diligent man stands out. Practicing diligence is an excellent way to stand out for Christ at home, in the workplace, and even at church. Today, complete each one of your tasks, however big or small, with diligence.
>
> DR. DAVID JEREMIAH

Diligence. My dad called it stick-to-it-iveness. Diligence is being persistent and hard-working, industrious, conscientious and thorough. Proverbs says that there are always rewards for diligence: "A slack hand causes poverty, but the hand of the diligent makes rich" (Proverbs 10:4 *ESV*). "Diligent hands will rule, but laziness ends in slave labor" (Proverbs 12:24).

More importantly, when we work diligently, we represent Christ. Whatever we're doing today, we're doing for His honor and His glory. If we live, it's to honor the Lord. And if we die, it's to honor the Lord. So whether we live or die, we belong to the Lord (see Romans 14:8, *NLT*).

Whatever you're about today, don't do it half-heartedly. Give it all you've got. You're working for Him. You bear His name, and you represent Him. It matters not whether you're typing, digging with a backhoe, caring for children, driving a truck or cooking a meal—whatever you're doing, you are working for the Lord.

How would things change in your workplace, in your home or even in your church, if everybody did what they did with diligence and to the glory of God?

Pit Stop
PRACTICE

"Today, complete each one of your tasks, however big or small, with diligence." And watch what a difference it makes in your life and in the lives you touch.

December 24

Every time you pick up a newspaper, every time somebody gives or writes the date, you're testifying to the fact that Jesus Christ was born over 2,000 years ago. We celebrate that fact. Jesus really is the reason for the season. I hope this is a wonderful time of celebration and joy for you.

Jesus Christ came to this earth for the purpose of giving His life so that you can have life and have it abundantly. As you prepare to celebrate His birth, I want you to take stock of where you are spiritually. Listen to these words from John's first letter: "If we claim we have no sin, we're only fooling ourselves and not living in the truth. But if we confess our sins to him, he is faithful and just to forgive us our sins and to cleanse us from all wickedness. If we claim we have not sinned, we're calling God a liar and showing that his word has no place in our hearts" (1 John 1:8-10, *NLT*).

Take inventory of your life today. Be honest with yourself. Look in the mirror; and if there is sin in your life, confess it to God. Just say, *Lord, I blew it. I shouldn't have done it. And I ask You to forgive me.* He wants to do that. He wants to come into your life. He wants you to live clean and pure. I want to echo what John wrote just a few verses later: "I am writing to you who are God's children because your sins have been forgiven through Jesus" (1 John 2:12, *NLT*).

Oh, my friend, confess your sins to God, experience forgiveness, and enjoy an intimate relationship with the King of kings and Lord of lords. Then have a wonderful, joyous celebration of Jesus' birth.

Pit Stop
POINT TO PONDER

This is the message of glad tidings and great joy: Jesus came to this earth to rebuild the bridge between God and humanity. Now you can enter into His presence without blame, and you can find there all the joy and completeness that your heart craves.

December 25

Isaac Watts originally wrote his hymn "Joy to the World" to celebrate Christ's return. But it has since become a traditional Christmas carol celebrating Christ's first appearance on earth:

> Joy to the World, the Lord is come!
> Let earth receive her King;
> Let every heart prepare Him room,
> And Heaven and nature sing,
> And Heaven and nature sing,
> And Heaven, and Heaven, and nature sing.
>
> Joy to the World, the Savior reigns!
> Let men their songs employ;
> While fields and floods, rocks, hills and plains
> Repeat the sounding joy,
> Repeat the sounding joy,
> Repeat, repeat, the sounding joy.
>
> He rules the world with truth and grace,
> And makes the nations prove
> The glories of His righteousness,
> And wonders of His love,
> And wonders of His love,
> And wonders, wonders, of His love.

Today, repeat the sounding joy, for He has come!

Pit Stop
PRAISE

The wonders of Your love, Lord! Oh, the wonders of Your love!

December 26

Have you ever been told you're impatient? Do you find it hard to wait? Let me tell you about an experience I had one day. I don't remember where I was driving to that day, but a woman in front of me was not moving as fast as I would have liked. Now, I didn't say any bad words; but in her rearview mirror, she could see the expression on my face. And she read it correctly. She got out of my way so that I could hurry to wherever I was going.

I didn't realize it, but she was a lady from our church. The next Sunday, she said to me, "I was in front of you the other day, and I could see that you were in a hurry!"

I had to pray, "Lord, help me to be more patient." The words of Psalm 27:14 are for me, I guess: "Wait for the Lord; be strong and take heart and wait for the Lord."

I really do believe that if I would just take those words to heart, things would often go so much better for me. I even get impatient with the Lord. He might speak to me about something, and I just rush right out to do it *right now*. But I know there are times when I should wait on His timing, rather than run out in front of Him.

Waiting on the Lord doesn't mean you just sit around and twiddle your thumbs. He wants you to be productive, but you need to wait on Him, trusting His plan, knowing that His ways are far better than your ways.

From Psalm 27:11, I pray for you and me both: "Teach [us] how to live, O Lord" (*NLT*).

Pit Stop PRAYER

Father, I do trust You, and I am certain that my future is in Your hands and that You will work out Your plans for me. Yet I get impatient and run ahead of You. Forgive me for this lack of trust. Teach me to live so that I have more patience in all things.

December 27

My mom used to say, "Son, if you can't say something good, just don't say anything."

That's good advice. I still need to heed that advice today, because it's so tempting at times to speak words of cursing. Not four-letter kinds of curses, but things that tear down instead of build up.

Here's a challenge for all of us: "Do not let any unwholesome talk come out of your mouths, but only what is helpful for building others up according to their needs, that it may benefit those who listen" (Ephesians 4:29).

James talks quite a bit about that little instrument called the tongue (see James 3:1-12). Like a little spark that can set a forest ablaze, the tongue is a small thing that has the power to set a life on fire. It holds the power to bless and the power to curse. But, asks James, can a spring bring forth both fresh water and salt water?

God wants us to live so close to Him that our tongues are under His control and serve as a blessing. Don't let any unwholesome talk come out of your mouth. Guard your tongue. Watch what you say. Be careful and choose to speak only words of blessing and encouragement.

God wants you to use your mouth to offer praise to Him and exalt His name and build others up. That's why you are in this world, my friend.

Let blessing come out of your mouth today.

Pit Stop
POINT TO PONDER

"Do not repay evil with evil or insult with insult, but with blessing, because to this you were called so that you may inherit a blessing" (1 Peter 3:9). Your mouth, your hands and feet, your entire self, can be used for good or for evil, for blessing or for cursing. But your calling, child of God, is to spread goodness—even in response to evil. And God will bless you in return.

December 28

In the New Testament, there are two Greek words used for the word "kindness." In Acts 28:2, Luke is writing about one of Paul's missionary journeys, and he says, "the islanders showed us unusual kindness." The original Greek word used here refers to hospitality, acts of kindness, and thinking of others.

The other word for "kindness" in the New Testament is found in Galatians 5:22, in the list of fruits of the Spirit. The original Greek word translated here as "kindness" means gentleness in dealing with others, goodness in action, and sweetness of disposition.

I love that definition, "sweetness of disposition." Would those around you every day use that phrase to describe you? I want to be a person of sweet disposition. Sometimes a person will call somebody else a sourpuss. I'd much rather have someone say, "You know, he has a sweet disposition about him."

As much as I want that, I know it cannot come from me, from my own nature. It will only come from God. Kindness is a gift of the Spirit, a fruit of the Spirit who is doing His work in me.

My friend, "letting the Spirit control your mind leads to life and peace" (Romans 8:6, *NLT*). Allow the Holy Spirit to produce His fruit in you and guide you into life and peace.

Pit Stop
PRACTICE

Open yourself up to the Spirit of Christ and His power. Only He can produce His character in you. Ask Him to transform your mind and guide you into life and peace. He has begun His work in you and He will continue!

December 29

Paul closes one of his letters to the Thessalonians with some advice on how to live: "See that no one pays back evil for evil, but always try to do good to each other and to all people" (1 Thessalonians 5:15).

Don't pay back wrong for wrong. But following that instruction is sometimes a really difficult challenge.

Remember Jesus' words about turning the other cheek? "If somebody curses you, bless them," Jesus said (see Luke 6:28). I have to tell you, that's not a natural reaction. If somebody does something wrong to me, everything in me says, "Get 'em back!"

But Jesus calls us to live on a higher plane. When that aggressive driver cuts you off or that person at work is unkind or says things to you that are inappropriate, Christ wants you to choose to react in a way that is not a "payback." I don't think He meant that you should let people run over you or that you should not confront wrong. But He is saying that you are to respond with kindness.

Look for ways to live out kindness today, at home, at work—wherever you go.

Pit Stop
PRAYER

Lord Jesus, show me ways I can follow this teaching of Yours. I know that I cannot do this in my own strength. You know that everything in my old nature wants to give back evil for evil, but Your promise is that I don't have to be a slave to those old ways of thinking and behaving. I want to live Your way, so I will depend on Your strength and wisdom to do things Your way.

December 30

Always be humble and gentle. Be patient with each other, making allowance for each other's faults because of your love. For there is one body and one Spirit, just as you have been called to one glorious hope for the future.

EPHESIANS 4:2,4, *NLT*

The word for today is "patience." As we approach the end of another year, I'm sure all of us could list disappointments of the past year: people we've been disappointed in, frustrations we've had to deal with, and unexpected conflicts in relationships, among other things.

But I want to remind you that we're to walk humbly before the Lord. You have been bought with a price; you're no longer your own; you are His. You can put your trust and your hope in Him.

Be patient with other people. There's one Body, one Spirit and one glorious hope for the future. No matter who or what has disappointed you, you can rest in God's plan and His care. He gives you hope in the midst of distress and discouragement.

If you have some concerns about the coming year, focus on God and trust Him. He has promised He will meet your needs.

I pray that God will help you live in trust and that you will walk humbly before your God, giving Him praise and honor and glory.

Pit Stop
POINT TO PONDER

Consider these words from Martin Luther's hymn "A Mighty Fortress Is Our God": "And though this world, with devils filled, should threaten to undo us, We will not fear, for God hath willed His truth to triumph through us." No matter what you encounter in life—disappointments, conflicts, frustrations, opposition, persecution—God's plan and truth will triumph. You are part of His plan! Hold fast to that assurance.

STEVE WINGFIELD

December 31

This is New Year's Eve. We're saying goodbye to another year and hello to a new, unknown year. I pray that it will be a year filled with His blessing. In Romans 8:20-21, we read these words:

> With eager hope, the creation looks forward to the day when it will join God's children in glorious freedom from death and decay (*NLT*).

What a day that's going to be! We, too, wait with eager hope. There's going to be a glorious day when our Lord will return and we'll join Him in the glory of heaven. We'll be free from death and decay forever and forever.

We enter this New Year with eager hope. God has a job for us to do until Jesus does come back. He wants to use us to reach this generation with the gospel of Jesus Christ. We've been chosen and called to be His representatives to the world and to live lives that bear the fruit of His righteousness. His Spirit lives in us to teach, guide and strengthen us, and His mighty power is present in every breath of every day!

God bless you as you walk humbly with Him, and may you have a happy and prosperous New Year.

Pit Stop
PRAYER

Let these words from Washington Gladden's hymn "O Master, Let Me Walk with Thee" serve as your prayer as you get ready to start a new year: "In hope that sends a shining ray far down the future's broadening way, in peace that only Thou canst give, with Thee, O Master, let me live."

Endnotes

1. Charles H. Spurgeon, *Lectures to My Students* (Peabody, MA: Hendrickson Publishers, 2010), p. 185.
2. John Ortberg, *When the Game Is Over, It All Goes Back in the Box* (Grand Rapids, MI: Zondervan, 2007), p. 212.
3. A. W. Tozer, *The Knowledge of the Holy: The Attributes of God: Their Meaning in the Christian Life* (New York: HarperCollins, 1978), p. 23.
4. Peace Pilgrim, *Peace Pilgrim: Her Life and Work in Her Own Words* (Santa Fe, NM: Ocean Tree Books, 1998), p. 59.
5. Francis A. Schaeffer, *No Little People* (Wheaton, IL: Crossway Books, 2003), p. 211.
6. Octavius Winslow, *The Sympathy of Christ with Man: Its Teaching and Its Consolation*, vol. 1 (London: James Nisbet and Co., 1862), p. 215. (Available online at http://books.google.com/books.)
7. Ibid., p. 216.
8. Henri Nouwen with Michael J. Christensen and Rebecca J. Laird, *Spiritual Direction: Wisdom for the Long Walk of Faith* (New York: HarperOne, 2006), p. 111.
9. Dallas Willard, *Hearing God: Developing a Conversational Relationship with God* (Downers Grove, IL: InterVarsity Press, 2012), p. 242.
10. John Wesley, *How to Pray: The Best of John Wesley on Prayer* (Uhrichsville, OH: Barbour Publishing, Inc. 2007), p. 5.
11. David Brainerd and Jonathan Edwards, *The Life and Diary of David Brainerd: With Notes and Reflections* (Cedar Lake, MI: ReadaClassic, 2010), p. 56.
12. Ibid., p. 47.
13. Billy Graham, *Hope for Each Day: Morning and Evening Devotions* (Nashville, TN: Thomas Nelson, 2012), January 6-Evening.
14. A Monk of the Eastern Church, *Orthodox Spirituality* (Crestwood, NY: St. Vladimir's Seminary Press, 1978), p. 51, quoted in Gary Thomas, *Holy Available: What If Holiness Is About More Than What We Don't Do?* (Grand Rapids, MI: Zondervan, 2009), p. 17.
15. *John Calvin: Writings on Pastoral Piety*, ed. Elsie Anne McKee (Mahwah, NJ: Paulist Press, 2001), p. 272.
16. Oswald Chambers, *My Utmost for His Highest* (Uhrichsville, OH: Barbour Publishing, 2000), April 11.
17. Oswald Chambers, *My Utmost for His Highest* (Uhrichsville, OH: Barbour Publishing, 2000), December 24.
18. Jonathan Edwards, *The Works of Jonathan Edwards, A.M.*, vol. 2 (Google eBook), p. 217.